DEMOCRACY, SOVER
EUROPEAN

MICHAEL NEWMAN

Democracy, Sovereignty and the European Union

HURST & COMPANY, LONDON

First published in the United Kingdom by
C. Hurst & Co. (Publishers) Ltd.,
38 King Street, London WC2E 8JZ
Copyright © 1996 by Michael Newman
All rights reserved.
Printed in England

ISBNs
1-85065-256-2 (cloth)
1-85065-255-4 (paper)

PREFACE

In different ways both academics and politicians are asking similar questions about the future of the European Union: Does it still make sense to talk of the 'sovereign state' or is power now moving upwards in the direction of a political union and downwards to a regional level? What are the implications of any such trends for democracy? Controversy over what *is* happening and what *should* happen has engulfed the whole European Union, and the discussion will intensify as the 1996 Intergovernmental Conference approaches. Such issues are clearly of crucial importance. However, this book originated with a feeling of dissatisfaction about the ways in which the debates are often conducted. Much of the political discussion seemed to be largely polemical, with a deliberate distortion of both information and concepts; and the academic one was often unduly esoteric and removed from the most fundamental normative questions about democracy and social justice. This book is therefore an attempt to clarify some of the most important issues in a debate which has both theoretical and practical significance.

I am well aware of having only scratched the surface of a highly complex subject, and said nothing about some key policy areas. I have not discussed the external policies of the Member States, or the impact of the EU as a whole upon the autonomy of other states. Nor have I examined all the major areas in domestic policy. In particular, I have omitted the critical issue of environmental sustainability because I lacked the expertise and did not wish to cover it superficially. But I hope that the book provides a stimulating exploration of concepts, an analysis of the nature of the EU as a set of relationships, and a consideration of its impact upon certain crucial policy areas, which have been chosen because of their central importance in relation to the theory and practice of democracy. For the underlying assumption is that democratisation is the fundamental goal, and that both states and the EU should be judged as means to this end.

Several people have helped me to write this book. I was fortunate in that Valerio Linter, a friend and former colleague, was equally interested in the subject. This led to many discussions and in

1994 we jointly organised a conference on 'The Nation-State, Supranationalism and Democratic Control: Economic Policy and the European Union' (published by the Federal Trust as *Economic Policy-Making and the European Union*). This conference, and all those who contributed to it, were enormously beneficial in stimulating my own thinking about the economic problems. My colleagues Frank Brouwer, Dave Edye and Peter Gowan have all influenced my arguments in different ways, even though none of them might agree with my conclusions. Ben Wynne, the Library and Information Officer at the European Documentation Centre at the University of North London, has also been extremely helpful in providing me with relevant EU data – often at a moment's notice. I am also very grateful to Christopher Hurst for accepting my book proposal so readily and to the University of North London for granting me a sabbatical semester in which to write it. But, above all, I have two debts of gratitude. The first is to Ines for reading and criticising each chapter, and improving the whole book. The second and more general one is to the students of European Studies at the University of North London. Over the years I have benefited far more from our seminars and tutorials than they have realised, and it is to them that this book is dedicated.

London, January 1996   M. N.

CONTENTS

TABLES

ABBREVIATIONS

CAP	Common Agricultural Policy
COR	Committee of the Regions
COREPER	Committee of Permanent Representatives
COSAC	Conference of the European Affairs Committees of the national parliaments and European Parliament
ECB	European Central Bank
ECJ	European Court of Justice
ECSC	European Coal and Steel Community
ECU	European Currency Unit
EEC	European Economic Community
EFTA	European Free Trade Association
EIB	European Investment Bank
EMS	European Monetary System
EMU	Economic and Monetary Union
EP	European Parliament
EPC	European Political Co-operation
ERDF	European Regional Development Fund
ERM	Exchange Rate Mechanism
ESCB	European System of Central Banks
ESF	European Social Fund
ESPRIT	European Strategic Programme for Research and Development in Information Technology
EU	European Union
EURATOM	European Atomic Energy Community
EUREKA	European Programme for High Technology Research and Development
IGC	Intergovernmental Conference
JCWI	Joint Council for Welfare of Immigrants
MEP	Member of the European Parliament

MS	Member State(s)
OECD	Organisation for Economic Co-operation and Development
QMV	Qualified Majority Voting
SEA	Single European Act
SEM	Single European Market
SIS	Schengen Information Service
TENS	Trans-European Networks
UNICE	European Union of Employers' Confederations

1

CONCEPTS AND CONFUSIONS

The Treaty agreed at Maastricht in December 1991, and signed two months later in the same city, began with a confident proclamation:

> By this Treaty, the High Contracting Parties establish among themselves a European Union, hereinafter called 'the Union'. This Treaty marks a new stage in the process of creating an ever closer union among the peoples of Europe, in which decisions are taken as closely as possible to the citizen.[1]

However, the optimism was premature. Instead the Maastricht Treaty reactivated a long-term destabilising debate about the relationships between the Member States and the European Union. On the one side were those who insisted that Maastricht was a step too far and that democracy and sovereignty must be defended against the encroachment of 'Brussels'; on the other were those who claimed that sovereignty was now anachronistic and that the way forward was to recognise the importance of the Union, while simultaneously democratising it. In Britain, the issue dominated Parliament and led to votes of confidence in July 1993 and November 1994. This perhaps was to be anticipated given the divisions within the Conservative Party and Britain's traditionally semi-detached attitude to 'Europe'. Of greater significance was the fact that in the French referendum in September 1992 there was the narrowest of majorities in favour of the Maastricht Treaty (51.05% to 48.95%) and 'Euroscepticism' has continued, and in Germany public opinion was also generally negative and, in October 1993, the Constitutional Court imposed some very rigorous constraints about future developments.[2] However, it was in Scandinavia that

---

[1] Title 1, Article A in *Treaty on European Union*, Luxembourg: Office for Official Publications of the European Communities, 1992, p. 7. (This book refers to the 'Maastricht Treaty' rather than to the official title.)

[2] This led to a revision of the Basic Law, with the inclusion of a new Article 23, laying down that any further transfer of powers to the European Union will require the approval of the Bundestag and Bundesrat, with a two-thirds majority in both houses.

the results of the disputes over the EU have been the most dramatic. In the referendum in June 1992 the Danish people rejected the Treaty by 50.7% to 49.3%, bringing the incipient crisis over Maastricht to a head, and plunging the EU into a long period of uncertainty, from which it has not really recovered. And while the Danish government secured sufficient concessions to reverse the result in a second referendum the following May (with 56.8% voting in favour), the Norwegians rejected membership (by 52.3% to 47.8%) in a referendum in late November 1994, repeating the decision they had taken twenty-two years earlier.[3] Once again the whole project of 'ever closer union' was called into question.

The issues in these disputes are crucially important both for the individual countries and for Europe as a whole. But it is far less evident that the terms in which the debates are conducted necessarily illuminate the real nature of the problems involved. This is particularly the case when 'sovereignty' is invoked as a justification for a particular policy. For example, on the same day that the Norwegian 'no' voters prevailed in the referendum, Conservative 'Eurosceptic' rebels in the House of Commons were disciplined (by the withdrawal of the party whip) for voting against the government on Britain's contribution to the EU budget. They, like the Norwegian opponents of EU membership, were proclaiming that they were defending sovereignty and democracy. But how much did they really have in common with their Scandinavian counterparts? The Norwegian 'no' voters were generally defending a high level of welfare expenditure, high environmental standards, and high subsidies to protect the traditional fishing industry in the far north of their country.[4] The British 'Eurosceptics' came from the Thatcherite

---

[3] It had been agreed that Denmark would not participate in the single currency, or be bound by the rules applying to Stage III of monetary union. Nor would Denmark participate in the aspects of the Common Foreign and Security Policy which had defence implications. There were also 'clarifications' of the Treaty designed to reassure Danish voters.

[4] For a brief discussion of Norwegian concerns, see Lars Mjøset, 'The Nordic Economies and their External Challenges' in Frank Brouwer, Valerio Lintner and Michael Newman (eds), *Economic Policy Making and the European Union*, London: Federal Trust, 1994. See also John Redmond (ed.), *Prospective Europeans*, Brighton: Harvester Wheatsheaf, 1994; Lee Miles, *Enlargement of the European Union*, London: University of North London Press, 1995. For longer term perspectives, see Valter Angell (ed.), *Norway Facing a Changing Europe*, Oslo: Norwegian Foreign Policy Studies 1992; Lars Mjøset *et al.*, *Norwegian Political*

wing of the Conservative Party, and wanted to restrict all forms of government expenditure and controls in favour of neo-liberal economics.[5] Opponents of the EU in the Norwegian Labour Party and British Conservative Party justified their positions with similar slogans, but their political priorities were quite different.

Of course, it is well-known that those involved in such campaigns use political terms in an emotive way so as to mobilise support from a wide range of opinion. It is easier to generate opposition to the Maastricht Treaty or to entry into the European Union by suggesting that the 'nation-state', 'sovereignty' and 'democracy' are in danger than to concentrate on detailed technical issues. And the power of each of these concepts – nation, state, sovereignty, democracy – is enhanced by their conjunction. Yet it is surely clear that analysis is being obscured rather than illuminated in this discourse? In particular, there is no necessary connection between the 'nation' and the 'state' or between either of them and 'democracy'. However the 'nation' is defined – and this itself is extremely contentious – we know that some nations do not possess a state, and that states do not necessarily represent, or represent equally, all nations within their borders.

However, the 'Euro-sceptics' have no monopoly in using concepts emotively. Consider the evolution in the terminology used to describe the EU. The first term was the 'Common Market'. This suggests an economic organisation, characterised by commerce and competition. The second designation, after the merger between the EEC, the ECSC, and EURATOM in 1967 was the 'European Communities'. This implied a move beyond economics, since a 'community' suggests a group or society characterised by solidarity and co-operation. And this image was furthered when the three 'Communities' became known as the 'European Community': after all, one community is more cosy than three. Transformation from

Economy, Report of the Institute for Social Research, Oslo, 1994; and David Arter, *The Politics of European Integration in the Twentieth Century*, Aldershot: Dartmouth, 1993.

5 D. Baker, A Gamble and S. Ludlam, 'Conservative Splits and European Integration', *Political Quarterly*, 4, 1993; D. Baker, A Gamble and S. Ludlam, 'The Maastricht vote and Conservative MPs', *Parliamentary Affairs*, 2, 1993; D. Baker, A. Gamble and S. Ludlam, 'The Parliamentary Siege of Maastricht, 1993: Conservative Divisions and British Ratification', *Parliamentary Affairs*, 1, 1994.

a 'Community' to a 'Union' is no doubt intended to change attitudes
once more by suggesting a single, united, entity. But, of course, it
is highly debatable whether any such entity exists.

Those involved in political action may thus deliberately use terms
in particular ways so as to promote particular beliefs among those
whom they seek to influence. However, it is also possible that they
believe their own rhetoric because of the conceptual framework
through which they have developed their political outlook. Concepts help us to analyse politics through elucidating complex
relationships, but they also convey particular types of analysis which
lead us to particular interpretations of the world. Nowhere is this
more true than in the typical terms in which debate about the
European Union has been conducted, not only in political circles
but also in academic ones. Indeed because they are working within
different conceptual frameworks, those who are professionally involved in analysing the EU are as divided in their interpretations of
its nature and significance as are politicians and political parties.

The title of this book thus contains three terms – 'democracy',
'sovereignty', and the 'European Union' – which are all contestable
in the sense that each of them may be viewed in very different ways.
In the case of 'democracy' this is a commonplace observation. Since
it now has positive connotations throughout the world, almost all
regimes proclaim themselves as 'democratic' irrespective of their
actual nature and, as many analysts have shown, there are also a great
number of contending concepts of democracy – direct or representative, participatory or 'elitist', local or centralised, liberal or
social, and so on.[6] Some of these controversies will be explored in
later chapters. However, 'sovereignty' and even the 'EU' are hardly
less problematic. This chapter therefore explores the confusing
nature of these two terms and explains the attitudes that are adopted
to them in this book.

Sovereignty

As already noted, opponents of the European Union have cus-

[6] David Held (ed.), *Prospects for Democracy*, Oxford/Cambridge: Polity Press, 1993;
John Dunn (ed.), *Democracy – The Unfinished Journey*, Oxford University Press,
1992; Anthony Arblaster, *Democracy*, Milton Keynes: Open University Press,
1987; James L. Hyland, *Democratic Theory: The Philosophical Foundations*,
Manchester University Press, 1995.

tomarily argued that it threatens 'sovereignty', while proponents have normally taken one or more of the following positions: either that 'sovereignty' had already ceased to exist in the contemporary world, or that it *should* be superseded, or that the EU leads to 'pooled' or 'shared' sovereignty. The debate has been bitter and prolonged, but it is doubtful whether it has clarified the issues. There are two reasons for this: first, the term 'sovereignty' is inherently ambiguous; secondly, each side in the debate has often been intent on using the word to justify its aims rather than to explain anything. Let us consider these points in turn.

The ambiguity of sovereignty. The formation of European states in the modern era emerged from conflicts which involved dual processes. On the one hand, the sections of the nobility who gained control prevailed over rivals *within* the territory; on the other, they secured ascendancy against *external* forces which claimed rights over the territory. In particular, monarchs needed to defeat rival contenders internally and to break free from the claims of the Papacy to rule in the name of Christian universalism. Such conflicts matured over centuries with complex economic, military, political and religious/ideological issues involved. The emergence of the concept of sovereignty provided a means of legitimising the power of the states which triumphed in these battles.[7]

The first notion of sovereignty – theorised most fully by Jean Bodin (1529-96) and Thomas Hobbes (1588-1679) – was essentially the claim that power should be vested in a single source which was free from external and internal constraints.[8] It was intended to demonstrate the need for power to be located in the state and to undermine the claims of others to dispute this on the basis of such justifications as ancient privileges or Christian universalism. It may

[7] For a full historical analysis of the doctrine, see F.H. Hinsley, *Sovereignty*, Cambridge University Press, 2nd edn, 1986. See also Joseph A. Camilleri and Jim Falk, *The End of Sovereignty*, Aldershot: Edward Elgar; David Held, 'Democracy, the Nation-State and the Global System' in David Held (ed.), *Political Theory Today*, Oxford/Cambridge: Polity Press, 1991; Andrew Vincent, *Theories of the State*, Oxford: Blackwell, 1987.

[8] Jean Bodin, *Les six livres de la république*, Paris, 1583 (see Jean Bodin, *On Sovereignty*, ed. and transl. Julian H. Franklin, Cambridge University Press, 1992); Thomas Hobbes, *Leviathan*, 1651 (see Hobbes, *Leviathan*, ed. and intro. C.B. Macpherson, Harmondsworth: Penguin, 1968).

therefore be termed the *doctrine of state sovereignty*. In theory, this doctrine need not have led to 'absolutism'. However, since it had no specifically democratic content, there was no guarantee against despotism and in practice, of course, Monarchical absolutism developed during the late seventeenth century with *state sovereignty* as a justification.

A later, and closely related, doctrine was *legal sovereignty*. Its major theorist was John Austin (1790-1859) who argued that all laws were commands of a sovereign who was habitually obeyed by society without owing obedience to any other authority.[9] Such commands were binding because the sovereign had the power to enforce penalties, but no external body had the ability to impose penalties on the sovereign authority. Thus, for example, there could be no international law because there was no sovereign to enforce it. This doctrine of *legal sovereignty* has been enormously influential, both as a justification for state power and as a basis for opposition to supranational notions.

Neither *state sovereignty* nor *legal sovereignty* has any necessary connection with democratic ideas. However, sovereignty is often equated with democracy. Indeed, even though Hobbes sought to define sovereignty in terms of a single person, it was simultaneously being claimed by parliament, and he was forced to admit the possibility of an assembly as the location for sovereign power. Embodied in this was the argument, developed by John Locke (1632-1704) that 'sovereignty' did not reside in states, but in the 'people'.[10] Certainly, Locke's conception of the 'people' was highly restricted – predominantly comprising landowners who were opposed to monarchical absolutism. Nevertheless, in embryonic form, this was a democratic claim that the people rightfully held power and it was up to them to decide the institutional form through which it should be wielded. This was a third concept of sovereignty, which may be termed the *doctrine of popular sovereignty*.

The relationship between these doctrines was (and remains) ambiguous. *Popular sovereignty*, developed more fully in the work of Jean-Jacques Rousseau (1712-78) and in the claims of the Third

[9] John Austin, *The Province of Jurisprudence Determined*, New York: Humanities Press, 1965 (originally published 1832).
[10] John Locke, *Two Treatises of Civil Government*, 1690 (ed. and intro. Thomas I. Cook, New York: Hafner, 1969).

Estate during the French Revolution, could challenge *state sovereignty* by setting the claims of the people against the claims of the state.[11] But it could also strengthen a state which claimed, as did Napoleon III, to embody the popular will.[12] In this case the power of the state was legitimised by combining the arguments which underlay both doctrines, and this combination has been so potent that it is necessary to use a different term to distinguish it from its two sources: *popular state sovereignty*. At its most extreme, this doctrine has been used to justify the claim that the unity between state and people is so complete that no separate institutions are necessary to represent the people. It has thus been adopted by twentieth century Fascist and Stalinist regimes.

If the idea of *popular sovereignty* could either challenge the power of the state or buttress it through the doctrine of *popular state sovereignty*, this was even more clearly the case with the notion of the people as a 'nation'. Once nationalism became dominant as a mobilising force in the nineteenth and twentieth centuries, states which could mould or exploit such sentiments drew additional strength, while other states were weakened, and often disintegrated under the pressure. Moreover, while claims about the existence of a 'national will' could be combined with claims about *popular sovereignty*, they could also be used to suppress this essentially democratic notion.[13] Once again, a successful attempt to distort these claims in a bogus combination could provide legitimation for the most extreme form of 'totalitarianism' – hence Hitler's claim to personal power on the basis of embodying the 'volk'. In effect, this combined *popular state sovereignty* with the notion of a 'national will', with the 'nation' defined in racist terms. But of course the idea of the state representing a 'nation' is also the dominant organising

[11] Jean Jacques Rousseau, *Du Contrat Social*, 1762 (see Jean Jacques Rousseau, *The Social Contract*, ed. and intro. Charles Frankel, New York: Hafner, 1974).

[12] David Thomson, *Democracy in France since 1870*, Oxford University Press, 1977, chapter 1.

[13] There is now a vast literature on this, but the argument is expressed most succinctly in some of the inter-war and wartime writings. See, for example, Harold Laski, 'Nationalism and the Future of Civilization' (1932) in *The Danger of being a Gentleman and other Essays*, London: Allen and Unwin, 1939; E.H. Carr, *Nationalism and After*, London: Macmillan, 1968 (originally 1945); Alfred Cobban, *The Nation State and National Self-Determination*, London: Fontana, 1968 (originally 1944).

principle of the twentieth century, based on the claim that we live
in 'nation-states' and that such states uphold *national sovereignty*. But
what is the relationship between this doctrine of *national sovereignty*
and the other doctrines of sovereignty? In particular, can it be a
democratic notion, in harmony with *popular sovereignty*?

Liberal-democratic supporters of the idea of *national sovereignty*
argue that this is possible when the internal organisation of the state
is itself democratic. The whole liberal tradition of political thought
has been based on the idea of dividing and limiting powers and it is
suggested that this is quite compatible with the doctrine of sovereignty.[14] Proponents of this view thus argue that it is possible to
have democratic institutions through which citizens may express
their political demands and preferences, to divide power between
executive, legislative and judicial branches of government, and also
to decentralise responsibilities within the state, while maintaining
national sovereignty. This may be termed a *doctrine of divided
sovereignty*.[15] Finally, a variant of this idea may be termed the *doctrine
of shared sovereignty*. This is believed to encapsulate the situation of
federal systems, in which power is not only territorially divided, but
also overlapping between the central and sub-central tiers of government. On this view it may be maintained that the state, though
constitutionally and territorially divided, maintains its sovereignty –
or national sovereignty – in relation to the external world. The
requirement is that there should be a 'decision-making system'
within a territorially defined state, but this does not imply a single
centre of power.[16]

The following uses of the term 'sovereignty' have been distin-
guished above: *state sovereignty*; *legal sovereignty*; *popular sovereignty*;
popular state sovereignty; *popular state sovereignty in combination with*

---

[14] This was the position originally taken by Locke in his *Second Treatise on Civil
Government* (chapters 12 and 13) and is endorsed by many contemporary theorists.
See for example, Hinsley, op. cit., chapter 6.

[15] It may be argued that the term 'parliamentary sovereignty' is more appropriate
for this view. However, this may imply that all sovereignty is, or should be, vested
in parliament. If so, it is perhaps more appropriate to regard this as a form of
popular sovereignty, in which the people delegate their right to rule to parliament.
If, however, it is accepted that power is, and should be, divided between different
institutions, the term *divided sovereignty* indicates this more clearly.

[16] See, for example, Preston King, *Federalism and Federation*, Beckenham: Croom
Helm, 1982, chapter 11.

*various forms of 'totalitarian' claims; national sovereignty; divided
sovereignty and shared sovereignty.* From this it may at least be concluded that the term is now inherently ambiguous. If someone refers
to 'sovereignty', without further clarification, we cannot be sure
what s/he is talking about. But, before considering the implications
of this ambiguity, it is necessary to look at some of the arguments
against sovereignty.

The end of sovereignty?   The suggestion that the doctrine of sovereignty has outlived its purpose and should now be confined to the
'dustbin of history' is not new. The idea has long existed in federalist
and anarchist theories, and in the first quarter of the century many
pluralist thinkers also took this line.[17] However, the viewpoint has
now entered the mainstream of political analysis, particularly with
reference to the EU. The first proposition, which purports to be
based on empirical evidence, argues that sovereignty is a myth which
bears no correspondence with reality, while the second, which is
overtly normative, suggests that the doctrine is in some sense
'dangerous'. These may be discussed in turn.

   –Sovereignty as a myth. Those who argue this case normally begin
with essential elements in the doctrines of *state sovereignty* and *legal
sovereignty*: that is, first that the state is rightfully ascendant within
the territory, and secondly that it is not answerable to external
forces.[18] They dispute both aspects of these claims.
   The argument about the domestic sphere proceeds in a similar
way to those endorsing the doctrine of *divided sovereignty*. In other
words, it notes that in no society does the state actually hold a
monopoly of power, and that in liberal-democracies some degree
of dispersion of power is institutionalised and explicitly advocated.
But the opponents of the doctrine of sovereignty are normally more

---

[17] For federalist and anarchist theories, see King, op. cit.; for pluralist theories see
David Nicholls, *The Pluralist State*, London: Macmillan, 1975; Paul Hirst, *The
Pluralist Theory of the State*, London: Routledge, 1989; and Vincent, op. cit.,
chapter 6.

[18] Camilleri and Falk, op. cit., Paul Hirst, *Associative Democracy*, Oxford/Cambridge:
Polity Press, 1994; see also various writings by David Held, in particular
'Democracy, the Nation-State and the Global System' in Held, *Political Theory
Today*, op. cit.; 'Democracy: From City-States to a Cosmopolitan Order?' in
Held, *Prospects for Democracy*, op. cit.; *Democracy and the New International Order*,
London: Institute for Public Policy Research, 1993.

concerned to demonstrate the extent to which the *external* claims
are bogus. In reality, they argue, states are highly constrained by
international forces in an increasingly interdependent world. If,
therefore, the doctrine of sovereignty is able to describe neither
internal nor external reality, what purpose is served by maintaining
the concept? Is it not solely a myth – a vestige of a bygone age?

The validity of the apparently empirical argument will be discussed below. However, the proponents of this viewpoint are not
motivated simply by their concern that sovereignty no longer
describes reality. The more fundamental consideration is almost
always normative: the alleged dangers of the doctrine.

– *Sovereignty as a danger.* At their most extreme, these dangers are
seen as follows: the *internal* risk that the so-called sovereign state will
seek to assume absolutist powers even within a liberal-democracy,
and the *external* danger that sovereignty (particularly when reinforced by nationalism) legitimises aggression, expansion, and dis-
regard for others in the name of a single interest defined by the state.
Less dramatically, the opponents of sovereignty may argue that the
dangers are more insidious. Because it is based on an illusion that
the state has real power, it diverts attention from the solutions to
urgent world problems. The pressing dangers of militarism, economic
insecurity, deprivation, inequality, and ecological catastrophe cannot, it is argued, be resolved by the state since the real solutions are
inevitably international.[19]

Critics of the doctrine of sovereignty therefore advocate its
rejection on the basis of alternative values. These may be that
domestic power should be divided, that the needs of the world
community should be recognised or, more specifically, that the
demands of the EU should supersede those of the 'nation-state'.
Those who advocate an 'end to sovereignty' thus believe that they
are doing much more than arguing about the continuing relevance
of a term. For the term, at the very least, legitimises a situation which

---

[19] Camilleri and Falk, op. cit. For a powerful statement of the moral argument, see
Charles R. Beitz, 'Sovereignty and Morality in International Affairs' in Held,
Political Theory Today, op. cit., and 'Cosmopolitan liberalism and the states system'
in C. Brown (ed.), *Political Restructuring in Europe: Ethical Perspectives*, London:
Routledge, 1994. The combination of moral and empirical arguments was also
a pronounced feature of Harold Laski's theories of sovereignty. See Michael
Newman, *Harold Laski – A Political Biography*, London: Macmillan, 1993.

impedes the solution to real problems. Thus, while there is clearly an empirical aspect to the case – concerning the location of power in the contemporary world – the main purpose of the argument is to 'de-legitimise' the state.

One way in which defenders of the doctrine of sovereignty respond to such arguments is by disputing the empirical content. There is thus a lively debate – which will be considered later – as to whether the undoubted tendency towards 'globalisation' has actually weakened states. Some theorists have presented strong arguments to suggest that it has not had this effect and that some states are far more powerful than they have ever been. They therefore suggest that the parameters may have shifted, but that this does not mean that the doctrine no longer has validity.[20]

A second response is to point to the fact that sovereignty exists in the sense that 'sovereign states' are recognised – for example, by membership of the UN.[21] Moreover, the UN and other international institutions have attempted to elaborate the implications of recognition by defining sovereignty in terms of such principles as 'sovereign equality', and non-intervention.[22] And Anthony Giddens explores the political characteristics of internationally recognised states as follows:

> Of what does sovereignty consist? The following elements might be listed as most important – in effect, definitive of what sovereignty is. A sovereign state is a political organisation that has the capacity, within a delimited territory or territories, to make laws and effectively sanction their up-keep; exert a monopoly over the disposal of the means of violence; control basic policies relating to the internal political or administrative form of government; and dispose of the fruits of a national economy that are the basis of its revenue.[23]

---

[20] For a recent collection which presents a range of arguments in defence of sovereignty, see Robert H. Jackson and Alan James (eds), *States in a Changing World: A Contemporary Analysis*, Oxford: Clarendon Press, 1993.

[21] This is essentially the argument in Hinsley, op. cit., chapters 5 and 6.

[22] The relevant articles are quoted and analysed in Gershon Baskin, *Jerusalem of Peace: Sovereignty and Territory in Jerusalem's Future*, Jerusalem: Israel/Palestine Centre for Research and Information, 1994.

[23] Anthony Giddens, *The Nation State and Violence*, Berkeley, CA: University of California Press, 1985, p. 282.

The defenders of sovereignty are surely justified in arguing that the fact of international recognition carries some distinct advantages. To deny this would be to argue that the search for statehood by Palestinians or Kurds or Scots is to pursue a goal which is entirely illusory. Perhaps, on normative grounds, it would be preferable to envisage a world in which it became immaterial whether or not a people possessed a state. But this is very different from suggesting that, in current conditions, 'sovereignty' is irrelevant. For the existence of a state means that at least some people within a territorially bounded area possess some power.

The state remains the dominant form of political organisation in the contemporary world, and it cannot be assumed that the possession of 'sovereignty' (in the sense of recognition) is to possess an empty shell without significant content. This needs to be examined empirically.

Nevertheless, I regard sovereignty as an unhelpful concept. Why is this?

Sovereignty as an unhelpful doctrine.   If it were generally agreed that 'sovereignty ' should be understood in the rather narrow sense associated with international recognition it might have some limited use as a term. To describe a state as 'sovereign' would tell us that it was in a different category from an entity which simply aspired to 'statehood'. Similarly, it might be argued that it is useful to distinguish between a 'sovereign' state and a state that is not fully 'sovereign' in the sense that it is entirely dependent on an external protector. However, even if this were acknowledged, it would follow that to describe a state as 'sovereign' provides us with no indication as to the *amount* of power it wields. The United States and Guatemala are both recognised as 'sovereign states' by the United Nations but they are vastly unequal in all other respects. The problem is that sovereignty is not generally understood in this way. On the contrary it is often assumed that it is a tangible entity which could be measured in quantities of power. Certainly, would-be states normally need certain *kinds* of power to achieve recognition – in particular, sufficient control over the territory which they purport to rule. However, neither the extent nor the components of such power are constant throughout history or between different states in the same era. For example, as noted above, John Austin – following Bodin – saw 'legal sovereignty' as the basis of state power. But since state power is multi-dimensional and far more extensive than *legal sovereignty*, there is no reason why the transfer of some aspects of legal competence from the state should necessarily reduce its power. Indeed there could be circumstances in which states chose to transfer some aspects of their competences in the belief that their overall power would nevertheless be enhanced. This observation has immediate relevance for the debates about the EU. That is, while it is often argued that the transfer of certain competences from the state to the EU constitutes a 'loss of sovereignty' – or a 'pooling of sovereignty' – these are not very helpful descriptions of the process. It could instead be viewed as a transfer of certain competences which were formerly regarded as integral to state power, but which are no longer viewed in this way. And the way in which the process is described has very considerable implications for the way it is interpreted. Thus if sovereignty is regarded as a *quantity* of powers, the transfer of some forms of legal competence may be seen as *reducing* the power of the state. If, however, it is seen as a definitional attribute of statehood, there is no necessary reason to assume that the transfer of certain legal competences reduces overall state power – it may even increase it if it brings other gains. In other words, the implication that 'sovereignty' has empirical components beyond those required to secure recognition as a state may then suggest a particular, and arguable, interpretation of the process of European integration.

Yet the problem is not simply that sovereignty, when treated as more than a formal attribute of statehood is misleading. It is also that the term is being used as a doctrine of *legitimation* – as indeed it was in its origins. And, while the ambiguities noted earlier detract from the clarity of the concept, they reinforce its legitimating functions.

In my view, there is not a single usage of the term, discussed above, which cannot be expressed more clearly in other ways. If we want to talk of *state sovereignty*, we can examine the specific justifications for state power over society; if we want to talk of *popular sovereignty*, we can more usefully discuss this in terms of 'democracy'; if we want to consider *divided sovereignty* or *shared sovereignty*, we can understand these more fully by analysing the kinds of constitutional/institutional relationships within states. And so on. The only remaining use would be the formal legal sense involved in recognition as a state. But if this is really a definitional attribute of statehood

– since all states that are recognised as such are 'sovereign' and all bodies that are 'sovereign' are recognised as states – it is not even clear that this usage is particularly helpful.[24]

It may be argued that the advantage of the term 'sovereignty' is that it suggests a link between all the ideas discussed above, which might otherwise seem separate. *But it is this very attempt to link them that is problematic.* For, by failing to specify the usage, opinion may be mobilised on bogus grounds as if sovereignty constitutes some holy order. For example, Right-wing nationalists seek to rally support by talking of the threat to 'sovereignty' and implying that this has something to do with 'democracy'. But their real intentions may have far more to do with *state sovereignty* or *popular state sovereignty* than with *popular sovereignty* or *shared sovereignty*. Use of the term 'sovereignty' (deliberately?) blurs all these crucial distinctions. It diminishes clarity rather than adding to it.

To argue this is *not* to take a position against those who wish, in particular circumstances, to defend a state against forms of supra-nationalism. For example, it is possible to feel great sympathy with Norwegian opponents of the EU, who feared that membership could threaten their democracy and high welfare expenditure. But it would be preferable to conduct the argument in these terms than to invoke sovereignty as a justification.

More generally, this book is based on the view that exploration of the relationships between the Member States and the EU is of great practical and theoretical importance. It analyses these interactions in terms of power and democracy, seeking to elucidate both empirical evidence and normative considerations. Such issues are often dealt with, both in academic and political discourse, with reference to the term 'sovereignty'. Indeed this word is so deeply embedded in discussions of these questions that it has been used in the title of the book to indicate the subject matter. Yet, as argued above, the concept of sovereignty is so ambiguous and distorted that

---

[24] 'In all body-politics...it is the state which wields sovereignty, and that structure, notional or tangible, which possesses it is by definition the state.' Hinsley, op. cit. p. 220. This also suggests that the notion of 'sovereignty' does not really help us to distinguish between a 'sovereign state' and one that is not fully 'sovereign'. If the state in question has achieved external recognition, it is *ipso facto* a state in a formal, legal sense even if its autonomy is severely constrained, and if has not been recognised internationally it will not be so regarded. It might then be termed a 'puppet state' or an 'aspirant state', in accordance with the specific circumstances.

it is now a barrier to analysis. It will therefore not be used except when quoting from other sources.

The European Union

It may appear bizarre to suggest that the EU is a contestable notion. Surely it is a designation for a legal entity, with its own budget, institutions, staff, and representation throughout the world? All this is certainly true, but does not eliminate the conceptual difficulties in characterising the EU. Nor are these simply the result of the fact that the Maastricht Treaty complicated the structure by creating a three-pillar organisation, in which two of the pillars –Justice and Home Affairs and the Common Foreign and Security Policy – remain largely outside the Community. This may add to the confusion, but is not the major cause of it. The fundamental problem, which has bedevilled interpretations of the integration process ever since the establishment of the European Coal and Steel Community in 1952, is to decide what sort of entity it is. Viewed from differing conceptual frameworks, it actually appears very different. Such frameworks may be extremely complex, taking the form of consciously articulated theoretical paradigms, or they may be much looser – sets of assumptions which underlie attitudes and interpretations. But in either case they constitute different notions of the 'reality' of the EU. This can be illustrated by contrasting the two most extreme positions.

The EU as an embryonic federation. The Federal vision has been a deeply rooted aspiration amongst many of the most active campaigners for a 'European Union'. It was perhaps expressed most eloquently by Altiero Spinelli (1907-86) in 1941, when held as a prisoner of Fascism, in the so-called Ventotene Manifesto:

> The absolute sovereignty of the nation states has caused each one of them to try to dominate the others, because each feels itself threatened by the power of the others. Moreover, each tries to extend its sphere of influence over an ever larger area, so as to allow itself freedom of action and to ensure for itself the means of subsistence without having to depend on others. The inevitable result of this desire to dominate is the hegemony of the strongest state over all the others, which are subjected to it. . .
> The forces of reaction have men and leaders able and educated

to command who will fight obstinately to maintain their supremacy. They will know how to disguise themselves in a crisis, proclaiming themselves lovers of liberty, of peace, of the general welfare, of the poorer classes. . .

The fulcrum on which these elements will try to lever themselves into power will be the restoration of the nation state. . .

If this aim is achieved the forces of reaction will have conquered. Even if these [reconstructed] states are democratic and socialist in appearance, the return to power of the reactionaries will merely be a matter of time. National jealousies will re-emerge and every state will once again think in terms of using force of arms to satisfy its particular demands. . .

The problem which must first be solved is the final abolition of the division of Europe into sovereign national states. Without this, any progress made will be appearance only...

The manifold problems which bedevil the international affairs of the continent have become insoluble: definition of the boundaries in areas of mixed populations, protection of rights of ethnic minorities, outlets to the sea for inland countries, Balkan question, Irish question, etc. All of them could most easily be resolved by a European Federation. Historically, similar problems arising between the petty principalities which went to make up the larger national units lost their bitterness on being transformed into relations between one province and another.[25]

This vision has been kept alive by Federalists ever since, with Spinelli continuing to play a major role until his death. Most of them have been dissatisfied by the actual process of European integration, and most acknowledge that the European Union is not yet a Federation because the governments of the Member States (MS) remain far too strong, with the supranational powers of the EU conversely too weak. However, the Federalist perspective generally holds that the EU is in *the process of becoming a Federation*.[26] It is argued

[25] From *Comunita europee*, December 1973 in Richard Vaughan, *Post-War Integration in Europe*, London: Edward Arnold, 1976, pp. 14-16; see also Lucio Levi (ed.), *Altiero Spinelli and Federalism in Europe and the World*, Milan: Franco Angeli, 1990.

[26] See, for example, Murray Forsyth, 'Federalism and Confederalism' in Brown (ed.). *Political Restructuring in Europe* op. cit.; John Pinder, *European Community – The Building of a Union*, Oxford University Press; Michael Burgess, *Federalism and European Union: Political Ideas, Influences and Strategies in the European Community, 1972-1987*, London: Routledge, 1989; and Lucio Levi, 'Recent

that crucial competences have been passed to the Union level, while states are also challenged from below by regional and local forces, and by nations seeking self-government. The way forward is thus seen as recognition of the fact that the old state-centred world has passed, and the introduction of a new, democratic constitution, specifying the appropriate powers at EU, 'national', and sub-state levels. Academic studies of the EU, which are influenced by the Federalist perspective, thus tend to interpret the EU as a wholly new entity which is in the process of superseding the Member States, and which now needs strengthened democratic institutions at EU level.

Realist theory. In modern academic terms, realist theory is a school of thought in International Relations. However, this has been influenced by earlier theorists, such as Niccolò Machiavelli (1469-1527) and Thomas Hobbes. Basically realists such as E.H. Carr (1892-1982) and Hans Morgenthau (1904-1980) have viewed states as the irreducible element in international politics and, since these are fundamentally self-interested and competitive, the underlying condition is perceived as one of conflict.[27] However, like Hobbes's self-interested individuals, each state also seeks security rather than a situation which will lead to constant war. From this perspective, the EU is therefore regarded as a means of managing potential conflict and competition so as to enhance security.[28] But it could never transcend the Member States in the sense suggested by Federalists, for those states are basically using it to promote their own interests. Thus while Federalists might condemn governments for opposing the construction of a full political union, realists will argue that this is to be expected: states remain the 'real' actors which operate the international institutions that they establish.

Federalists may be more overtly 'normative' in outlook than realists as they openly proclaim that they want to construct a new system, while realists claim that they are simply analysing the world

---

Developments in Federalist Theory' in Levi, *Altiero Spinelli*, op. cit.

[27] H.J. Morgenthau, *Politics Among Nations*, New York: Knopf, 1960; E.H. Carr, *The Twenty Year Crisis: An Introduction to the Study of International Relations*, London: Macmillan, 1962.

[28] See, for example, Hedley Bull, *The Anarchical Society: A Study of Order in World Politics*, London: Macmillan, 1977; Raymond Aron, *Peace and War: A Theory of International Relations*, New York: Doubleday, 1966; Hinsley, op. cit.

rather than taking an attitude towards it. However, this difference
is probably less significant than it appears. After all, Machiavelli and
Hobbes also claimed that they were simply observers of the situation,
but they clearly sought to justify power politics on the basis of their
apparently scientific approach. Modern theorists also disguise the
normative basis of their operating assumptions, but some of the
realists have been disparaging about the 'illusions' of those who have
sought to justify supranational ideals. These attitudes have obviously
implied something about their own values.[29] However, the more
relevant point is that Federalists and realists – whatever their motives
– *perceive* the EU quite differently. Thus while Federalists will call
for democratisation *of the EU as a whole*, realists will regard this as an
illusion. For if the state is the only real actor, democratisation at
supranational level is a forlorn hope.

Federalism and realism constitute the two extremes in academic
analysis of the EU and most contemporary theorists fall somewhere
between them. Although there are important distinctions between
all the other theories and their operating assumptions, they may be
grouped into two 'families', which have some resemblance either
to Federalism or realism. The first, with the family resemblance to
Federalism, may be termed 'integration theories', and the second,
with a family resemblance to realism, may be termed 'international
relations theories'.

Integration theories.   In the past forty years, there have been a number of integration theories and they have undoubtedly become
increasingly sophisticated.[30] The most important has been 'neo-

[29] Hinsley, *Sovereignty*, op. cit., pp. 211, 226-35; Alan Milward, *The European Rescue of the Nation-State*, London: Routledge, 1992, chapter 6. For a forceful critique of realist assumptions, see Camilleri and Falk, op. cit., chapter 2.

[30] For an explanation and critiques of the major theories up to the early 1980s, see Paul Taylor, *The Limits of European Integration*, Beckenham: Croom Helm, 1983; for more recent work, see William Wallace, 'Introduction: the dynamics of European integration' and Robert O. Keohane and Stanley Hoffmann, 'Conclusions: Community politics and institutional change' in William Wallace (ed.), *The Dynamics of European Integration*, London: Pinter/RIIA, 1990; Clive Church, *Integration Theory in the 1990s*, London: University of North London Press, 1995; and the following unpublished papers presented at the 2nd European Community Studies Associations-World Conference Brussels 5-6 May 1994: Janne Haaland Matlary, 'Integration Theory and International Relations Theory: What does the Elephant Look Like Today and How Should it be Studied?' and Mehmet Ugur,

functionalism' and this itself has undergone various changes over time.[31] Others include co-operative federalism, neo-federalism and also a non-specific form of economic determinism which is often applied to the EU.[32] There are a number of important differences between such theories but in this writer's view, there are two common elements which justify grouping them with each other, and with Federalism.

The first is the belief that the EU is unique – or at least so much more important than any comparable experiment that it needs its own explanatory framework. It cannot therefore be treated in the same way as any other 'international organisation' because it is so much more than this. The density of the interactions between the MS, the sophistication of the institutional framework, the extent of supranationalism, the range of EU competences and policy areas –all these render it a distinct entity.

Secondly, and perhaps of still greater importance, such views are linked by the fact that they all suggest *directionality* : that is, they all suggest that the EU is 'going somewhere' and will ultimately become more supranational, with the Member States becoming less important. Certainly, neo-functionalism became much less confident about the smoothness of this progress after the set-backs to the integration process from the mid 1960s to the early '80s, and most of its adherents now accept that integration will proceed in 'fits and

---

'Integration Theory Re-Visited: State-Society Relations as Key for Understanding European Integration'.

[31] The major early works were Ernst B. Haas, *The Uniting of Europe: Political, Social and Economic Forces, 1950-1957*, Stanford University Press, 2nd edn, 1968, and Leon Lindberg, *The Political Dynamics of European Economic Integration*, Stanford University Press, 1963. For shifts in the positions of both authors, see Ernst B. Haas, *The Obsolescence of Regional Integration Theory*, Berkeley: University of California Press, 1975, and Leon Lindberg and Stuart Scheingold, *Europe's Would-Be Polity*, Englewood Cliffs, NJ: Prentice-Hall, 1970. For a useful brief explanation, see Stephen George, *Politics and Policy in the European Community*, Oxford University Press, 1985, chapter 2.

[32] For co-operative federalism, see Emil Kirchner, *Decision-Making in the European Community: The Council Presidency and European Integration*, Manchester University Press, 1992; for neo-federalism, see John Pinder, *European Community – the Building of a Union*, Oxford University Press, 1991 and 'European Unity and Nation State: A Case for New-Federalism?', *International Affairs*, 1986, no. 1. For a brief critique see Michael Newman, *The European Community – Where does the Power Lie?*, London: University of North London Press, 1993.

starts' rather than 'ever upward'. The EU may be a 'journey to an unknown destination', but it is still a journey.[33]

In other words, these integration theories (or the looser set of assumptions associated with them) hold that the EU is qualitatively different from other international entities, and that the features which have made it so distinct will become more pronounced as time goes on. This does not mean that all these theorists would agree with the fully Federalist proposal of a new constitution for the EU, but they would accept that both democratic theory and practice need to recognise the qualitative changes that have taken place and will continue in the future.

International relations theories.   Most international relations theorists now recognise that realism is over-simplified, given the vast increase in international organisations of all kinds, and the extent of the transactions now conducted at an international level by non-governmental organisations. New approaches such as neo-realism, regime theory, and liberal-institutionalism have thus attempted to take account of these changes and to incorporate such phenomena into an explanatory framework.[34] There are important differences between these approaches. For example, while 'neo-realists' saw the US–Soviet conflict as a major cause for West European Integration and have therefore been somewhat pessimistic about the future of the EU with the ending of the Cold War, liberal-institutionalists believe that there are other factors which give it an enduring stability.[35] However, despite the important differences between

---

[33] Andrew Shonfield, *Europe: Journey to an Unknown Destination*, Harmondsworth: Penguin, 1972.

[34] For 'neo-realism', see R. Gilpin, *War and Change in World Politics*, Cambridge University Press, 1981; K.N. Waltz, *The Theory of International Politics*, Reading, MA: Addison-Wesley, 1979; for regime theory, see Robert O. Keohane and Joseph Nye, *Power and Interdependence*, London: HarperCollins, 2nd edn, 1989; for liberal-institutionalism, see A. Moravcsik, 'Preferences and Power in the European Community: A Liberal Intergovernmentalist Approach', *Journal of Common Market Studies*, no. 4, 1993; P. Van Ham, *The EC, Eastern Europe and European Unity*, London: Pinter, 1993. For a brief explanation of these paradigms applied to Europe, see Hugh Miall, *Shaping the New Europe*, London: Pinter/RIIA, 1993.

[35] Peter van Ham, 'The European Community after Hegemony: The Future of European Integration in a Multipolar World', *International Relations*, 5, 1993.

them, they also form a 'family' group with realism, on the basis of three common elements.

First, while they may agree with integration theorists that the EU is more highly developed than any other international organisation, they do not regard it as unique. The dense and complex interactions between states and non-governmental organisations in the contemporary world are seen as arising from shifts in the international system and particularly in the international economy. The EU is a specific, and particularly complex, example of a more general tendency. Secondly, there is much less sense of *directionality* in the International Relations approach. Some, as noted, believe that the EU will now endure, but disintegration is regarded by many as at least as probable as further integration. Thirdly, despite agreement about the EU being a complex system, the fundamental emphasis is still on the state as the major actor. Thus the supranational elements within the EU are taken much less seriously than they are by integration theorists, and inter-governmentalism is regarded as the enduring feature of the system. The implication of this is again scepticism about democratisation of the EU as a whole, and a greater emphasis upon the Member States.

The approach in this book. It was suggested earlier that attitudes towards the EU are influenced by the conceptual framework through which it is 'perceived'. But, as argued above, views about democracy in relation to the EU, also depend upon the paradigm through which one analyses it. Those who believe that they are living in an enduring state-dominated world will remain sceptical about 'democratising the EU', while those who believe that the EU is an 'embryonic Federation' will regard the whole question differently. It is therefore necessary to say a little about the approach adopted in this book. It does not adopt a highly theorised position about the integration process, but follows a rather eclectic approach. However, certain theoretical and ideological beliefs certainly condition the analysis. It might therefore be helpful to make these explicit by explaining my personal views.

The *values* professed by Spinelli in the Ventotene Manifesto are attractive. The attempt to supersede antagonistic nationalisms, to demystify the 'nation-state', and to build a viable supranational order based on peace and democracy appear to be crucial goals. Similarly, the hostility of European Federalists towards the xenophobia which underlies the attitudes of some of those who cling to the state in the name of 'sovereignty' and 'the nation' is shared by this writer. The Federalist vision is therefore a compelling one particularly when, as in the work of Spinelli, the European Federation is seen as a stage towards 'a more distant future when the political unity of the entire globe becomes possible.[36] However, one can also be very sceptical about many of the claims made by Federalists and their 'family' associates who adhere to integration theories. The implicit or explicit emphasis on 'directionality' seems unwarranted. How many experts, after all, foresaw the disintegration of the Soviet bloc? Yet *disintegration* is surely easier to predict than the construction of a new Federation or even 'ever closer union'? It also seems that the history of the EU has been dominated by an 'official version', which has paid too much credence to the elevated ideals *professed* by the politicians who helped to construct it. Alan Milward, and some of his associates, have recently written revisionist accounts of the origins of the EU, which emphasise the extent to which it was designed to safeguard the 'nation-state' rather than to transcend it.[37] Sometimes this version might be too intent on iconoclasm, but the sceptical attitude appears quite valid. Nor is this only of relevance to historical accounts: much of the EU's own analysis is inevitably propagandist, and some of those who write about it appear to accept its own claims too readily. It cannot be assumed that the EU is a new entity which has superseded the MS because the EU institutions present it as such. Clearly, the States – or some of them – remain major international actors in their own right and, in my view, they are likely to remain so for the foreseeable future.

Overall, then, the emphasis will be upon the complexity of the relationships between the EU and the MS. The Federalist and integrationist family are correct in believing that the EU is, in some senses, an entity which is more than the sum total of its components, and that there is a partially autonomous process at work in the dense network of institutional interactions. There is an erosion of the separateness between the 'domestic' and the 'external' in the MS' relationships with the EU. On the other hand, International Rela-

---

[36] Ventotene Manifesto, in Vaughan, *Post-war Integration*, op. cit., p. 16

[37] Alan Milward, *European Rescue of the Nation-State*, op. cit.; Alan Milward *et al.*, *The Frontier of National Sovereignty – History and Theory*, London: Routledge, 1993.

tions theorists seem justified in emphasising the extent to which the governments – or some of them – remain dominant within the EU, and continue to operate separately from it. And, as already noted, the notion that the EU is necessarily moving in any one direction is dubious.

Democracy and the EU

The eclectic interpretation of the EU will naturally also have implications for the discussion of democracy. Those who are sure that the EU is moving – and should continue to move – towards Federalism can be quite confident that the EU is now a 'polity' which requires fully democratic institutions. Those who are equally convinced that the states are – and should remain – dominant will contest this viewpoint. But the more 'mixed' interpretation suggested here will obviously mean that the operation of democracy is also seen as highly complex. Nor is this book written on the assumption that either the states or the EU can be categorised in terms of a single value based on simple polarities – vice *or* virtue, positive *or* negative, progressive *or* reactionary. It appears more productive to begin with a set of goals which need to be attained in practice. It is then possible to consider the EU in relation to the contribution which it makes – or might make – to the realisation of these goals.

The analysis therefore considers some of the topics – the economy, social policy, regions, citizenship, and control and accountability – which are of central importance in the theory and practice of democracy. In each case it seeks both to elucidate the current position, and to define policy goals. Because these are inevitably normative, the argument will sometimes be controversial. However, before considering any of the specific areas, it is necessary to examine the EU decision-making system.

2

THE E.U. AS A POLICY-MAKING SYSTEM

Opponents of the EU are keen to present 'Brussels' as a powerful supranational organisation which can make almost instant policy decisions which will sweep aside cherished local traditions in the interests of bureaucratic centralisation. On the other hand, those who have despaired of their own governments have sometimes looked to the EU as an agency of salvation. While these two views are in most ways diametrically opposed to one another, there is one similarity between them: both imply that the EU is a decisive and autonomous policy-making body.

The main purpose of this chapter is to counter this idea and to argue that the EU is, on the contrary, a system characterised by a tendency to 'immobilism'. It seeks to demonstrate this in three ways. In the first section it suggests that John Locke's notion of a 'social contract' provides a useful model for understanding the original institutional structure in the EU, and this was a basis for a relatively weak policy-making apparatus. The second section summarises the evolution of the EU, with particular emphasis upon the recent period. It explains the additional pressures on the institutional system which have arisen both as a result of the behaviour of certain governments, and because of the increasing complexity of the EU. The third section then examines the key policy-making institutions, and highlights the tensions within and between them. Finally, a brief conclusion draws out the implications of the main arguments.

The origins of the policy-making system and the Social Contract model

The contemporary EU is obviously vastly different from the original Communities established by the 'Six' – the European Coal and Steel Community (ECSC) in 1952 and the European Economic Community (EEC) and European Atomic Community (EURATOM) in 1958. And yet the fundamental institutional structure of the current EU was largely prefigured in the ECSC. The *history* of these early phases of integration is complex and controversial. However, understanding of the institutional system is facilitated by two fundamental factors. First, the new structures were established as a result of definite decisions and agreements reached by governments. Secondly, those agreements were articulated in precise and extensive treaty form. These two factors provide an essential insight into the nature of the system which was established in the 1950s.

The institutional set-up of the Communities had the following crucial elements which are still evident.[1]

- a treaty statement defining some concrete objectives;
- two institutions (the Commission and the Court of Justice [ECJ]) which were to play a key role in ensuring that these goals were attained, and which were simultaneously both partially autonomous from the MS and tied to them by nomination and appointments; and
- one institution, comprised of the governments of the MS (the Council of Ministers), which maintained decisive powers in crucial respects.

In other words, the founding treaties built a structural tension into the relationships between the new institutions. On the one hand the MS provided the Commission and ECJ with an important degree of autonomy; on the other hand, they sought to ensure that these supranational institutions were restricted in their scope. Why was this contradiction incorporated into the institutional relationship? Social Contract theory provides an insight into this feature of the new system.

Differing versions of social contract theory were used by Hobbes, Locke and Rousseau as a means of explaining the origins of states. In effect, they suggested that people in a pre-political society were able to agree a contract between themselves, and between themselves and their putative rulers, to create a basis for government. Such notions provoked a well-known refutation by David Hume (1711-76), who argued that we have no knowledge of any such contract but much evidence that existing governments had acquired their power by force and fraud. There was therefore no point in maintaining an intricate theory that was difficult to understand and still more difficult to defend.[2] However, Hume's objection does not

---

1
  The description is based on the EEC, which was – and remains – easily the most important of the Communities.
2
  David Hume, 'Of the Origin of Government' in *Essays Moral, Political and Literary*,

apply to the origins of the EU because there *was* a contract embodied in the founding treaties. If, therefore, the MS are substituted for individuals, social contract theory is helpful as an explanatory model for the EU institutional system. Locke's version is of primary relevance, but it is instructive to begin by considering why the other two theorists' models are *not* appropriate.

Hobbes's argument in *Leviathan* (1651) was that in a state of nature without government, there was no security for anyone and life was a war of all against all. The only means of escape was for everybody to agree to yield all their individual power to a state which would then be able to promulgate laws and create a situation of order. Even if this led to a situation which some might describe as 'tyranny', it would be preferable to living in a stateless society in which there was no security at all. The transfer of power was therefore rational for each individual. This Hobbesian contract is *not* applicable to the EU, since it would suggest that the MS had agreed to abandon their rights to self-government and to hand all their power to a new supra-state which could rule over them. This new Leviathan would then also possess full law-making powers throughout the Union, and the MS would be reduced to being passive recipients of its decisions. This is clearly not true either in practice or in the original institutional set-up.

Rousseau's version in the *Social Contract* (1762) is a little more helpful. This was based on the supposition that individuals could suppress their individual selfish wills so that a 'general will' could emerge, which would define the overall social interest. The policy and legislation of the state would then reflect this general will. Some may hold that this idea provides an appropriate representation of the EU, and that each MS seeks to suppress individual self-interest in a search for the general good. However, this would be a highly idealistic version of the reality of the decision-making process. In any case, Rousseau's Social Contract suffers from the same defect as Hobbes's for he too was suggesting that the individuals create a new state which then has full power. Rousseau's version differed, in the sense that he was arguing that the people were active participants in defining the policies of the state but, like Hobbes, the result was a state of undivided and unrestricted power. Once again, therefore,

---

discussed in John Plamenatz, *The English Utilitarians*, Oxford: Basil Blackwell, 1958, chapter 2.

Rousseau's social contract is an inadequate representation of the EU system, for the MS were certainly unwilling to establish this kind of super-state.

Of far greater relevance is the notion of the Social Contract contained in Locke's *Second Treatise on Civil Government*, (1690). His starting point was that the inhabitants of pre-political society, who were fundamentally self-interested individuals, already had a conception of their rights and of the law. The point of establishing the state was not to bring about any total transformation but to introduce some benefits, which were unattainable in the state of nature. In particular, the state would be able to enforce the existing law in a more effective and equitable manner so as to safeguard and promote the existing interests of the members. However, the condition was that this new political order would be answerable to the members of society who created it, and would respect their existing rights. Furthermore, the members would determine the extent of power wielded by the new political entity: the state could not, ultimately, decide its own prerogatives.

This Lockeian Social Contract provides a helpful insight into the nature of the EU. First, for Locke, the new state was really an instrument to *facilitate* the attainment of existing interests. This was also the basis for the EU. Secondly, he was arguing that, although members of society were able to define their own goals, *it was necessary to establish new legal and political institutions so that these goals could be attained more effectively*. Again, this is parallelled by the establishment of the treaties to provide a legal system, with the ECJ to preside over it, and the European Commission to suggest policies which would help in the attainment of the aims. In other words, the underlying assumption was that the individual MS would not be able to attain their goals without new institutions which possessed some degree of independence from their creators. But thirdly, it was nevertheless axiomatic that the people (through a legislature) retained the ultimate right to determine the law and the extent of the power wielded by the new executive. This again is suggestive of the relationship between the MS and the 'executive' – that is, between the Council of Ministers and the Commission. As in the Lockeian contract, there was a tension between the need to establish institutions with sufficient *independence* to achieve the aims which had been defined, and the need to ensure that they were ultimately in a relation of *dependence* on the governments that had created them.

However, there is one feature of the EU system which is more sophisticated than that suggested in Locke's Social Contract.

While Locke talked of the 'people' and the need for the state to rest on consent, he actually constructed his political system primarily in the interests of those who already had power in the pre-political society.[3] In reality, it was their rights which were to be protected and their consent which was sought. On the assumption that the MS (rather than their citizens) constituted the 'society' that originally created the EU system, it was more progressive in this respect than the Lockeian system. For it simultaneously recognised the inequality between the MS and moderated it within its own institutional structures. Thus while the larger states were granted greater weight in the decision-making process, there was also a partial re-distribution of power, since the smaller states were accorded a stronger role (in votes in the Council, in the appointment of Commissioners, and in representation in the European Parliament) than that warranted purely by their population sizes or resources.[4] Locke's system contained no mechanism for securing the consent of those without power in society, but the founding treaties of the EU were designed to accommodate the individual interests of all the MS.

If the Social Contract provides a useful analogy for the foundation of the EEC, what was the purpose of the Treaty of Rome – the original contract? Although it would be simplistic to suggest that this may be reduced to the attainment of a single objective, it is clear that the most fundamental aim was to create a customs union – and ultimately a full common market. It is for this reason that the treaty pays far more attention – in terms of concrete obligations – to economic and commercial matters than to any other issues. This is not to say that none of the participant governments attached importance to such matters as political unity or social policy, but the

[3] There is controversy amongst experts on Locke as to the extent to which he based his system entirely on the interests of property owners. This interpretation is influenced by C.B. Macpherson, *The Political Theory of Possessive Individualism*, Oxford University Press, 1962. For a different view see John Dunn, *The Political Thought of John Locke*, Cambridge University Press, 1969.

[4] This may be illustrated by comparing the two extreme poles among the current EU members. In 1991 Luxembourg had a population of 400,000 and a GDP of 7 billion ECU, while Germany's population was 79.3 million and its GDP 1269 billion ECU. Luxembourg has one Commissioner and six MEPs, while Germany has two Commissioners and 99 MEPs. Luxembourg has two votes within the Council of Ministers and Germany has ten.

treaty represented the concrete 'contract'. Viewed in this way, the balance of power between the institutions is not difficult to understand.

The establishment of a common market was held to be in the long-term interest of all the MS, on the underlying assumptions that economies of scale, competition and comparative advantage would maximise benefits. However, while each government accepted that this would be beneficial in the long-term, each had domestic interests (for example less competitive industries) which would suffer by the creation of the market.[5] Simultaneously each was aware that all other governments also had such interests and would be tempted to protect them. Nor was it solely a matter of protecting weaker industries for, as each government was primarily supportive of its own domestic interests, each would also be likely to seek competitive advantages against the other MS. In these circumstances, it would be extremely difficult for any substantial progress to be made if the governments *simply* made an agreement amongst themselves to work towards a common market. There was thus a need for *partly* autonomous agencies which would propel them towards their goal (and this would have the additional advantage of strengthening the hands of governments against domestic interests they wished to withstand). The four principal components of this autonomy were:

– the establishment of a very extensive and detailed 'contract' in the sense that the Community was based on a Treaty with the status of 'law';
– an agreement that such law would be incorporated within the domestic legal systems of the MS and supersede existing laws in the event of conflicts;
– the establishment of the ECJ to ensure compliance with Community law by MS and their nationals; and
– the appointment by the MS of a European Commission to suggest the legislation that would be necessary to bring about the goals of the Community and to act as its guardian.

The objective was thus to ensure that the Commission and ECJ had sufficient *independence* to promote the original objectives of the

---

[5] See, for example, Roy Willis, *France, Germany and the New Europe*, Stanford University Press, 1968; Robert Marjolin, *Architect of European Union: Memoirs, 1911-1986*, London: Weidenfeld and Nicolson, 1989; Milward, op. cit.

Treaty, while also ensuring that they remained *dependent* upon the MS. This tension was built into the institutional relationships, and has been present ever since. Indeed it has been one of the EU's defining characteristics and, as such, provides an overall context for its policy-making. *However, neither Locke's Social Contract nor the Treaty of Rome are models for dynamic institutional decision-making.* They are designed to transfer power in limited realms to new institutions, while leaving the existing power-holders free in other spheres. Obviously, the Social Contract is only an analogy for the EU system, but it provides an important insight into its tendency towards immobilism.

Yet there was an unpredictable element inherent in the situation, which meant that the EU could not be contained within the terms of the original contract. One early example of this concerned agriculture. Thus while the Common Agricultural Policy (CAP) had only been set out in general terms in the Treaty of Rome, it proved to be the main economic obstacle in the negotiation of the customs union. It was settled in stages, with a major crisis in 1965, and the establishment of the 'own resources' financing system in 1969.[6] But the CAP, which was effectively a concession to farming interests as part of the bargain necessary to secure agreement for the removal of tariffs on industrial goods, became the most fundamental common policy of the Community. The CAP accounted for 60-70% of the budget until the 1988 reform and remains easily the biggest item of expenditure (scheduled still to take 46% of the total budget even in 1999).[7] Similarly the CAP has led to a vast committee and policy-making apparatus. However, the whole policy was really a necessary by-product of the construction of the EU rather than a primary goal.

More generally, the development of the EU has led it to grow in various directions which have introduced ever greater complexity into the system, exacerbating the problems of effective policy-making. This evolution is now summarised.

---

[6] Milward, op. cit.; Hans von der Groeben, *The European Community: The Formative Years: The Struggle to Establish the Common Market and the Political Union (1958-1966)*, Luxembourg: Office for Official Publications of the European Communities, 1987; Desmond Dinan, *Ever Closer Union? An Introduction to the European Community*, London: Macmillan, 1994.

[7] Neill Nugent, *The Government and Politics of the European Union*, London: Macmillan (3rd edn), 1994, chapters 12 and 13.

EU institutional development

Only three institutions were of real importance in the early years of
the EEC: the Council of Ministers (Council), the Commission, and
the ECJ.[8] The ECJ steadily advanced the process of integration by
judgments establishing the supremacy of Community law, thereby
increasing the penetration of the Community into the 'domestic'
systems of the MS.[9] Some of these judgments – in particular those
on gender equality – were to make the role of EC law very visible
(see Chapter 4). Much more of the ECJ's work was relatively 'low
profile', but extremely important in consolidating the status of the
new legal system, particularly by bringing about a situation in which
domestic Courts accepted the ECJ's role as the ultimate interpreter
and arbiter of Community law. Given the supremacy of EC law in
the event of possible clashes with domestic legislation, this was of
crucial significance. Moreover, the ECJ's role was of particular
importance when the general impetus towards EU development was
lacking because political problems were impeding process. In these
circumstances, the apparently more technical and neutral nature of
the ECJ enabled it to maintain the process of integration.[10] Indeed
some of its most important judgments on issues of gender equality
were in the period of so-called 'Eurosclerosis' during the 1970s.
Such work by the ECJ not only clarified the legal position, but
helped build up campaigns for new forms of EU action in the area
of social policy, thereby also extending the integration process. The
role of the ECJ as a supranational actor has therefore undoubtedly
been of great significance. Nevertheless its position is necessarily
circumscribed by the two bodies which have explicit policy-making
prerogatives. The rest of this section therefore concentrates upon
the Commission and the Council in a situation of increasing
complexity.

   As already noted, the structural tension in the dependence-

---

[8] For full examinations of the institutions, see Dinan, op. cit., and Nugent, op. cit.
(Dinan provides greater historical and contextual analysis and Nugent more detail
on the institutions themselves).
[9] Josephine Steiner, *A Textbook of EEC Law*, 4th edn, Blackstone Press, 1994;
Nugent, op. cit., chapter 8.
[10] J.H.H. Weiler, 'Journey to an unknown destination: A Retrospective and
Prospective of the European Court of Justice in the arena of political integration',
Journal of Common Market Studies, 31, 4, December 1993.

independence relationship between the Commission and the Council of Ministers was built into the system.[11] The Treaty of Rome thus established the Commission as a crucial actor in all aspects of policy-making, implementation, and 'policing'. There were also constitutional safeguards for its position as the motor of the integration process. It was granted initiating power (Article 155), and it was stipulated that Council members could amend a Commission proposal only when they were unanimous (Article 149). If unanimity was not achieved, the governments had only two options – acceptance or outright rejection. The treaties also stipulated that the Commission shall 'be completely independent' and 'neither seek nor take instructions from any Government or from any other body'.[12] In theory, the Council had no initiating role but Article 152 gave it the right to 'request the Commission to undertake any studies which the Council considers desirable for the attainment of the common objectives, and to submit any appropriate proposals'. This provided it with leverage over the Commission's policy-making role. Moreover, as the primary legislative body, the Council had to approve all important Commission proposals.

The latent tension between the two institutions came to a head in 1965. The first President of the Commission, Walter Hallstein, wished to see the Commission evolve into a more powerful institution in a more supranational Community. He therefore deliberately linked the development of the CAP (which de Gaulle wanted) with moves towards Supranationalism to which the French leader was bitterly opposed. De Gaulle, the supreme advocate of a 'Europe of States', was determined to thwart any such pretensions by 'stateless', denationalised' Commission officials.[13] France thus operated a boycott of Community institutions during the summer of 1965 and in September de Gaulle escalated the conflict by announcing that

[11] Peter Ludlow, 'The European Commission' in Robert Keohane and Stanley Hoffmann (eds), *The New European Community: Decisionmaking and Institutional Change*, Boulder, CO: Westview Press, 1991; G. Edwards and D. Spence (eds), *The Commission of the European Communities*, Harlow: Longman, 1994; E. Kirchner, *Decision-Making in the European Community: The Council Presidency and European Integration*, Manchester University Press, 1992; S. Bulmer and W. Wessels, *The European Council*, London: Macmillan, 1987.

[12] Art 10.2. of the Treaty Establishing a Single Commission of the European Communities (Merger Treaty), 8 April 1965.

[13] Dinan, op. cit. p 55.

France would not accept a provision of the Treaty of Rome, due to come into effect, which would have introduced qualified majority voting into the Council of Ministers on a limited range of issues. The result of the conflict, in January 1966, was the so-called Luxembourg agreement. In theory, this was a compromise between de Gaulle and the other MS, for it did not lead to any amendment of the Treaty to establish unanimity as the operating system within the Council.[14] In practice, however, it constituted a victory for de Gaule in two major respects. First, it ensured that, in practice, unanimous decision-making would be the rule whenever a particular state declared that it had a major interest at stake. Secondly, the confidence of the Commission was crushed and it became very wary, until the late 1970s, about taking the initiative unless it was fairly sure that it would secure the Council's support. De Gaulle had thus pushed the balance very much towards the dependency relationship: EU institutions and policies could not develop beyond the wishes of the MS and, in the final analysis, beyond those of the most reluctant State.

During the 1970s the elevation of the governments over the Commission was intensified. In the 1970s a new, and purely inter-governmental institution, European Political Co-operation (EPC) was established outside the framework of the Community institutions to bring about foreign policy co-ordination.[15] Moreover, in 1974 the European Council of Heads of Government was also set up to formalise the increasing use of summit meetings to define policy objectives. In theory, this did not supersede the Council's role but, in practice, it developed into an increasingly powerful

[14] The relevant part of the agreement of 28-29 January 1966 stated: 'I. Where, in the case of decisions which may be taken by majority vote on a proposal of the Commission, very important interests of one or more partners are at stake, the Members of the Council will endeavour, within a reasonable time, to reach solutions which can be adopted by all the Members of the Council while respecting their mutual interests and those of the Community, in accordance with Art.2 of the Treaty. II. With regard to the preceding paragraph, the French delegation considers that where very important interests are at stake the discussion must be continued until unanimous agreement is reached. III. The six delegations note that there is a divergence of views on what should be done in the event of a failure to reach complete agreement. IV. The six delegations nevertheless consider that this divergence does not prevent the Community's work being resumed in accordance with the normal procedure.'

[15] Simon Nuttall, *European Political Cooperation*, Oxford: Clarendon Press, 1992.

body.[16] In a situation of economic recession, and political instability following the Middle East war and the oil embargo, the Community and its institutions appeared to be entering a phase of crisis. To an extent, this was alleviated by the close relations between France and West Germany, under Giscard d'Estaing and Schmidt. But this did not help the Commission as neither of them had much respect for its position and Giscard, in particular, went out of his way to snub its President.[17] Roy Jenkins, who became President in 1977, eventually succeeded in partly restoring the prestige of the Commission, but he had no illusions about Giscard's attitudes, believing that he really wanted 'to cut down the power of the Commission, to reduce or eliminate our political role' and to 'make us all servants of the European Council'.[18] The accession of the Conservative government in Britain in May 1979 accentuated the difficulties for the Commission. In effect, it meant that no major policy initiatives were possible until Britain secured a satisfactory budgetary settlement (eventually agreed in June 1984).[19]

Yet, while the subordination of the Commission to the governments remained clear throughout the period, it would be misleading to suggest that the Community was frozen and simply controlled by MS. First, the economic interdependence between the countries was steadily developing and was leading to new developments. The first attempt at Economic and Monetary integration in the early 1970s had come to nothing, but the European and Monetary System (EMS) began in 1979 and proved very effective.[20] Secondly, an increasing number of demands were now made for Community policies, which would previously have been considered solely domestic affairs. In particular, from the early 1970s there were more active demands for more interventionist forms of social policy.

[16] See pp. 43ff. for a discussion of the relationship.

[17] Dinan, op. cit., p. 93.

[18] 'Giscard's Plan to Hobble the Commission', 14 September 1978, in Roy Jenkins, *European Diary, 1977-1981*, London: Collins, 1989, p. 311.

[19] John W. Young, *Britain and European Unity, 1945-92*, London: Macmillan, 1993, chapter 6.

[20] Valerio Lintner, 'Monetary Integration in the European Community' in Valerio Lintner and Sonia Mazey, *The European Community: Economic and Political Aspects*, Maidenhead: McGraw-Hill, 1991; M. Artis, 'The European Monetary System' in A.M. El-Agraa (ed.), *Economics of the European Community*, London: Philip Allan, 1990.

Regional policies, which had effectively begun as a 'sop' to Britain in 1974, also now became a necessary part of the Community's agenda as compensation to 'weaker' areas. Thirdly, as already noted, the ECJ continued to strengthen the domestic impact of Community law. Fourthly, the first directly elected European Parliament (EP) in 1979 made this body far more 'visible'. Having already secured some limited budgetary powers in 1970 and 1975, the EP – though relatively weak – now provided a focus for demands for new policy competences and institutional changes.[21] Fifthly, the very failures of the 1970s – particularly the general downturn in economies, accompanied by a growth of non-tariff barriers – created pressures for the development of new initiatives by the EU. Finally, there was a widely shared conviction that the current institutional system was impeding progress. This point has particular relevance and merits further explanation.

The original treaty had assumed that the MS would be able to agree about the policies that would be necessary to ensure their common goals. The advent of the Thatcher government, with a demonstrable willingness to block progress on all matters until Britain's budgetary rebate was agreed, introduced a completely different element into the situation, for it implied that the most reluctant MS could dictate the pace of development. Moreover, it was clear that the difficulties of decision-making within the Council of Ministers were likely to increase with the EU's enlargement to the South, which began with the entry of Greece in 1981, and would be followed in 1986 by that of Portugal and Spain. Such enlargements not only increased the number of MS to be accommodated, but also introduced countries with quite different levels of economic development from the original 'six' (this had also been the case with the entry of Ireland in 1973). This would further complicate the decision-making process, inevitably making agreement more difficult to reach. All these considerations meant that there was growing pressure, from several sources, for institutional reforms. With the settlement of the British budgetary dispute in June 1984, the European Council, under the French Presidency, therefore established the Dooge committee to improve co-operation. How-

---

[21] Social Policy is discussed in chapter 4, Regional Policy in chapter 5, and the European Parliament in chapter 7.

ever, political arguments were not, in themselves, the catalyst for change.

During the recession of the 1970s, the first inclination of governments had been towards national retrenchment, accompanied by a growth of non-tariff barriers, in an attempt to maintain domestic employment. By the early 1980s a coalition of business interests and European governments, working on neo-liberal economic doctrine, interpreted the situation quite differently. The answer, they felt, was a much faster move towards a Single European Market so as to modernise European industry and withstand competition from Japan, the United States and Newly Industrialised countries. The fact that the Thatcher government was committed to neo-liberalism, while other governments sought institutional change, made the conditions ripe for a breakthrough. Moreover, the appointment in January 1985 of Jacques Delors to the post of President of the Commission provided a further impetus.[22]

The result of this favourable conjunction was the Single European Act (SEA), which was agreed in December 1985 and implemented after the ratification process in July 1987.[23] The central feature of the SEA was an amendment of the Treaty of Rome, defining the internal market as an 'area without internal frontiers in which the free movement of goods, persons, services and capital is ensured', and setting a time-table for its achievement by the end of 1992. This constituted an assault on the proliferation of non-tariff barriers in such areas as public procurement policies and the service sector, and specified that the majority of harmonisation measures necessary for the attainment of the single market (and certain other economic policies) would be subject to qualified majority voting within the Council. The SEA also amended the existing treaties in such areas as social policy, economic and social cohesion, research and development, and the environment, and enjoined the states to co-operate to ensure a convergence of economic and monetary policy, taking account of the experience of the EMS. Foreign policy was now also partially brought within the competence of the Community although it still operated on an entirely inter-governmental basis.

[22] Dinan, op. cit., chapter 5; Andrew Moravcsik, 'Negotiating the Single European Act' in Keohane and Hoffmann, op. cit.; George Ross, *Jacques Delors and European Integration*, Oxford/Cambridge: Polity Press, 1995.

[23] Clive H. Church and Dermot Keogh (eds), *The Single European Act – A Transnational Study*, Dublin: Erasmus Bureau, 1992.

Under the SEA the Commission was also given greater scope in implementation, particularly in measures relating to the attainment of the Single Market, and the EP gained some significant new powers, primarily on legislative proposals to promote the internal marked, which gave the Council an incentive to reach accommodation with the EP in this area. (see chapter 7 for further details).

The SEA undoubtedly introduced new dynamism into the EU, and brought about greater institutional change than any previous developments, but it was an unstable compromise which was soon to reveal a deep rift between the British government and the prevailing consensus. The EP, the Commission, and some member States, had seen it as a preliminary to far greater change, while the UK's interest was to restrict the process to the agreement that had been reached – essentially guaranteeing an open market without significant intervention in social or monetary policies, and without major institutional reform. With varied motivations and interests, the other major actors sought to propel the Community further forward. The tensions mounted during 1987 as the poorer EU countries, backed by Delors, sought additional regional aid to offset some of the negative effects of the Single Market on their economies, and Thatcher resisted any increase in expenditure. But the 'Delors 1 budgetary package' was finally accepted in a compromise in February 1988.[24] However, the conflicts then mounted again and made the subsequent phase of development more complex than any other in the EU's history.

An important stage in the continuing dispute was the decision of the European Council in Hanover in June 1988, to establish the Delors committee to prepare a report on economic and monetary union. The conflict between the British government and the apparent Community consensus then broadened to encompass the social dimension, Economic and Monetary Union (EMU), institutional reform, and policy towards the post-socialist states in Eastern Europe. In June 1989 Britain was isolated in its attitude to the Delors report, and in December in Strasbourg the European Council decided (against Thatcher's wishes) to establish an intergovernmental conference to prepare an amendment of the Treaty so that the

---

[24] The official title of the budgetary package was 'Making a Success of the Single Act'. It sought to conciliate the British government by proposing reductions in CAP expenditure and budgetary discipline while satisfying the four poorest MS by doubling the social and regional funds. Dinan, op. cit., pp. 152-4.

EMU could be implemented. All the other governments also accepted the Social Charter, to which Thatcher was bitterly opposed, so Britain appeared to be completely alone.

The recalcitrance of the British government was the most visible manifestation of the increasing difficulties within the policy-making system. Nevertheless, it was far less significant than the dramatic changes in 1989-90, with the collapse of the Soviet system in Eastern Europe. In particular, the unification of Germany consolidated the shift in the balance of power within the EU which had gradually been taking place. During the 1960s and '70s France and Germany had been a 'privileged partnership' and developments within the EU had normally been based on their prior agreement.[25] However, having finally achieved the long-term goal of unification, it was evident that Germany's economic dominance would now be accompanied by a greater political assertiveness.[26] There was thus widespread concern that the new Germany could become a hegemonic power in Europe. The wish to 'contain' it within a strengthened EU provided impetus for further integration in 1990-91.[27]

For some time, the EP had been insisting that monetary union could not be considered in isolation from political union – a view which was shared by Delors. The position was strengthened very considerably in April 1990 when Mitterrand and Kohl sent a joint letter to the President of the European Council proposing that a second inter-governmental conference should be held on political union.

> ...to strengthen the democratic legitimacy of the union, render its institutions more efficient, ensure unity and coherence of the union's economic, monetary and political action and to define and implement a common foreign and security policy.[28]

[25] Haig Simonian, *The Privileged Partnership: Franco-German Relations and the European Community, 1969-84*, Oxford: Clarendon Press, 1985.

[26] The extent of the long-term preoccupation with unification is documented in Timothy Garton Ash, *In Europe's Name: Germany and the Divided Continent*, London: Cape, 1993.

[27] Lily Gardner Feldman, 'The EC and German Unification' in Leon Hurwitz and Christian Lequesne (eds), *The State of the European Community: Policies, Institutions and Debates in the Transition Years*, Boulder, CO: Lynne Rienner, 1991; Keohane and Hoffmann, op. cit.

[28] Reproduced in Finn Laursen and Sophie Vanhoonacker (eds), *The Intergovernmental Conference on Political Union*, Maastricht: Martinus Nijhoff, 1992, p. 276.

This was endorsed in a Dublin meeting of the Council in June, which established a parallel intergovernmental conference

...to transform the Community from an entity based mainly on economic integration and political co-operation into a union of a political nature, including a common foreign and security policy.[29]

It was then widely anticipated that the two inter-governmental conferences (IGCs), on monetary union and political union, which worked throughout the next year would bring about further major stages in the integration process, although it was equally clear that the underlying conflicts had not been resolved. Nor was there co-ordination between the two IGCs. Many of the governments, including those of France and Germany, and the Commission were committed to EMU, but the ideas about political union were much less clearly defined. Moreover, while Delors had wanted to increase the Commission's responsibilities he actually found it difficult even to sustain its current role, and denounced 'an enterprise to demolish the Commission' or put it 'on the sidelines'.[30] Agreement was finally reached in Maastricht in December 1991 (and signed in February 1992), leading to the convoluted Treaty of European Union.[31]

The first notable point about the treaty was that monetary union was its central feature. The procedures, mechanisms, and convergence criteria were set out in considerable detail, and EMU was explicitly justified as an integral part of the EU's commitment to a competitive open market. Yet although monetary union lay at the heart of the treaty, the British explicitly 'opted out' of the commitment to the final stage of irrevocably fixed exchange rates (and the Danes were hold a referendum on the issue). Perhaps it was assumed that all would eventually join, but it was unprecedented to initiate a treaty in which the central core was not binding on all its members. Secondly, the agreements signed at Maastricht were highly complex. Instead of incorporating all aspects of the accord into the Com-

[29] Quoted in Dinan, op. cit., p. 166.

[30] Quoted in Ross, op. cit., p. 149.

[31] For a full analysis, see Richard Corbett, *The Treaty of Maastricht: From Conception to Ratification: A Comprehensive Reference Guide*, Harlow: Longman, 1993. For a full explanation of the changes introduced by the Maastricht Treaty, see C. Church and D. Phinnemore, *European Union and European Community*, Brighton: Harvester Wheatsheaf, 1994.

munity, the result was to introduce 'three pillars'. One pillar comprised amendments to the EC treaties, and used full Community procedures (with elements of reform). But the two other 'pillars' – Common Foreign and Security Policy, and Justice and Home Affairs –remained largely *outside* those procedures. The Commission was to be involved, but there was to be very little accountability to the EP or to the ECJ. Thirdly, all the members, except Britain, signed a separate protocol – the Social Chapter. This could not be incorporated into the Treaty because it would have involved amending the Treaty of Rome and Britain would not agree to this. Instead, the other members stated that they could adopt a variety of measures – some by Qualified Majority Voting, and others by unanimity – without the presence of British ministers. However, Britain would still be involved in decision-making on aspects of social policy which were based on the Treaty of Rome or the Single European Act. It was probably anticipated that Britain would join at a later date and that the Social Chapter could then be incorporated into the Treaty, but this did not make the procedure any less obscure. It was also significant that the European Council was now explicitly recognised as the driving force in the new European Union. As this body had been created in 1974 at the height of the intergovernmentalist era and had no basis in the Treaty of Rome, this appeared to downgrade the original EC procedures.

However, it would be wrong to imply that the Maastricht Treaty simply constituted a new step towards a 'Europe of States'. The new Committee of the Regions, which was now established, gave some comfort to those who believed that sub-state power was finally being recognised. (see Chapter 5). Maastricht also widened the scope of the EU by including references to consumer protection, public health, culture, education, industry, development and trans-European networks. It also extended the use of qualified majority voting to some aspects of these policies, and to vocational training policy and certain features of environmental policy. The European Parliament also secured yet another legislative procedure, although this led to no fundamental alteration in power relationships (see chapter 7). But the main point about Maastricht was that it reinforced the enormous complexity in the EU's current stage of development, which was reflected in its institutional system.

This trend has continued since then. The defeat of the Danish government in the referendum in June 1992 thus led it to decide not to participate in the single currency, not to be bound by stage three of monetary union, and not to participate in any aspects of the Common Foreign and Security Policy, which had defence implications.[32] These concessions (plus clarifications over subsidiarity and citizenship) brought about a favourable vote in the second referendum in May 1993, but further complicated the decision-making system. Moreover, the two currency crises in the summers of 1992 and 1993, which almost destroyed the EMS, made it doubtful whether EMU would be attained, at least in accordance with the original timetable, and with all MS included. Such events, coupled with the EU's failure in the Yugoslav crisis, the continuation of economic recession, the end of the Cold War, and the growth of nationalism and instability throughout Europe, checked the impetus towards further integration. The Commission became more circumspect in its behaviour long before Delors' 'reign' finally came to an end in January 1995 and Jacques Santer, who then took over as President, was likely to be much weaker than his predecessor.[33]

Enlargement added to the complications. Because qualified majority voting had now become the dominant decision-making procedure in the Council, the British government sought to protect its existing blocking minority even after the new states joined. France, Germany, Italy and Britain have 10 votes each; Spain 8; Belgium, Greece, the Netherlands and Portugal 5; Denmark and Ireland 3; and Luxembourg 2. Out of this total of 76 votes, 54 constituted a qualified majority, and this meant that the five larger states could not outvote the smaller seven. Similarly, two large states could not constitute a blocking minority alone. When the enlargement negotiations were concluded, it was agreed that Austria and Sweden would be granted four votes each, and Norway and Finland three. This raised the total number of votes in the Council to 90 and in March 1994, despite British opposition, it was agreed that the blocking minority would be raised from 23 to

---

[32] For a full explanation of the concession to Denmark, see 'The Referendums' in Juliet Lodge (ed.), *the European Community and the Challenge of the Future*, London: Pinter (2nd edn, 1993, appendix).

[33] This is not necessarily because either Santer himself or the Commission as a whole are less effective. But as the second-choice President (after Major had vetoed the original candidate, Jean-Luc Dehaene) from the smallest MS, in a very difficult situation for the EU, Santer started his term of office with severe disadvantages.

27.[34] After the Norwegian rejection of membership, the blocking minority was reduced to 26, meaning that a qualified majority currently constitutes 62 out of a total of 87 votes.

This conflict was probably dictated mainly by the internal politics of the British Conservative party. Nevertheless, it indicated the likelihood of further controversies in the event of further enlargement, and indeed, over any proposals to increase the use of qualified majority voting in the Council. As comparatively small countries with high living standards, Sweden, Austria and Finland, which joined the EU in January 1995, were also relatively easy to absorb in economic terms. However, as they may be expected simultaneously to demand high standards in environmental and social policies, while wishing to maintain the right of veto, they will probably add to the complexity in the decision-making process. If further enlargement to the East takes place, to which the EU is pledged, the economic and political difficulties will be far greater. These would probably lead to an intensification of pressures which would necessitate major institutional reform.[35]

The argument thus far may be summarised as follows. The 'social contract' model of the original treaties limited the opportunities for dynamic decision-making by the new institutions by circumscribing the autonomy of the Commission (and the ECJ). This was then reinforced by attempts to strengthen the role of the governments, particularly by de Gaulle, and by the subsequent establishment and development of the European Council. Moreover, the successive enlargements of the EU have increased both the range of its policy competences and the diversity of interests that need to be reconciled. In other words, while the Lockeian 'social contract' was not designed for a decisive policy-making, the complexity of the current EU is vastly greater than it was in 1958, and this reinforces the difficulties. This may now be illustrated further by considering the major policy-making institutions in a little more detail.

---

[34] However it was conceded that if 'members of the Council representing a total of 23 to 26 votes indicate their intention to oppose the adoption by the Council of a decision by qualified majority', then 'a reasonable time' would be allowed to elapse to see if agreement could be found before the new blocking figure was used. Nugent, op. cit., p. 448.

[35] Miles, op. cit.

Co-operation and conflict: The Commission and the governments

The Commission may be weak in terms of its democratic legitimacy (see Chapter 7) but, given the current institutional set-up, a strong Commission is normally a necessity if the EU is to adopt an active role. Otherwise there is likely to be a tendency towards passive policy-making through the 'lowest common denominator' of MS interests, except when the larger states have an urgent agenda to promote. Yet the Commission is not well equipped to play the roles entrusted to it by the treaties.

In the first place, it is inevitably a relatively incoherent body. Its members are appointed by the governments without any clear criteria of selection, and are therefore ideologically and nationally diverse, and lack experience of working together. Moreover, it is evident that the MS tend to choose those whom they believe will be 'reliable', and this 'national' perspective is reinforced by the fact that the individual Commissioners then normally appoint their compatriots to the increasingly powerful *cabinets*. It is therefore extremely difficult to generate a common ethos and sense of purpose amongst the Commission. These problems are exacerbated by its relations with the Council 'above' and its own organisation 'below'.

Some of the larger MS tend to believe that they should secure full control of the policy-making process. There have therefore been periodic attempts to reorganise the institutional structure so as to confirm the Commission's subordination to the governments.[36] Even though these have so far been resisted the Commission's position is circumscribed in various respects. In particular, the Council has its own secretariat, which has become increasingly powerful in recent years, and the MS have ensured that their own bureaucracies are well represented in all the forums in which policy-making and implementation is carried out.[37] Moreover, there is the additional difficulty that the Presidency of the Council is on a six-monthly rotating basis, and this means that the Commission does not even have a very consistent policy-making environment

---

[36] Ross, op. cit., pp 148-9; Dinan op. cit., pp. 180-1; 219.

[37] The Council Secretariat, which has a staff of approximately 2,000 (of whom nearly two-thirds are interpreters and translators), serves the country which occupies the Presidency. Since the Presidency organises and chairs the meetings of both the European Council and the Council of Ministers, the Council secretariat serves both bodies.

in which to work. This is partly alleviated by the so-called troika system (in which the previous and subsequent Council Presidents work with the current one), and by close liaison with the Secretariat of the Council. However, the element of unpredictability in the situation renders the Commission's task difficult.

Its own structure reinforces these problems. The total staffing is less than 13,000, including 3,200 working in joint research centres, and 3,000 translators.[38] This is clearly inadequate in respect of the vast increase in responsibilities which have grown with the expansion of EU competences. But the problems are compounded by the Commission's division into twenty-three separate Directorate Generals (DGs), further undermining its cohesiveness and effectiveness, without the DGs even having the merit of coinciding with the portfolios held by the Commissioners. In 1991 Delors established a review to lead to fundamental reorganisation so as to enhance co-ordination, but this has not been implemented.[39] Moreover, the DGs often have strong inclinations of their own, which may be reinforced by the national and ideological composition of their senior staff. These may clash with one another – for example there have been major conflicts between the neo-liberal DGIV (Competition), particularly when controlled by Leon Brittan, and the more interventionist DGIII (Internal Market and Industrial Affairs), DGV (Employment, Industrial Relations and Social Affairs) and DGXIII (Telecommunications, Information Technologies and Industries).[40]

It is thus exceptionally difficult for the Commission to succeed in maintaining its credentials as the 'motor' of European integration. It probably has a chance of doing so only when, as in the case of Delors, it is led by an assertive major politician – normally from one of the larger countries – who is prepared to stand up to political leaders in the Council and, with the help of his own *chef de cabinet* and the Secretary-General of the Commission, is able to impose authority on the organisation.

While the growth in the Commission's staffing has not been commensurate with its increasing responsibilities, the bureaucracies which serve the Councils and the MS have shown a sharp increase in numbers since the establishment of the EEC. Whereas the

[38] Dinan, op. cit., p. 213.
[39] Ross, op. cit., pp. 161-5.
[40] Ross, op. cit., pp. 115-24, 129-35, 172-81; Dinan, op. cit., pp. 370-1.

Council of Ministers meetings in the early days were comparatively simple affairs, staffed by relatively few officials, there is now a complex structure in Brussels, dealing with vast amounts of business on a daily basis.

At the apex is the European Council, the twice-yearly meetings of the Heads of Government. The country that holds the Presidency also represents the EU internationally (with the President of the Commission), and chairs both the European Council meetings, and also those of the various Council of Ministers (see below). The Presidency also works through the Council's secretariat, headed by the Secretary-General. This body, as already noted, works closely with the Commission, but there are also elements of rivalry and mutual suspicion between them, stemming from their differing roles. In theory, the task of the European Council itself is to provide a sense of strategic direction to the EU and, as noted earlier, major new developments normally depend upon agreement at this level. However, the European Council is just as often preoccupied with ironing out disagreements between the MS which have not been resolved elsewhere in the system.

In the founding treaties, the highest intergovernmental body was not the European Council, but the Council of Ministers. In fact there are now over twenty such Councils, arranged in an unofficial hierarchy. The highest, whose members are the Foreign Ministers, is the General Affairs Council. This deals with the 'high policy' issues of economic and political integration and meets monthly (except in August). Just below it is ECOFIN, comprising Finance ministers. This also meets monthly (with a twice yearly retreat) and has become still more important with the development of the EMS, the prospect of EMU, and the currency crises of 1992-3. Other key Councils, which meet very frequently, are those of Agriculture and the Internal Market.

All these are served by the two Committees of Permanent Representatives (COREPER). COREPER 2 deals with the high policy areas that are considered by the General Affairs Council, and ECOFIN, while COREPER 1 considers most other matters (although agriculture is sometimes dealt with by a separate committee and ECOFIN sometimes by-passes COREPER and liaises directly with a special monetary committee drawn from national finance ministries).[41]

[41] Dinan, op. cit., p. 251.

Each COREPER meets at least weekly, serviced by at least ten working groups of national officials, meeting daily. The COREPER system was not based on the original founding treaties and was originally viewed with suspicion by the Commission. However, it was officially recognised in 1965 and has subsequently played an integral and increasingly important role in policy-making. Building on a decision of the 1974 Paris summit that the permanent representatives should act as a filtering system for the Council, the COREPERs categorise all items as either 'A' (ready for automatic approval) or 'B' for discussion. This obviously heightens their own decision-making role. However, it would be misleading to suggest that this is necessarily in opposition to that of the Commission, for there is also much co-operation between the national and EU bureaucracies in Brussels.

Indeed the potential conflict between intergovernmental and supranational elements is only one of the tensions within the policy-making system. Another is caused by the hierarchy between the MS, not only in the formal voting system, but in the whole way in which the Councils operate. The larger and wealthier states have far bigger civil services, wider international involvements, and generally more 'clout'. Their leaders often have a correspondingly elevated view of their historical importance. It is therefore more likely for policies to be initiated successfully when one of the major states (particularly France or Germany) controls the Presidency.[42] While it would be wrong to imply that there is any general alliance between the smaller states, it is true that some of them have seen the Commission as an ally in maintaining their own position against potential Great Power hegemony. This lack of unity between the MS in relation to the status of the Commission leads to a final, more general point, which is of crucial importance.

It is deeply misleading to represent the Council of Ministers or the European Council simply as EU institutions, for the MS are rivals as well as partners.[43] In other words, they are often intent on competition rather than co-operation. This is the reason for the growth of COREPER and the increasingly sophisticated organisations within some of the *domestic* bureaucracies, which are designed

[42] Kirchner, op. cit., p. 110.

[43] R.Morgan and C.Bray (eds), *Partners and Rivals in Western Europe: Britain, France, Germany,* Aldershot: Gower, 1986.

to handle the range of issues with an EU dimension.[44] The major objectives of such administrative 'streamlining' are to ensure that policy makers understand the perceived 'national' interests and are in the best possible position to ensure that these prevail. This does not, of course, preclude compromise, but it is important to stress that, in general, the representatives of the MS enter the Councils to advance a view that has been constructed through 'national' policy-making processes. Moreover, domestic bureaucracies often have an ethos of collective purpose, which the ideologically and nationally divided Commission and Councils may find it difficult to emulate.

Yet even this account of the intersecting relationships does not indicate the full complexity of the system. For the final element is the relative openness of the Commission to lobbying by pressure groups, particularly those of powerful farming, industrial and financial interests.[45] Many of these groups also operate on the national level, so that some of their demands – for example for the single market and monetary union – enter the EU policy-making system through two routes simultaneously – through the MS and through the Commission.

Policy-making within the EU is thus now best represented as a highly complex web of interactions. As the first Secretary-General of the Commission wrote as long ago as 1971,

> Being based on dialogue, the Community system bears little resemblance to the concept of government in the traditional sense of the word. The Community does not have a single head or a single leader. Decisions are collective and taken only after much confrontation of view points. The Communities have in fact been transformed into a vast convention. They are a meeting place for

[44] The extent of internal co-ordination varies considerably. In Italy and Germany it has been weak in comparison with the re-organisation that has taken place in France and Britain. It is argued that the British civil service has been the most co-ordinated of all the bureaucracies. David Hine, *Governing Italy: The Politics of Bargained Pluralism*, Oxford University Press, 1993, chapter 10; Simon Bulmer, 'The European Dimension' in G. Smith, W.E. Paterson, P. Merki (eds), *Developments in West German Politics*, London: Macmillan, 1989; David Spence, 'The Role of the National Civil Service in European Lobbying: The British Case' in S. Mazey and J. Richardson (eds), *Lobbying in the European Community*, Oxford University Press, 1993; Colm O'Nuallain (ed.), *The Presidency of the European Council of Ministers: Impacts and Implications for National Governments*, London: Croom Helm, 1985.

[45] Wyn Grant, 'Pressure Groups and the European Community: An Overview' in Mazey and Richardson, op. cit.

experts, ambassadors and ministers at hundreds and even thousands of meetings.[46]

But is it possible to identify the location of decision-making in this 'vast convention'? Many authors have implied that it is, so long as the analyst approaches the question in an appropriate way. This, it is argued, should not be based on the assumption either that full leadership lies with the governments or that it lies with the Commission or that these two bodies are in an adversarial relationship. Rather the Council-Commission relationship embodies a mixed system of decision-making in which the 'national' and EU perspectives are intermingled.[47] This is no doubt so, but it is debatable where this could be regarded as a dynamic policy-making system.

Since the governments of the MS are still embedded in both domestic concerns and in bilateral and alliance relationships outside the EU, they are inevitably seeking to balance a whole range of considerations emanating from the various environments in which they are operating. Their agreement is necessary before the EU can take any major policy initiatives, but no government is *exclusively* concerned with the development of the EU. Of course, the major states may seek to steer the EU in particular directions, but this is not the same as a clear policy-making system *within* the EU. Whatever its organisational weaknesses and the constraints upon it imposed by the government, the Commission therefore remains the only body potentially able to take on the initiating role. The appointment of Delors as President in 1985, exactly at the propitious moment for the development of the EU, constituted an opportunity for policy 'leadership' of this kind.

George Ross, who was allowed to work as an observer in Delors' *cabinet*, has provided a remarkable account of the way in which Delors combined strategic insight with other personal qualities to exploit the available opportunities to help propel the EU forward.[48] Nevertheless, because the Commission suffers from the inadequacies noted above, Delors' institutional power was relatively weak and he

[46] E. Noel, 'The Permanent Representatives Committee and the Deepening of the Communities'. *Government and Opposition*, 6, 4 (1971), quoted in Ludlow, op. cit.
[47] Ludlow, op. cit.; Kirchner, op. cit.; Wolfgang Wessels, 'The EC Council: The Community's Decisionmaking Centre' in Keohane and Hoffmann (eds), op. cit.
[48] Ross, op. cit.

(and Pascal Lamy, his *directeur du cabinet*) sometimes compensated for this by acting highhandedly within the organisation. Commission morale was raised when the integration project seemed to be moving ahead fast, but collapsed when staff were left with an impossible workload in the post-Maastricht crisis. One perceptive analyst has thus argued that Delors was extremely effective both in his relations with the Council and within the organisation in his early years as President, but later appeared to be part of the problem rather than the solution.[49] Moreover, he had initially won support from the governments by promoting the Single Market – which was not his real enthusiasm – but made much less progress in institutional and social developments. He may thus have reinforced the neo-liberal impetus without achieving the compensating sociopolitical developments that he actually favoured.[50] Moreover, as Ross also suggests, there is a more general lesson to be derived from the Delors years. Because the Commission's opportunities for policy leadership are always fleeting, a strategically-minded President is bound to exploit them to the full. But this will ultimately also lead to institutional overload and negative reactions from some governments, precipitating further attempts to restrict the Commission's role. Because of this, and because of the changes in the general climate, it seems probable that Jacques Santer will be unable to act in such a forceful manner and that the Commission's role as a policy-maker will be weakened during his period in office. But even if circumstances shift so as to create a more favourable climate for active policy-making, both past experience and the structural constraints, make it safe to predict that the EU will develop incrementally rather than dramatically.

This chapter has advanced three arguments for suggesting that policy-making within the EU is inevitably relatively slow. First, the Lockeian Social Contract model, which the original system resembles, ensures that the autonomy of the supranational institutions is severely circumscribed. Secondly, the EU has become ever more complex in terms of membership, the policy areas encompassed, and the divergent interests involved. All these factors have had an impact on

[49] Dinan, op. cit., p. 216.
[50] Ross, op. cit., pp. 227-47.

the institutional structure – epitomised by the complications of the Maastricht Treaty. Thirdly, while there will be occasional injections of pace to break through an impasse, such occurrences are relatively rare and depend upon a favourable conjunction of circumstances. In normal times policy-making within the EU is best represented as taking place through a highly complex web of interactions from which decisions 'emerge', without always being traceable to a specific source.

To describe the complexity of the policy-making environment is not necessarily to suggest that it should be different. It may be that the current system is appropriate for an entity which develops by seeking consensus from a diverse range of states, governments and interests. The point is that it is important to appreciate that the EU has a tendency towards immobilism, for this forms an essential context for the consideration of specific policy areas.

3

A EUROPEAN SOCIAL MODEL: (1) THE ECONOMY

After the second world war, West European societies underwent a quantitative and qualitative change, characterised by historically unprecedented levels of social expenditure by the state.[1] The result, from the late 1940s to the early 1970s, was the 'welfare state', based upon near full-employment, and a wide range of social benefits. There was, in fact, no single 'European social model': the welfare systems were constructed in quite different ways in the various countries, and even the economic under-pinning – though normally described as 'Keynesian' – took widely divergent forms.[2] Nevertheless, despite these differences there was a general similarity in the 'model' based on historically high levels of growth, with government intervention to sustain a high level of employment and social benefits. Moreover, the post-war system was often regarded as constituting a qualitative change from 'liberal democracy' to 'social democracy'. Certainly, the inequalities of capitalist society continued but the new 'model' incorporated a social dimension which offered a significant improvement in the life-chances of the working-classes. However, from the perspective of the mid-1990s these years are now regarded as the 'golden age'. From the 1970s, growth rates underwent a general decline, with recurrent crises. Thus while the percentage increase in output per year was 4.9% between 1950 and 1973 in the OECD area, this fell to 2.7% between 1973-1990 and to just 1.2% between then and 1993.[3] By 1994 overall un-

[1]
A. Maddison, *Dynamic Forces in Capitalist Development*, Oxford University Press, 1991; D. Puchala, 'Western Europe' in Jackson and James (eds), op. cit.
[2]
G. Esping-Anderson, *The Three Worlds of Welfare Capitalism*, Oxford/Cambridge: Polity Press, 1991; Lars Mjøset, 'The Nordic Model Never Existed, but Does it Have a Future?', *Scandinavian Studies*, 64, 4 (fall 1992).
[3]
Andrew Graham, 'Did Keynesianism work?' in S. Pollard, Will Hutton, Robert Kuttner *et al.*, *Jobs and Growth: The International Perspective*, London: Fabian Society, 1994, p. 6.

employment in the EU12 stood at 11%, having averaged close to 10% for a decade, with youth unemployment 20% and long-term unemployment 45% of the total.[4] Far greater numbers were in temporary and insecure work and, in addition, there were more than 52 million people living below the poverty line, with growing inequality on the basis of class, gender and ethnicity. Social expenditure had reached historically high levels, amounting to one quarter or one third of the GDPs of the individual MS, but this expenditure was swollen by unemployment benefits and support for an ageing population, and was failing to prevent poverty and social exclusion.[5] Moreover, the system was being questioned by those who argued that, in the face of external competition, the 'European social model' was too expensive.

Yet the post-war system had not been regarded as a luxury when it had been established. On the contrary, it had been seen as a necessity so as to stabilise liberal-democracy against the threats of Communism and Fascism. This may have been a pragmatic reason for state intervention in the economy, but many also saw it as the only form of capitalism which could be justified on democratic grounds. The same basic arguments surely apply in the mid-1990s, with the rise of fascist and extreme Right-wing movements, coupled with new forms of poverty and deprivation? There are thus again prudential reasons for suggesting that economic and social security must be re-established if the liberal-democratic system is to be viable. And, as in 1945, there are also moral arguments for claiming that this is the only form of society that could be justified as a meaningful form of democracy. As J.K. Galbraith said in a lecture in 1994,

> The discomfort and social disarray from unemployment and economic deprivation must always be in mind, as, also, the measures for their mitigation. The good society does not allow some of its people to feel useless, superfluous and deprived.[6]

[4] *European Social Policy: A Way Forward for the Union*, Brussels: European Commission White Paper, COM (94) 333 final/2, Brussels, 27 July 1994, chapter 1.

[5] Social Policy White Paper, op. cit., chapter 6. In 1992 the lowest percentage of GDP expenditure devoted to 'social protection' in the EU12 was in Portugal (16.6%) and the highest was in the Netherlands (31.6%). The average was 25.9%, with Britain just above it at 26.1%. Source: EUROSTAT, Brussels: 1994.

[6] J.K. Galbraith, 'The Good Society Considered: the economic dimension', *Annual Lecture of the Journal of Law and Society*, Cardiff Law School, 26 Jan. 1994.

But even if it were agreed that the goal should be the establishment of a 'good society', this would leave two fundamental issues
to be resolved. First, how could this now be achieved and secondly,
at what governmental level might effective policies be implemented?
The main purpose of this chapter is to consider the second question,
but it is necessary to begin by clarifying the position which will be
adopted in relation to the first one. For it is unsatisfactory to discuss
the level at which policies might be implemented without some
prior indication of their *nature*.

Neo-Liberalism versus social regulation

There has been bitter controversy as to how – or indeed whether –
the 'golden age' could be restored. This book does not suggest that
there are any easy solutions. But it is necessary to make my position
explicit in relation to one fundamental dispute which has characterised the policy debate in the capitalist world in recent years: that
between 'neo-liberalism' and 'social regulation'.

Neo-liberalism holds that a market economy is not only a
prerequisite for democratic political system, but is itself a vehicle for
democratic decision-making. For the market, it is argued, provides
consumers with the freedom to choose what to purchase with their
disposable income, and allows entrepreneurs and financiers to make
their investment decision on the basis of profitability – itself determined by consumer choices.[7] It also allows both consumers and
investors the right of 'exit' from any particular market. Interference
with these mechanisms by public authorities will, at best, lead to a
misallocation of resources, which will ultimately undermine economic
success or, at worst, bring about authoritarian or totalitarian rule.

It is unnecessary to emphasise the current salience of these ideas
and their importance in justifying an extension of competitive
principles into areas of public policy, previously shielded from
market conditions. Among EU governments, the British Conservative administration has espoused such thinking the most explicitly,
but it has made an impact throughout Europe, although not fully
implemented in practice anywhere.

[7] F.A. Hayek, *The Road to Serfdom*, London: Routledge and Kegan Paul, 1944;
Milton Friedman, *Capitalism and Freedom*, Chicago University Press, 1962;
Robert Nozick, *Anarchy State and Utopia*, Oxford: Basil Blackwell, 1974.

Such ideas have been effectively criticised elsewhere but, since the following arguments are based on a rejection of neo-liberal thinking, it may be helpful to summarise the objections to it which appear particularly relevant.[8] First, there are the obvious limitations of the 'perfect competition' model, which does not take account of such issues as monopoly power, externalities, co-ordination, and other 'imperfections' in the market. Secondly, while it is no doubt valid to argue that the economic realm cannot be controlled *completely*, it does not follow that no aspects of it can be regulated. In fact, states which have introduced so-called free market systems have introduced a whole range of regulatory laws so as to proscribe some forms of activity, while encouraging others. Neo-liberalism is not therefore opposed to controls *per se*, but to controls with particular aims. Thirdly, while it may be accepted that the 'market' may play a constructive role in resource allocation, individual choices about consumption cannot be regarded as a democratic mechanism. Some individuals may prefer spending money on videos to paying taxes to maintain a free public library service, but this does not mean that resource allocation for society as a whole should be based on such preferences. Not even those who choose to buy the videos may believe this, for they see their decisions as purely individual. But democracy involves conscious decision-making about such issues as the proportion of total available resources which should be devoted to library provision. Fourthly, the 'market' is not an abstract mechanism, which allocates goods and services in an impersonal way. It operates in a real situation of social, economic and political relationships and reflects the existing power relationships. Thus in a situation of existing inequalities, the less the market is controlled (for example, by progressive taxation and social expenditure), the more those inequalities will be reinforced. Similarly, if competitive activity prevails in a wide range of public services, unprofitable areas of social provision will be jettisoned and there will be a growing disparity between 'private opulence and public squalor'?[9] In fact, the prevalence

[8] William Keegan, *The Spectre of Capitalism: The Future of the World Economy after the Fall of Communism*, London: Vintage, 1993; Alan Haworth, *Anti-Libertarianism: Markets, Philosophy and Myth*, London: Routledge, 1994; Will Hutton, *The State We're In*, London: Cape, 1995.

[9] J.K. Galbraith, *The Affluent Society*, London: Hamish Hamilton, 2nd rev. edn, 1969, p. 227.

of neo-liberal economic thinking is at least *partly* responsible for the growing inequality and social exclusion currently facing the EU.[10] The arguments here are based on the alternative view that it is possible and necessary for public authorities to influence aspects of the economic activity both to enhance performance and for social purposes. There is clearly a wide range of viewpoints which would agree that such regulation of the market is necessary, even though the various schools of opinion will differ both in their *motives* for favouring such intervention and in the *extent* that they would accept it. However, the whole spectrum is at least united in the belief that regulation of the economy must be an integral part of the theory and practice of modern democracy.

The assumption in this chapter is thus that the conditions of the so-called 'golden age' could be restored – and hopefully surpassed – only with the help of conscious intervention by the appropriate public authorities. Yet the EU is now beset by severe economic problems. It is clear, for example, that Western Europe faces a very serious competitive challenge, particularly from the Pacific Rim, while the welfare demands upon it are constantly escalating.[11] Similarly, the whole nature of economic activity and organisation has been transformed in fundamental ways, with the growth of

[10] Britain has simultaneously shown marked increases in socioeconomic inequality and in the length of the working week. In 1979 the percentage share of total disposable household income (net after housing costs) of the poorest fifth of the population was 10% and that of the richest fifth was 35%. By 1991-2 the respective figures were 6% and 43%. In 1983 the average working week, including overtime, was 42.3 hours but by 1992 this had increased to 43.4, compared with the EU average of 40.3. The second longest working week in 1992 was in Portugal, with 41.3 hours, and in general working hours had declined since 1983. Sources: EUROSTAT, Brussels, 1995; *Social Trends 25*, HMSO, 1995.

[11] A particular problem is that the EU has been experiencing the phenomenon of 'jobless growth' in recent years and between 1990 and 1993 the ratio of the numbers employed to the population of working age declined still further. A major question is therefore whether even economic recovery will lead to a sufficient growth in employment – particularly of secure, high quality jobs. South East Asian and Japanese economies have been characterised by substantial employment growth. Although the United States has also shown a rapid increase in employment, much of this has been in the temporary, insecure and low-waged sectors. 'Unemployment in Europe', European Commission COM (94) 381 final, 14 Sept. 1994. See also Luc Soete, 'Economic Integration and Strategies for Employment' in Brouwer, Lintner and Newman, op. cit., Hutton and Kuttner, op. cit.

computer technology and new information systems. Such changes, and others discussed below, mean that the Keynesian demand management systems which underpinned the post-war economy will not be recreated in exactly the same way. Nor would it necessarily be desirable to re-establish such systems even if it were possible. The specific pattern of relationships established after the Second World War belonged to a particular era, which has now passed, and new systems of public/private enterprises will need to recognise the vast changes that have taken place, particularly in the spheres of culture, communications and social interactions. The assumption is only that extensive public intervention is necessary and desirable – not that it must take a predetermined form.

There is one final preliminary issue which needs to be clarified: the relationship between the *economic* and *social* aspects of a 'socially regulated economy'. It is often implied that the two are quite distinct: that the first goal is to create a dynamic economy, and that the social issues are then secondary. However, in the final analysis this distinction appears both untenable and based on an essentially neo-liberal framework. On this interpretation, such goals as full, high quality employment and equality between women and men and different ethnic groups, are all subordinate distributional issues. Moreover, this dichotomy between the 'economic' and the 'social' can all too easily be used to imply that there is an active economic sector and an essentially parasitic social one. Not only is this an ideologically-loaded misrepresentation of the situation, but it is also misleading to suggest that the social sector is not contributing economically. In fact it provides employment and services with multiplier effects on the economy, and also often has a direct impact on production. For example, it has been argued that the Danish health service contributed directly to the success of the pharmaceutical industry by providing secure public sector demand.[12] However, as long as it is recognised that there are mutually beneficial interactions between the 'social' and the 'economic' and that there is no absolute distinction between them, there are some analytical advantages in dividing them.

[12] C. Edquist and Bengt-Åke Lundvall, 'Comparing Small Nordic Systems of Innovation' in Richard R. Nelson (ed.), *National Innovation Systems*, Oxford University Press, 1993, cited in Lars Mjøset, *The Irish Economy in a Comparative Institutional Perspective*, Dublin: National Economic and Social Council, 1992, p. 279.

This chapter therefore concentrates on the 'economic' aspects of the subject. It considers the argument that the 'socially regulated economy' could no longer be established at state level and the alternative suggestion that the EU is now the appropriate level for such regulation. Chapter 4 then considers the EU as an actor in social policy. However, there is a very close relationship between the two chapters which are, in effect, both asking at what level a 'European social model' might now be established.

The argument that the EU is now the appropriate level for economic management

The erosion of confidence in state management of the economy. Part of the reason for the declining confidence in 'national' management has been the record of left-of-centre governments in practice. The failure of the British Labour government in 1974-9 and, perhaps still more, the *volte face* of the French Socialist government between 1981 and 1983, shattered the beliefs of many about the possibility of 'Keynesianism in one country'.[13] More generally, the record of Socialist and Social Democratic administrations in Europe and other parts of the world has appeared to demonstrate their ineffectiveness in maintaining welfare goals in the face of recessionary pressures.[14] Indeed the recent evidence of retrenchment in the Nordic states – once regarded as the model for Social Democrats elsewhere – suggests a fundamental problem in maintaining the Keynesian consensus.

There is now a widespread belief that the demand management techniques, which underpinned social regulation, arose from specific conditions in the period of post-war reconstruction and the so-called 'long boom'. These, it is argued, have now been eroded by a number of changes related to 'globalisation'. Over 30% of world trade is currently carried out within the international transactions of the top 200 transnational companies and such operations account for 60% of trade among developed economies.[15] This means that

---

[13] Donald Sassoon, 'A New Political Order? The Agenda for Social Democracy' in David Miliband (ed.), *A More Perfect Union? Britain and the New Europe*, London: IPPR, 1992.

[14] Lawrence Wilde, *Modern European Socialism*, Aldershot: Dartmouth, 1994.

[15] Camilleri and Falk, op. cit., p. 70; Miall, op. cit., p.31.

such companies can determine substantial proportions of both the trade and production of the countries in which they are located. At the same time, capital of all kinds now moves freely throughout the world and, underpinned by information technology, there is round-the-clock trading on a single global market. A trillion dollars of foreign exchange is now traded daily, of which about 90% is for speculative purposes, and only 10% finances real commercial transactions.[16] Many analysts have therefore concluded that such changes mean that 'governments no longer possess the autonomy to pursue independent macroeconomic strategies effectively, even if they were to seek to do so.'[17]

These points are of *general* application, but there are some further factors, which apply particularly to the EU. For the MS have consciously adopted policies which reduce their individual policy-making possibilities in respect of one another, on the assumption that, in so doing, each 'national economy' will gain more than it loses, and that the overall EU economy will benefit. Above all, the objective of every stage has been to ensure that no MS can resort to any form of protectionism against his partners. Originally, the main element in this involved trade policy, followed by competition policy (with severe restraints on government subsidies to particular regions or enterprises), but this has gradually been extended to embrace policies involving capital, financial services, non-tariff barriers (for example, product specification and public procurement), and labour.[18] The constraining impact of EMU on the theoretical range of national economic policy options would be still more marked, not only because it would preclude competitive devaluations but, far more seriously, because it would necessitate a far greater convergence of economic policy than has hitherto been the case.[19] Indeed, the rise in interest rates following German

[16] Robert Kuttner, 'Where the Macro meets the Structural' in Hutton, Kuttner *et al.*, p. 40.

[17] G. Garrett and P. Lang, 'Political Responses to Interdependence: What's Left for the Left?', *International Organization*, 45, no. 4, p. 543, quoted in David Held and Anthony McGrew, 'Globalization and the Liberal Democratic State', *Government and Opposition*, 28, 2, spring 1993; see also Falk and Camilleri, op. cit., chapter 4 and references.

[18] Dinan, op. cit., chapters 12 and 13 and references.

[19] Christopher Taylor, 'Sovereignty and European Monetary Arrangements' in Brouwer, Lintner and Newman, op. cit.; Ruth Kelly, 'A Framework for

unification, and the restrictive convergence criteria embodied in the Maastricht treaty have already reinforced the rigour of austerity measures in most countries in the EU.[20]

In any case, even without EMU it may be argued that each development in economic integration may also make it more difficult for an individual state to pursue a radically different economic strategy from that of the EU as a whole. From all this it may be concluded that EU states are constrained both by the general pressures from the global economy, and by the specific interdependence which they have developed. In fact it is extremely difficult to isolate the EU dimension from the wider phenomena. Many of the ways in which the EU restricts policy-making at state level are highly visible because they are based on treaties or subsequent legislation, and follow from the explicit objectives of the union. The more general constraints on national economic policies are less 'transparent'. Yet at times for crisis – for example over the ERM in 1992 and 1993 – the pressures were obviously global in character. And, in any case, many of the developments within the EU – for example, in freeing capital movements – have reflected world-wide tendencies. Each EU state is therefore simultaneously affected by a formal, institutional system, with a legal basis (the EU itself), and by the global network of financial and commercial transactions. It is therefore not surprising that it is difficult to disentangle the separate impacts of these two interlocking systems. However, it seems reasonable to suggest that the global economy is the more dominant since its constraining pressures would exist irrespective of the existence of the EU, and because the latter is, at least in part, an attempt to control some of them. In any case, it is indisputable that both forms of external pressure have combined to constrain the effectiveness of national economic management. This has led to an increasing tendency to look to the EU as the main instrument for social regulation.

Few would argue that the nation-state is completely redundant in an economic sense. Indeed most of those who envisage the EU

European Exchange Rates in the 1990s' in Jonathan Michie and John Grieve Smith (eds), *Unemployment in Europe*, London: Academic Press, 1994; M.J. Artis, 'The Maastricht Road to Monetary Union', *Journal of Common Market Studies*, 30, no. 3, Sept. 1992; Gerald Holtham, *Economic Integration after Maastricht*, London: IPPR, 1993.
[20] Holtham, op. cit.

as playing an important role, also specify the need for action on all other levels – national, regional and local. However, there is a growing body of opinion which implies that the EU level now has primary importance in the establishment of an advanced socially regulated economy.[21] As one proponent of this viewpoint puts it, 'The theory of national roads is bankrupt . . . the epoch of construction of social democracy in one country has come to a close.'[22]

The EU as the level for economic management.   There is clearly much force in the argument that, in theory, the EU as a whole possesses more of the prerequisites for an advanced socially regulated economy than does any individual state. By 1990 the EU and EFTA accounted for 58.6% of world trade (including intra-European trade).[23] Intra-regional trade has been growing fast and, by 1992, on average, 61.3% of the exports of each MS went to other EU states and 59.3% of its imports came from them.[24] Furthermore, whereas the main beneficiaries of direct investment opportunities during the early phase of integration had been US transnationals, the recent trend has been towards increased intra-European foreign direct investment.[25] Thus a market of almost 370 million, which accounts for approximately 25% of world economic output, would obviously have enormous advantages over the individual state in attempting an expansionist economic policy. Nor, according to some studies, would the EU as a whole incur the kind of balance of payments problems that would

[21] Stuart Holland, *The European Imperative: Economic and Social Cohesion in the 1990s*, Nottingham: Spokesman, 1993; *Put Europe to Work*, Report of the Parliamentary Group of the Party of European Socialists, Brussels, 1993; Valerio Lintner, 'National Economic Sovereignty and European Integration' in Brouwer, Lintner and Newman, op. cit.; Valerio Lintner, 'Monetary Integration, Recession and the Left', *Labour Focus on Eastern Europe*, no. 1, 1993.

[22] Sassoon, op. cit., pp. 108-9.

[23] GATT, International Trade, 1990-1, cited in Miall, op. cit., p. 30. By 1993, even excluding all intra-EU trade, the EU12 accounted for 19.2% of world imports and 20% of world exports. 'External Trade: Monthly Statistics', December 1994, EUROSTAT.

[24] EUROSTAT, 1994. In 1992 EFTA accounted for 16% total EU exports and imports. 'European Economic Area: Background Report', Commission of the European Communities, 13 Jan. 1994. The enlarged EU has thus consolidated its internal trading strength, although the European Economic Area agreement in 1992 had effectively led to the economic incorporation of EFTA in any case.

[25] Miall, op. cit., p. 34.

be faced by the individual state, since approximately 93% of production and consumption is covered by production within the EU area (as distinct from the much greater dependence of the national economies on the global economy).[26] There is therefore a strong case for arguing that universal expansion by the EU states as a whole could be mutually beneficial – by promoting intra-Union trade – while individual 'national' expansion could easily be threatened by balance of payments crises.[27] Similarly, the EU as a whole would have greater resilience against external competition and shocks, could guarantee more funds to finance research and development, and could devote more resources to education and training. In theory, the EU could also control multinationals and currency speculation more effectively than the individual states, and could use its greater economic power to uphold the extensive forms of welfare provision which would be required for advanced social regulation.

Such arguments have been propounded – albeit with differing emphases – by various authors.[28] However, while there is little doubt about the *theoretical* advantages of an EU strategy, there are many fundamental issues which need further examination.

The argument under scrutiny

States and economic power. In the first place, it is necessary to reconsider the argument that, in general, states have been rendered impotent in the face of global pressures. Certainly, the shifts in international economy have been remarkable and it is no doubt true that these have had a constraining impact even upon the most powerful states. However, it is misleading to imply that this puts all states into a similar category. Viewed in this way it might appear that the United States and Ethopia are both impotent victims of global economic pressures, and that there is only a difference of degree between them. Yet this must be an invalid representation of the situation, for the difference in wealth between the most ad-

---

[26] 'Putting Europe to Work', op. cit.

[27] Andrew Glyn and Bob Rowthorn, 'European Employment Policies'; John Grieve Smith, 'Policies to Reduce European Unemployment' in Michie and Grieve Smith, op. cit., p. 198, p. 261.

[28] Holland, op. cit. Lintner, 'Monetary Integration', op. cit.; Lintner, 'Economic Sovereignty', op. cit.; Wilde, op. cit.; Sassoon, op. cit.

vanced and the least developed economies is greater than at any time. Moreover, as Gurr argues, some of the more powerful states

'... command more resources, absolutely and in proportion to the capabilities of their societies, and have greater capacities to organise and deploy human and material resources in the service of state policies than any historical political systems, including the largest of empires'.[29]

More specifically, it has been argued that, despite the global pressures, the basic long-term trend has been one in which some states have become *less* dependent on the external environment because they are able to finance their activities from internal sources rather than by external borrowing. According to this analysis the erosion of *de facto* economic control varies with the size and level of development of the particular states, and also with the extent of international involvement and ability to adjust. While it is therefore true that even the United States cannot now conduct domestic monetary policy without considering its impact upon international financial flows, this only shows that particular activities associated with independent statehood are in a constant state of flux. Overall, 'the interdependence-independence relationship is dialectical and not one way'.[30] Similarly, many studies show that the relationships between transnational companies and states are far too complex and varied to be characterised in a way which suggests that all states are equally dependent upon the decisions of private corporations.[31] On the contrary, the home base of transnationals, including the government, derives far greater benefits from their activities than the recipients of inward investment.[32] Thus, to paraphrase George Orwell, if all states are equal in the face of global economic pressures, some are more equal than others.

Such observations also apply to the member states of the EU.

[29] Ted Robert Gurr, 'War, Revolution and the Growth of the Coercive State' in James A. Caporaso (ed.), *The Elusive State*, London: Sage, 1989, p. 50.

[30] Stephen D. Krasner, 'Economic Interdependence and Independent Statehood' in Jackson and James, op. cit., p. 318.

[31] Susan Strange, 'Supranationals and the State' in John A. Hall (ed.), *States in History*, Oxford: Basil Blackwell, 1986.

[32] Yao-Su Hu, 'Exploding the Globalisation Myth: Competitive Advantage and Corporate Nationality' in Harry Cowie and John Pinder, *A Recovery Strategy for Europe*, London: Federal Trust, 1993.

First, some of these are themselves major economic actors, with home-based transnational companies. Naturally, this applies, above all, to Germany, which accounts for approximately 25% of the GDP of the EU15.[33] But France, Britain and Italy are also major economies, and some of the smaller North European states are extremely wealthy in world comparative terms.[34] It is thus evident that these MS, viewed individually, are still in a relatively advantageous position – in comparison with the majority of states – to withstand some of the external pressures. Secondly, and more generally, the inequality of states in the world as a whole is obviously replicated by the inequality of states within the EU.[35]

Germany has far greater scope than any other country for developing and implementing its own policies. Indeed, a frequent charge, intensified after unification, has been that the perceived needs of the German economy have reinforced deflationary pressures throughout the EU as a whole, and have even dictated the nature of the project for EMU.[36] Yet it is also true that other MS possess some margin for manoeuvre, and conclusions about the extent of economic autonomy for each state would really require at least three levels of investigation: analysis of its role in the international economy; analysis of the specific impact of the EU; and analysis of the general impact of the EU on the economies of all MS. It is not clear that such studies are really possible given the extent to which all the variables are inter-dependent, but some relevant work has been done.

Valerio Lintner has attempted to trace a relationship between the size of the economy and the loss of economic autonomy arising from both EU membership and globalisation. In general, he concludes that medium-sized economies (such as that of Britain) experience the most difficulties because they have traditionally exercised far

---

[33] 1499 billion ECU out of a total of 5840.1 in 1992. Sources: EUROSTAT, 'Facts through Figures' (1994) and 'European Economic Area: Background Report', Commission of the European Communities, 13 Jan. 1994.

[34] In 1993 the wealthiest MS in GDP *per capita* was Luxembourg with a standard of living 68% above the EU average. Denmark, Sweden, Austria also have GDP *per capita* incomes well above the EU average. Six of the top ten trading countries in the world are in the EU and a seventh, Switzerland, is closely associated with it. *The Guardian*, 15 Dec. 1994; Paul Kennedy, *Preparing for the Twenty-First Century*, London: Fontana, 1994, p. 260.

[35] See chapter 5.

[36] Holthman, op. cit., Miall, op. cit., pp. 37-9.

greater autonomy which they can no longer maintain. Small economies, he argues, face fewer difficulties because they have never had illusions about their ability to influence the external parameters that constrain local decision-making.[37] This parallels the conclusions of Susan Strange that medium-sized economies experience the greatest difficulties in relation to supranationals because of the lack of a clear role of control or subordination.[38] However, others have argued that the extent of Britain's economic relations with areas outside the EU provide it with more autonomy than Lintner suggests.[39] It is also true that some smaller states – such as Austria, Switzerland and the Nordic countries – developed expertise over a long period in maximising the advantages they possessed so as to secure some autonomy.[40] Moreover, during the so-called 'golden age' different policy mixes appeared to 'work' in the various West European economies, and Mjøset has argued that, even among the five Nordic countries, there was considerable variation, with Sweden, Norway and Denmark following Keynesian policies and Finland and Iceland operating non-Keynesian devaluation cycle models.[41] The fact that this variation now seems to have ended reinforces the more general argument that the onset of neo-liberalism, in an era of increased 'globalisation', has circumscribed the extent of the autonomy that previously existed. But it does not mean that it has ended it entirely.

It is also important to emphasise that the share of GDP taken by government revenue varies between around 35% and 50% in the EU states.[42] Governments are able to influence the economy through employment, purchasing, taxation, social security systems, investment policies and, at present, through interest rate and currency changes. Obviously, the extent of their room for manoeuvre both

[37] Lintner, 'Economic Sovereignty', op. cit., p.17.

[38] Strange, op. cit., pp. 304-5.

[39] Taylor, op. cit.

[40] Mjøset, *The Irish Economy*, op. cit.; Peter Katzenstein, 'Small States in an Open International Economy' in P. Evans, D. Rueschmeyer and T. Skocpol (eds), *Bringing the State Back In*, Cambridge University Press, 1985.

[41] Mjøset, 'The Nordic Economies', op. cit., p. 72; F. Scharpf, *Crisis and Choice in European Social Democracy*, Ithaca, NY: Cornell University Press, 1991.

[42] Francis Cripps and Terry Ward, 'Strategies for Growth and Employment in the European Community' in Michie and Grieve Smith, op. cit., p. 252.

within the EU, and within the world as a whole, is dependent upon a whole range of variables and differs substantially from state to state. But even the smallest and weakest have some individual advantages to exploit. Thus, for example, Luxembourg has made the most of language restrictions for economic reasons, and even some of the micro states, such as Andorra, have used their distinctiveness effectively.[43]

There are further points about the EU itself which should induce caution about *over-stating* its impact upon the economic autonomy of the MS. First, the MS do not always comply with EU policies, and enforcement is difficult. For example, the abolition of non-tariff barriers following the SEM, has been uneven. In 1992 the Commission thus estimated that only 2% of public markets had been won by firms outside the home country, despite the attempt to outlaw national bias in public procurement policies.[44] Secondly, whatever their theoretical outlooks on competition policy, it is the four larger and more powerful states that have been responsible for an increasing proportion of total state aid to their own national enterprises within the EU, and the Commission has often ultimately accepted this.[45] In other words, MS sometimes attempt to use the external advantages of the EU as a bloc while exploiting their room for manoeuvre internally. Thirdly, even monetary and financial integration – which has often been viewed as the factor which is most constraining upon economic divergence – may not preclude some autonomy in the development of national policies. This is not only because some economies are already effectively in a Deutschmark zone, but in the more important sense that, even within monetary union, governments could promote separate policies designed to

[43] Bruno De Witte,'Cultural Legitimation: Back to the Language Question' in Soledad Garcia (ed.), *European Identity and the Search for Legitimacy*, London: Pinter, p. 155; Harvey W. Armstrong and Robert Read, 'Federalism and Subsidiarity: Lessons from European Micro-States and EC Autonomous Regions', paper at 2nd ECSA-World Conference, Brussels, 5-6 May 1994.

[44] Dinan, op. cit., p. 345. It was also notable that when British Telecom agreed a joint venture with Viag, the Munich-based chemicals group in January 1995, each took only a 37.5% stake and offered the rest to German institutions in order to improve the chances of securing the necessary licences to operate in Germany. *The Guardian*, 11 Jan. 1995.

[45] Dinan, op. cit. p.378. During 1994, for example, the Commission accepted state aid to Air France and to the German steelmaker, Eko Stahl.

influence the rate and type of investment, and these are ultimately of greater importance in relation to 'real' economic performance.[46]

Finally, because the failure of the expansionist strategy of the French Socialist government in 1981-3 has been so influential in eroding confidence about 'national' strategies, it is worth noting a recent revisionist interpretation of the events. Halimi, Michie and Milne argue that the French socialists had anticipated all the consequences of placing trade liberalisation and the ERM above expansion, and that they made a deliberate deflationary choice, which could have been avoided. They thus conclude:

> The failure of the 1981-83 French reflationary experiment cannot legitimately be used to justify the widespread claim that effective national macroeconomic and industrial policies are no longer viable.[47]

None of this contradicts the arguments in favour of a common EU strategy. Nor is it even intended to imply that any of the MS necessarily has sufficient autonomy to re-establish full employment and social welfare in isolation. It is simply to make the point that many EU states continue to retain considerable leverage over their economies and to discount the idea that they are now impotent as economic actors.[48]

Is the EU capable of economic management?   It has already been noted that the *theoretical* arguments in favour of the EU as the location for economic management are very strong. There is obviously room for disagreement as to whether even this body is of sufficient weight to influence the direction of the world economy, or whether real change would require agreement with the United States and Japan.[49] Nevertheless, there are good grounds for believ-

---

[46] Laurence Harris, 'Financial Integration and Economic Policy in Europe' in Brouwer, Lintner, and Newman, op. cit.

[47] Serge Halimi, Jonathan Michie and Seumas Milne, 'The Mitterrand Experience' in Michie and Grieve Smith, op. cit., pp. 114-15.

[48] See also Donald J. Puchala, 'Western Europe' in Jackson, and James, op. cit. For the Commission's own assessment of the EU economy as a whole, and that of the MS, see Commission of the European Communities, *1995 Annual Economic Report*, 1995 COM (94) 615 (final), 13 December 1994.

[49] Will Hutton and Robert Kuttner, 'Full Employment in a Free Society' in Hutton and Kuttner, op. cit.

ing that the EU would be sufficiently powerful both to make considerable headway alone, and to influence the other world economic actors into reaching international agreements on trade and labour policies. However, all this is purely academic because the EU currently does not operate as one economy. It is therefore necessary to 'unpack' arguments about EU effectiveness so as to understand exactly what is being proposed. Only then is it possible to assess the possibilities. For example, the most ambitious of such ideas would be the suggestion that the EU should now undertake the kinds of policies previously exercised by states at the height of the Keynesian era. This implies that it should act like an interventionist state, but as was shown in the last chapter, the EU does not possess this kind of power or policy-making apparatus. The suggestion therefore simply by-passes all the intractable political problems which would need to be resolved, by effectively envisaging a political union with strong central powers. It would therefore seem more plausible to envisage more limited approaches which might help to establish an EU dimension for economic intervention. A number of such proposals have been made, and some have been partially implemented.

Proposals for EU economic intervention. First, there is the approach which emphasises the arguments for infrastructural investment, for research and development, for skills training, and for coordinated labour market policies – for example, by reducing indirect labour costs to employers. Such policies were recommended in the Commission's December 1993 White Paper, *Growth, Competitiveness, Employment* and were generally endorsed at the Essen summit a year later.[50] The importance of infrastructural development was also recognised in the Maastricht commitment to the development of transnational networks in transport, telecommunications and energy (TENS). At the Edinburgh summit in December 1992 the European Council authorised a new lending facility of 5 billion ECU for the European Investment Bank (EIB), primarily to accelerate the financing of these projects, and this was raised by a further 2 billion ECU at the Copenhagen summit in June 1993.[51]

[50] *Growth, Competitiveness, Employment* COM (93) 700 Final, 10 Dec. 1993.

[51] The Copenhagen summit also allowed the EIB an additional 1 billion ECU for small and medium enterprises. Nugent, op. cit., p. 247.

Since the EIB normally operates within strict constraints acceptance of the importance of providing new financial arrangements for such developments constitutes a partial recognition of the need for intervention in the economy. However, this should not be exaggerated. At the Essen summit in December 1994, Delors insisted that a new EU borrowing instrument would be required to fund the planned £300 billion programme of investment in TENS, but the governments postponed this decision until there was sufficient evidence that the private sector and the European Investment Bank were unable to provide the funds.[52] In any case, 7-8 billion ECU constitutes a very modest step towards intervention at EU level.

A second approach, which has long been advocated by many, would be the development of an effective EU industrial policy to complement the CAP. Such policies have been pursued, to an extent, since the late 1960s, and reached their peak between 1981 and 1985, when Etienne Davignon, the Commissioner responsible for industrial affairs, sought Community-wide technological collaboration.[53] This led to the ESPRIT programme approved in June 1983 calling for collaboration on 'pre-competitive' research, and this was followed by a number of other programmes, including EUREKA – to develop European technology – in 1985. In theory, many such programmes could be developed both to identify potential EU 'champions' and to maintain a link with regional policy.[54] However, for reasons which will be discussed below, this has not happened on any large scale, and it is also notable that industrial policy was totally subordinated to competitiveness within the Maastricht Treaty. (Title XIII, art. 130)

A third proposal, taking a variety of forms, is to attempt to shift the priorities from the current deflationary bias, based on monetary policies, to a concern for the 'real' economy. One obvious suggestion would be that the system of central banks (ESCB) and the proposed European Central Bank (ECB) should be brought under

---

[52] *The Guardian*, 12 Dec. 1994. For a general analysis see Colin Turner, *Trans-European Networks: The Infrastructure for the Internal Market*, London: University of North London Press, 1994.

[53] Dinan, op. cit., Chapter 13.

[54] Malcolm Sawyer, 'Industrial Strategy and Employment in Europe' in Michie and Grieve Smith, op. cit.; Iain Begg and Barry Moore, 'Industrial Regeneration and Economic Redistribution' in Miliband, op. cit.

political control. However, the Maastricht Treaty is categorical on the subject:

> Neither the ECB, nor a national central bank, nor any member of their decision-making bodies shall seek or take instructions from Community institutions or bodies, from any government of a Member State or from any other body. The Community institutions and bodies and the governments of the Member States undertake to respect this principle and not to seek to influence the members of the decision-making bodies of the ECB or of the national central banks in the performance of their tasks (Title II, art. 107).

It has also been suggested that other economic indicators – perhaps reduction of unemployment – could be incorporated into the convergence criteria. Furthermore the narrow targets of price stability which characterise the Maastricht approach to EMU are, in theory, complemented by a much more progressive commitment to

> ... promote throughout the Community a harmonious and balanced development of economic activities, sustainable and non-inflationary growth respecting the environment, a high degree of convergence of economic performance, a high level of employment and of social protection, the raising of the standard of living and quality of life, and economic and social cohesion and solidarity among the Member States (Art. 2).

Stuart Holland has suggested that this could be exploited by the establishment of a new Medium Term Economic Policy Committee, which would enjoy equal status with the proposed Monetary Committee, to report on progress in these respects.[55] This is an ingenious suggestion for reconciling the goals of monetary stability with wider economic strategies. Unfortunately, it has not been accepted. The December 1994 Essen summit accepted Delors' plan for a 'competitive council' of senior industrialists to advise annually on what should be done to meet the challenge from American and Asian economies, but there is obviously no guarantee that this would counter the current neo-liberal bias.[56]

Finally, there is the most important suggestion: that there could

[55] Holland, op. cit., pp. 21-3.
[56] *The Guardian*, 12 Dec. 1994.

be a coordinated EU expansion based upon government expenditure on public services and infrastructure. Whereas states which attempted such policies individually would be 'punished' by rapid capital movements or balance of payments crises, the EU as a whole could, it is argued, undertake such a strategy successfully because of the high degree of trade between the MS.[57] While the primary instruments of this policy would still be at state and sub-state levels, the EU would obviously be a major coordinating 'actor' and, indeed, such an initiative would clearly change its whole orientation towards greater intervention.[58] However, it must again be noted that, so far, there is little sign of the EU governments moving in this direction.

All these arguments have clear importance and, if implemented, such policy recommendations would also provide the EU with an important role in supporting and sustaining moves towards a 'socially regulated economy', without calling for a quantum leap into quasi statehood. Nevertheless, there are some fundamental problems about the EU attempting even these, relatively limited, forms of intervention.

The most obvious practical difficulty is the insignificance of the EU budget in comparison with the overall GDP of the bloc. Following the Edinburgh summit of December 1992 the budget is set to rise to 1.27% of total EU GNP by 1999. Certainly, the absolute size of the budget – set to reach 84 billion ECU by 1999 – is very large in comparison with the economies of many poorer states in developing countries, and it also represents a much higher percentage of the GDP of the smaller economies within the EU. This means that, at the micro-level, EU regional and social expenditure may make a very substantial difference to its recipients (see Chapters 4 and 5). But, although the CAP expenditure is now declining as a percentage of total expenditure, it is still expected to account for 46% of the total by the end of the period. This reduces the available

[57] Glyn and Rowthorn, op. cit.

[58] Grahame F. Thompson, 'Unitary State, Federation or Confederal Public Power: What Principles for European Political Unity?', Paper at 2nd ECSA World Conference, 5-6 May 1994; Paul Hirst, 'Maastricht, the Missed Turning Point: The European Community Between Integration and Decline', paper at the Lothian conference 'Federalism and Subsidiarity', 17-18 Dec. 1993.

funds for industrial intervention or other forms of pump-priming and, as already noted, the EIB is constrained in its lending powers.[59] In any case, at the macro level, total EU expenditure is far too small to play a primary role in the economic development of the whole area and the limitation is not substantially altered by the limited lending powers of the EIB (although again this plays a significant role in the lower income countries and regions where the loans are mostly concentrated).[60] Nor is there any real prospect of a major increase in the size of the budget: on the contrary, it seems likely that the net contributors would now be *less* inclined to generosity than was the case at the time of the Edinburgh summit.[61] The emphasis has shifted to vigilance against abuses rather than discussion of expenditure needs. The bulk of the money required for investment in economic regeneration would therefore need to be raised by borrowing or taxation at state or sub-state level.

A second problem in transforming the EU into an instrument of economic intervention concerns the Commission itself. Delors' own prominence as an advocate of intervention made it appear as if the Commission as a whole was solidly behind his policies and that the MS were the sole barrier to progress on this front. However, this was certainly not the case. On the contrary, a battle has raged within the Commission, with DGIV (Competition) challenging almost every proposal for intervention and, particularly when controlled by Leon Brittan, often triumphing over DGIII (Industrial Affairs). In April 1993 the free market forces even succeeded in emasculating DGXIII (in charge of high technology and research), which had been closely associated with a *dirigiste* policy.[62] The same conflict has been fought over state aid to industry, and DGIV has been often triumphant in upholding competition policy.[63] One important reason for this is that, although the arguments may appear

[59] For a belief general explanation of the budget, see Michael Shackleton, 'The Budget of the EC: Structure and Process' in Lodge, op. cit. For the details of the 1994 budget, see Nugent, op. cit., chapter 12.

[60] Nugent, op. cit., p. 248.

[61] Michael Shackleton, 'The Community Budget after Maastricht' in Alan W. Cafruny and Glenda G. Rosenthal, *The State of the European Community: The Maastricht Debates and Beyond*, Harlow: Longman, 1993; Bruce Millan, 'View from the Commission' in Brouwer, Lintner and Newman, op. cit.

[62] Dinan, op. cit., p. 371.

[63] Ross, op. cit., pp. 115-24, 129-35, 177-8, 220.

to be based on economic theory or political values, battles between the MS are also being fought out within the Commission. Thus, for example, in 1991 when electronics firms were lobbying the Commission for support, those who favoured intervention (above all the French) were opposed by a coalition of member states which had no national champions in the field:

> Transcending north-south differences, Britain, Ireland, Spain and Portugal feared that protection of European industry would hamper foreign investment in their countries, harm consumers, and divert scarce Community resources to giant firms in France, Germany, and the Benelux.[64]

Of course, industrial intervention – at least in terms of maintaining state aid – sometimes triumphs, as was the case with Air France and the German steel industry in 1994. But such victories will always be denounced by others and, given the centrality of competition policy in the EU and DGIV's special status as its guardian, there will be strong grounds for denouncing such derogations as 'distortions'.[65] This raises a more fundamental problem about shifting the EU towards an interventionist strategy.

The nature and limitations of the EU as an economic actor.   As noted in Chapter 2, the primary purpose of the founding treaties was to create a Customs Union, followed by a Common Market. The underlying economic philosophy was essentially that of free market capitalism, on the assumption that, by abolishing tariff and non-tariff barriers and equalising competitive conditions, there would be efficiency gains. The idea was thus to create an economic area in which national distortions of the market would progressively be eliminated. It is true that, from the start, these aims were partially offset by other features of the EEC, some of which were avowed as principles, and the rudiments of a Social Policy commitment were also adumbrated in the founding Treaty.[66] The CAP was a clear departure from free, competitive principles and subsequent develop-

[64] Dinan, op. cit., p. 370.
[65] Michelle Cini, *European Community Competition Policy*, London: University of North London Press, 1992.
[66] For example, art. 2 of the Treaty of Rome avowed more general economic aims. (Social Policy is discussed in Chapter 4).

ments – particularly in social, regional and environmental policies – have indicated further elements of regulation. But should these be regarded as equally *embedded* in the EU or are they subordinate to the competitive principles? There is good reason to argue that, thus far, the development of the market economy has been the *fundamental* purpose. The other policies have developed primarily as part of the bargaining process by which particular states, or interests, have received forms of compensation for accepting the latest stage in the opening of the market. For example, the original development of a regional policy was primarily regarded as a palliative to help Edward Health secure domestic support for British entry, and the subsequent increases in the structural and cohesion funds in 1988 and 1992 (Delors I and II) have been designed to ensure compensation to the poorer EU countries in return for acceptance of the SEM and EMU commitments.[67] This is not to suggest that such policies are unimportant or to deny the constant expansion of competences. But at each stage, the primary rationale has been free competition in an open market, and the treaty obligations have been far more concrete in this respect than in other policy areas. This was quite evident in the Maastricht Treaty, where the general statement of goals in Article 2 was then given an unambiguous interpretation in Art. 3a:

1. For the purposes set out in Article 2, the activities of the Member States and the Community shall include, as provided in this Treaty and in accordance with the timetable set out therein, the adoption of an economic policy which is based on the close coordination of Member States' economic policies, on the internal market and on the definition of common objectives, and conducted in accordance with the principle of an open market economy with free competition.

2. Concurrently with the foregoing, and as provided in this Treaty and in accordance with the timetable and the procedures set out therein, these activities shall include the irrevocable fixing of exchange rates leading to the introduction of a single currency, the ecu, and the definition and conduct of a single monetary

---

[67] The main innovation in the Delors II proposal, accepted at the 1992 Edinburgh summit, was the establishment of a Cohesion Fund. The criterion for receiving funding was that per capita GNP was less than 90% of the EU average. Michael Shackleton, 'The Community Budget after Maastricht' in Cafruny and Rosenthal, op. cit.

policy and exchange-rate policy the primary objective of both of which shall be to maintain price stability and, without prejudice to this objective, to support the general economic policies in the Community, in accordance with the principle of an open market economy with free competition.

3. These activities of the Member States and the Community shall entail compliance with the following guiding principles: stable prices, sound public finances and monetary conditions and a sustainable balance of payments.

So far governments and economic elites have thus supported the EU as a framework through which economies have been opened on market principles, and this has been underwritten by the treaties and subsequent legislation.[68] Market opening, in the sense of the removing of barriers, is often described as 'negative integration' and proponents of the EU as a framework for social regulation of the economy often suggest that the time is now ripe for 'positive integration' through the provision of common policies.[69] However, if the above interpretation of the history of integration is valid, it is clear that this would involve a profound shift – perhaps greater than that which was necessary to bring about the 'Keynesian' era after the Second World War. For it would not only require a change of policy preferences, but would also probably involve a transformation in the institutions and legislation of the EU.

Of course the degree of change that would be necessary is dependent upon the type of policy which is envisaged. It would, for example, be possible, without any major transformation, to moderate the deflationary bias of EMU by introducing other economic indicators into the convergence criteria. Similarly, the MS could adopt some common policies for economic regeneration without departing from EU legislation. They might need to jettison the current orthodoxies about public expenditure limits but, if there were a common approach, it would be possible to maintain competition laws. However, there are two points which must be emphasised. First, if, as argued above, the EU has *primarily* been a framework for opening up economies to competition, it follows that

[68] For a full discussion, with a different interpretation, see W. Goldstein, 'The EC: capitalist or dirigiste regime?' in Cafruny and Rosenthal, op. cit.

[69] Holland, op. cit., pp. 12–13, following Jan Kindleberger, *International Economic Integration*, 2nd edn, Amsterdam: Elsevier, 1954.

it could not take on other tasks as an equal priority, without a thoroughgoing change in its ethos and a re-ordering of the hierarchies within the Commission. Secondly, no such change could come through the Commission itself which, as argued in chapter two, is inevitably constrained by the MS. If there were a major political shift within the MS, forces in the Commission (and, of course, in the European Parliament) would no doubt play their role in persuading the Council to adopt a programme for economic regeneration. But this suggests that any such development would initially need to come from the MS. If so, political processes within MS (or some of them) would be the *primary* cause of the change, which might, in theory, then be generalised through EU policies.

By the end of 1994 there was little sign that this kind of change was under way. The Maastricht Treaty, and particularly its concept of an EMU, had suggested an adherence to many of the tenets of neo-liberalism, and the post-Maastricht developments did not lead to any thoroughgoing re-evaluation of this position. Even after the ERM crises (of 1992 and 1993) most of the discussion seemed to concern the number of countries which would move towards EMU together rather than the economic principles on which the proposal was based. With the approval of the governments, the Commission thus issued information about MS progress in attaining the Maastricht targets and strictures against those which were lagging, and at the Essen summit in December 1994 the European Council declared that a strict interpretation of the convergence criteria was essential.[70] It is true that the Commission White Paper of December 1993, *Growth, Competitiveness, Employment* highlighted the problem of unemployment and, with the White Paper, *European Social Policy: Options for the Union* of July 1994, emphasised the importance of maintaining the 'European social model'.[71] But, while this constituted an important counter-balance to the deflationary emphasis of the Maastricht Treaty, some of the economic proposals – and particularly the stress on active labour market policies – were certainly influenced by neo-liberal thinking. Moreover, given the

[70] Agence Europe, 9-10 Dec. 1994. The British government began to question the criteria early in 1995, but its motives were mainly tactical and domestic, and it was not clear that this would generate a wider debate in the EU.

[71] *European Social Policy – A Way Forward for the Union*, COM (94) 333 final/2, Brussels, 27 July 1994. See chapter 4 of the present work for an extensive discussion of the content.

decision-making system within the EU, economic policy could only be transformed with great difficulty. Certainly, the EMU commitment could be allowed to lapse – as it was in the 1970s – but the construction of an alternative policy would be far more problematic, particularly as the development of extensive interventionist powers would require unanimity.

This chapter has argued that democracy requires social regulation of the economy, and that globalisation has limited the scope for such regulation at the level of the individual state. But it has also suggested that the EU lacks the powers necessary for *leading* this form of economic transformation, and that it would require a fundamental change for it to become a major actor in the establishment of a socially regulated economy.

The situation is characterised by relativities. All states are constrained, but they are not all helpless victims of international forces. All EU states are economic actors, but they are obviously not all of equal importance. The EU itself is an economic player in some respects, but is not able to initiate or implement fundamental change in the direction of social regulation. Some states are far more decentralised than others but, even in the most centralised states, local and regional economic initiatives are of crucial importance. In this indeterminate situation, the most important question is how a successful impetus for change might begin. For both practical and theoretical reasons, this surely cannot start at EU level, but must begin 'lower down' within the politics of the MS – perhaps within several MS. Yet even a change in one major country could have a decisive impact on the EU as a whole. As one study of employment policies concludes,

> The contagious impact of a major, public sector-led expansion of employment in a single country should not be underestimated. Just as the collapse of the Mitterrand expansion in 1983 seemed to signal the final collapse of traditional Keynesian policies, so a successful expansion of employment would do more than anything else to build up support for expansion.[72]

[72] Glyn and Rowthorn, 'European Employment Policies' in Michie and Grieve Smith, op. cit., p. 198.

4

A EUROPEAN SOCIAL MODEL: (2) SOCIAL POLICY

If full employment constituted one key aspect of the post-war 'golden age', the development of 'cradle to the grave' systems of welfare provision was the other. Indeed the establishment of 'welfare' states was probably the most important factor in transforming the political systems into more meaningful forms of democracy for the mass of the population, and therefore also legitimising them domestically. However, social policy has become an increasingly salient element in debates about 'Europe' since the late 1980s. This is partly because of the resistance of the British government to the efforts to enhance the 'social dimension' so as to offset the negative effects of economic integration, but also because EU activity in this area has undoubtedly become more significant in recent years. It is now a matter of real debate as to whether the EU can play an important role in upholding the social policy regimes that reinforced liberal democracy after the Second World War and, if so, in what ways.

The chapter is divided into three sections. The first summarises the evolution of EU social policy since 1958; the second summarises some of the lessons from experience so far; and the final one offers some conclusions on the role of the EU.

The evolution of EU social policy

'Social policy' is not a term that may be defined precisely, and the EU has used it to cover a wide range of issues, ranging from apparently technical 'health and safety' matters to 'quality of life' concerns, to much more politically sensitive areas, including industrial relations systems, and redistributive policies covering health, education, housing and social security. The November 1993 Green Paper, *European Social Policy: Options for the Union*, noted the ambiguity, but stated its intention to include the full range of policies in the social sphere, including labour market policies.[1]

In practice, social policy played a very subordinate role in the early stages of West European Integration. Since the EEC was established in the era of rapid economic growth which was sustaining the domestic welfare systems, and since the architects of the Community assumed that general living standards would rise as a result of free market conditions, there was little pressure for policymakers to accord a high priority to social policy issues at EEC level.

The main function of Community social policy was to facilitate the free movement of workers, and it was in this area that limited progress was made. In 1961 the first legislation was implemented and, during the next seven years, most forms of legal discrimination against migrant workers were gradually proscribed.[2] Building on the system already introduced by the European Coal and Steel Community, the European Social Fund (ESF) was also established with 'the task of rendering the employment of workers easier and of increasing their geographical and occupation mobility within the Community' (Art 123). The ESF became operational at the end of 1962 and, over the next six years, almost 1 million workers had benefited from it. However, its contribution was minimal in comparison with the outlays of the MS themselves, and there was far greater migration from non-EC areas than from within the Community (although there was significant movement from Southern Italy to France and Germany).[3] The final key element in this area of policy was to ensure that MS adopted 'such measures in the field of social security as are necessary to provide for the freedom of movement of workers' (Art 51). Action on this was almost immediate, with two Regulations passed in 1958, and a series of further measures between then and 1970.

None of this was 'high-profile'. In general, it was devised and implemented by restricted circles of officials, and even the ESF was criticised for being unimaginative and hierarchical in its procedures.[4]

[1] *European Social Policy: Options for the Union* (Green Paper), Luxembourg: Office for Official Publications of the European Communities, November 1993.

[2] Chris Brewster and Paul Teague, *European Community Social Policy: Its Impact on the UK*, London: Institute of Personnel Management, 1989, pp. 55-8.

[3] Brewster and Teague, op. cit., pp. 58-60.

[4] D. Collins, *The European Communities: The Social Policy of the First Phase*, London:

Yet the Treaty of Rome itself contained the basis for a much more active social policy if decision-makers chose to implement it. By far the most radical commitment was the requirement in Article 119 that:

> Each member State shall during the first stage ensure and subsequently maintain the application of the principle that men and women should receive equal pay for equal work...

This fundamental democratic principle had been incorporated within the treaty somewhat fortuitously. The French government had already accepted it at the end of the Second World War because it was simultaneously preoccupied by two problems: a declining population and a shortage of labour. The equal pay commitment had therefore been one aspect of a policy designed to provide conditions which would enable women simultaneously to raise children and remain within the labour force.[5] However, French employers feared that they would suffer a competitive disadvantage in a Common Market unless all other MS implemented a similar policy – hence the French government's insistence on Art. 119. However, in practice this remained a 'dead letter' in the first phase: the other MS ignored their Treaty obligation, and neither the Commission nor the French government took any action against them. It was, however, an issue which would play a major role in converting the EU into a major social policy actor in its second phase.

Most of the other social provisions were less securely based in law, but could also have significant effects if activated. In particular, following a general statement about the 'need to promote improved working conditions and an improved standard of living for workers' (Art. 117), Art. 118 charged the Commission with

> . . . the task of promoting close co-operation between Member States in the social field, particularly in matters relating to:
> – employment;
> – labour law and working conditions;
> – basic and advanced vocational training;

Martin Robertson, vol. II, 1975, cited in Brewster and Teague, op. cit., p. 61.

[5] Adrienne Clark, 'Some Are More Equal Than Others: A study of European Community gender equality policies with particular reference to women in the United Kingdom and women in France', unpubl. MA thesis, South Bank University, 1993.

- social   security;
- prevention of occupational accidents and diseases;
- occupational hygiene;
- the right of association, and collective bargaining between employers and workers.

However, there was no clear *commitment* in these areas. The Commission was to make studies, deliver opinions, and arrange consultations, but it was not evident that any firm action was expected and, as already noted, little concrete policy emerged in the first phase. Nevertheless, the specification of relevant issues provided some basis for later developments.

Finally, it is worth noting two other elements of the original treaty with potential social policy relevance. First, the Common Agricultural Policy included a social dimension in that Art. 39 stipulated that 'a fair standard of living for the agricultural community' must be ensured. However, as relatively wealthy farmers have always derived far greater benefits from the CAP than poorer ones, it will not be discussed here. Secondly, the Preamble to the Treaty professed an anxiety to reduce the 'differences existing between the various regions and the backwardness of the less favoured regions'; and Art. 92(3) permitted some derogations from competition policy to permit regional aid. Later on the regional policy was certainly to have relevance for social policy but, before 1970, this scarcely existed since it was also encompassed within free market assumptions.

Overall, it therefore seems reasonable to conclude that, during the first phase Community social policy existed mainly in embryo. However, it is significant that even in the 1960s the Commission was much more ambitious in its thinking on social policy, in the belief that this could convert the EC into a 'real' Community, while the governments thought that the Commission was far too close to the trade unions in this area. This led to mounting resistance from the MS and a complete breakdown in communications between the governments (except Italy) and the Commission by 1966. In December of that year a compromise was reached, which meant that the initiative in social policy passed from the Commission to the Council and the Commission's contacts with Trade Unions and Employers' associations were to be restricted.[6]

[6] Elizabeth Meehan, *Citizenship and the European Community*, London: Sage 1993, pp. 68-70.

During the second phase of development – from about 1970 till 1984 – Community intervention in social policy became far more active and extensive, and the 1966 compromise was superseded. There has been some debate as to the reasons for this, but most commentators agree that a crucial factor was the submission of a memorandum on social policy by Chancellor Willy Brandt to the Hague Conference in December 1969 which stated that co-ordination of economic integration with social harmonisation was vital. This, he argued, was necessary both because of the social upheavals that had followed the May 1968 'events' in Paris, and because any move towards EMU would need a counterbalancing set of social policies to protect those who were likely to suffer from such a development.[7] In other words, he saw a need to legitimise the Community by giving it a 'human face' – an idea shared by the Commission.[8] Moreover, this mission soon became more urgent, with the sharp downturn in economic performance and rise in unemployment in the early 1970s.

Despite Brandt's memorandum in 1969, little action was taken by the Council of Ministers until the Paris summit in 1972 which called upon the Commission to draw up an action programme by 1 January 1974 'providing for concrete measures and the necessary resources, particularly in the framework of the Social Fund'.[9] The Council of Ministers then adopted the (non legally binding) programme, which specified forty priority measures to be carried out during a three year period. The major headings have been summarised as:

1. the attainment of full and better employment in the Community;
2. the improvement of living and working conditions so as to make possible their harmonisation while the improvement is being maintained;

[7] Juliet Lodge, 'Social Europe: fostering a People's Europe?' in Juliet Lodge (ed.), *The European Community and the Challenge of the Future*, London: Pinter, 1989, p. 31.

[8] Michael Shanks, *European Social Policy Today and Tomorrow*, Oxford: Pergamon, 1977, p. 13, cited in Brewster and Teague, op. cit., p. 68.

[9] Sonia Mazey, 'European Community Social Policy' in Valerio Lintner and Sonia Mazey, *The European Community: Economic and Political Aspects*, Maidenhead: McGraw-Hill, 1991, p. 115.

3. the increased involvement of management and labour in the economic and social decisions of the Community, and of workers in the life of the enterprises in which they are employed.[10]

Inevitably, the results were 'mixed' (see below, page 86). In particular, although the reduction of unemployment – especially of youth and long-term unemployment – had been seen as the major priority, the Community's own resources were quite inadequate to make any *substantial* contribution to the resolution of the problem. The ESF was the most concrete policy instrument in this sphere, and it gradually became more focused – to help certain regions and certain sections of society such as migrant workers, the young unemployed, women, and people with disabilities. The resources available to it were also gradually increased. Similarly, the regional development fund (ERDF), which was established in 1975, was also expanded and became more coordinated with the ESF as time went on. Nevertheless, these funds were inevitably unable to make a major impact at a macro-Community level and unemployment grew from 2.6 million in 1973 to 6.5 million in 1980 and to 12.4 million (with the inclusion of Greece) in 1984.[11]

In 1981 it was the turn of the newly-elected French Socialist government to attempt to elevate the Community's role in social policy. Mitterrand's first government was committed to attempt domestic expansion and sought a complementary policy steer at EC level.[12]

With Margaret Thatcher blocking all progress until Britain's demands for budgetary rebates were settled and in a generally 'monetarist' international climate, the French initiative was ignored and the Socialist government soon embarked on its U-turn towards austerity policies. However, the proposals re-emerged three years later when the Fontainebleau summit (which approved the

---

[10] P. Venturini, *1992: The European Social Dimension*, Luxembourg: Office for Official Publications of the European Communities, 1989 p. 16, quoted in Mark Wise and Richard Gibb, *Single Market to Social Europe*, Harlow: Longman, 1993, p. 134.

[11] Wise and Gibb, op. cit., pp. 139-40.

[12] The new government thus submitted a memorandum to its partners, with three main objectives: 1. to place employment problems at the heart of Community policy; 2. to increase the 'social dialogue' between employers and employees at Community, national and company level; 3. to improve consultation and cooperation on matters of social protection. Wise and Gibb, op. cit., p. 146.

budgetary settlement) approved a new social action plan with the rationale that the Community would not be able to compete internationally unless it also strengthened its social cohesion.[13] This was then reinforced by Delors' appointment to the European Commission and his immediate declaration that the goal was not only Economic and Monetary Union, but a 'Social Europe'.

By now the British government had already blocked a series of Directives in the social policy area and it appeared unlikely that Margaret Thatcher would agree to any new legal basis for social policy.[14] However, the Single European Act (Art. 118a) eventually incorporated a significant advance by putting health and safety legislation on the same decision-making basis (qualified majority voting) as matters necessary for the attainment of the Single Market. This subsequently led to various disputes, with the British government arguing that Commission proposals should be based on social policy, where unanimity was required, rather than health and safety. (Indeed it even took this line in May 1989 in an attempt to veto the introduction of compulsory health warnings on cigarette packets!) However, the new treaty basis for decision-making in health and safety undoubtedly constituted a major breakthrough in the social policy area and has led to some important Directives on working conditions and related matters, such as maternity leave.

Following the signature of the Single European Act, it was apparent that the conflict over social policy was continuing. At first it seemed as if the British government might secure the initiative, for in December 1986 it secured approval by the other MS for an 'Action Plan for Employment Growth', which had a distinctly de-regulationist emphasis.[15] However, the next year, under the Belgian Presidency, the emphasis shifted back towards social protection, and early in 1988 the Delors 1 package was finally accepted. This had important social implications as it proposed a co-ordination of the ESF and ERDF and doubled the budgets of each of these funds. Then in September of the same year the Vice President of the Commission, Manuel Marin, put forward an extensive memorandum on the social dimension of the international market, which foreshadowed the Social Charter.[16]

[13] Wise and Gibb, op. cit., p. 147.
[14] Brewster and Teague, op. cit., pp. 82-4.
[15] Ibid., pp. 97-9.
[16] For an extensive summary of the proposals, see Mazey, 'EC Social Policy', op.

However, this was not a definite commitment and during the next year the conflict over social policy intensified.[17] Finally, in May 1989 the Commission put forward the first draft of the Social Charter.

This was less extensive than the kind of 'social constitution' which some had sought, and it was in the form of a 'solemn declaration', rather than a legally binding document. But it was clearly also a firm rejection of Britain's minimalist position. However, the bargaining continued for six months, with concessions made (primarily by the French) in an abortive attempt to secure British adherence. The Social charter adopted in December 1989 sought to define the basic social rights of EC citizens as

- freedom of movement of EC citizens within the Community;
- equitable wages sufficient to enable a decent standard of living;
- rights for part-time and temporary workers;
- improved living and working conditions involving the progressive Community-wide harmonisation of holiday periods and so on;
- adequate social protection for both those in and out of work;
- freedom of association and collective bargaining;
- the right to vocational training;
- equal treatment for men and women;
- adequate participation of employees in the affairs of the companies that employ them;
- satisfactory health and safety at work;
- protection of children and adolescents at work;
- proper retirement pensions; and
- the integration of disabled persons into the world of work.

The Social Charter was not really a new departure. Apart from the fact that the Council of Europe had already possessed a rather similar document in 1961, it was clear that many of the social rights were derived from the original Treaty of Rome, and some of the

---

cit., pp. 123-4.

[17] The Commission and most of the MS occupied a position somewhere between the two extremes of the Trade Unions and European Parliament majority, which sought a legally binding charter to counter-balance the internal market, and the European Union of Employers Confederations (UNICE) and the British government, which wanted no further social policy initiative. Paul Teague and John Grahl, *Industrial Relations and European Integration*, London: Lawrence and Wishart, 1992, p. 120.

items had long existed in the form of draft proposals. Nor was the action programme to implement the Social Charter, which the Commission produced, particularly radical. It is true that it included some proposals on holiday and sickness pay, health and safety and the mutual recognition of qualifications, which had not been included in the original Charter, but there were also some important omissions. Thus whereas Articles 14-16 of the Charter had laid down rights to freedom of association and collective bargaining, the action programme explicitly ruled out any concrete EC initiatives on the grounds that the MS retained responsibility in this area. And although the Charter referred to a 'decent wage', following lobbying by Ireland and Portugal, no legally binding instrument establishing a minimum wage was included.[18] Yet despite this dilution, progress was painfully slow. Although the aim had been to implement the Charter by the end of 1992, very little of it had even been converted into legislation by the end of 1991, while 200 (out of the total of 282) single market measures had been adopted, and 168 were already in force.[19] By the start of 1993 only just over half of the Commission's proposals had been adopted by the Council and, by the end of 1994, the pace had not increased, largely as a result of British policy.[20]

The high point in expectations about social policy came in 1989, and the subsequent crisis over the integration process has left it in an acutely difficult position. The Maastricht Treaty itself contained no significant new elements in this sphere because of the British attitude, and the so-called Social Chapter (officially the 'Social Agreement' in the Protocol on Social Policy) signed by the other eleven (and subsequently adhered to by the three new Members in 1995) stated that it wished to implement the 1989 Social Charter on the basis of the *acquis communautaire*. It also clarified the policies that could be introduced by unanimity – areas such as social security,

---

[18] Teague and Grahl , op. cit., p. 123.

[19] Wise and Gibb, op. cit., p. 181.

[20] The Social Action Programme adopted in November 1989 foresaw twenty-one proposals for directives. By July 1994 the Commission had proposed all of these and thirteen had been adopted. (European Social Policy, White Paper, op. cit., p. 21). On 6 December 1994 the British government vetoed the Directive which would have given part-time workers protection against unfair treatment by employers. (On 22 September 1994 Britain also vetoed a Directive to introduce a right to unpaid paternity leave, but this had not been a part of the Social Action Programme).

termination of employment, and third-country worker protection – and those that could be introduced by a newly calculated qualified majority – proposals on working conditions, consultation of workers, and equality between men and women with regard to labour market opportunities and treatment at work. Britain would not be present for such discussions.

It was always clear that this arrangement would be unwieldy and probably unworkable. The other MS were obviously concerned that Britain would be able to under-cut the rest of the EU by maintaining a low-wage, unregulated economy, and these fears appeared plausible when Hoover announced re-location plans from Brittany to Scotland before Maastricht had even been ratified.[21] On the other hand, the British government also had reasons for anxiety: as there was no absolute demarcation between the policy areas specified in the Social Agreement and those in the Treaty, it could be subjected to decisions which it had not discussed. It was also extremely difficult to see how Britain would be able to evade any employment agreements in multinationals which operated in both Britain and other parts of the EU.

The most significant concrete development in the immediate post-Maastricht period was the compromise agreement on the Delors II package at the Edinburgh summit in December 1992, leading to a further increase in the cohesion funds, available to the ESF and ERDF. However, the publication of the Green Paper, *European Social Policy: Options for the Union* in November 1993, and the subsequent White Paper the following July, *may* represent a significant new stage in EU social policy-making. Before considering this it is necessary to consider some of the lessons that may be derived from the experience so far.

Successes and failures: a brief evaluation of EU social policy, 1958-93

The following is an over-view, divided into three sections: areas in which the EU may be regarded as successful; gender equality, in which it may be regarded as partially successful; and areas in which it has been wholly unsuccessful.

[21] ' The Hoover affair and social dumping', *European Industrial Relations Review*, 230, March 1993.

SUCCESSES

Information.   It is hardly surprising that the Community has found it relatively easy to make a positive contribution in areas which are the least politically sensitive. In general, data collection and analysis is in this category and the EU has become an indispensable source on comparative statistics and interpretation over a vast range of social policy issues. It is true that the collection of data or the request for reports are often ways in which decision-makers seek to avoid actual policy-making, and this has certainly been the case with the EU. Yet even when this may have been the intention, the research itself has been valuable in prompting further action. For example, it is possible that few government ministers were aware that relative poverty had *increased* between 1957 and the early 1980s until the Commission presented them with this evidence in the first anti-poverty programme.[22] Similarly, the EU's extensive investigations into the extent of gender inequality could not have been carried out without the resources of the Commission and they have certainly provided insights into the multiple sources of discrimination throughout the area which would otherwise probably have remained hidden (see further, page 90). Obviously, information is not equivalent to action or even policy, but it has a close relationship, with the second form of 'success'.

Cross-national awareness and networking.   EU information has facili-tated cross-national comparisons. Naturally, this can inform policy-making at state or sub-state level in a search to emulate 'best practice' when the political will exists. But in any case it has been very beneficial to campaigning groups, which have been able to 'network' to make common demands on the basis of lessons derived from the EU as a whole. The Commission has often facilitated such activities and the EP has also served as a focus for articulating particular views at the EU level. Various womens' and equal opportunities networks have been outstanding examples of this kind of lobbying activity.

Health and safety.   The involvement of the EU in Health and Safety legislation has advanced considerably, particularly since the Single European Act. Despite the recurrent conflicts between the British

---

[22] Mazey, 'EC Social Policy', op. cit., p. 119.

government and the Commission over the legal basis for some of the proposals, there has been a general willingness to accept the necessity for maintaining standards in this area. The risk that the Single Market could drive down safety levels and result in a politically unacceptable accident has led to agreement that protection is necessary. This has meant that Health and Safety has become an area of *supranational* regulation.[23] While the effects of this are less significant in the countries that already had relatively high levels of protection, and also naturally depend upon the effectiveness of domestic enforcement, one expert has pointed out that the Commission has acquired considerably autonomy in this area and that the EU has therefore introduced some measures which exceeded those in any of the MS. In this area the EU has not only been able to avoid the customary process of harmonising at the lowest level, but has even superseded the highest.[24]

The ESF and ERDF.   In the EU budget for 1994 the ERDF was granted an allocation of 9 billion ECU (or 12% of the total expenditure) and the ESF 6.5 billion (or 9% of total expenditure). This represents a further increase in allocation since the doubling of the structural funds in 1988 (the respective percentages in 1989 were thus 9.6% and 7.2%). Within the severe financial constraints within which they operate, both funds have become more focused and beneficial than in the early years of their operation, and some of the criticisms of the administration of the funds which are addressed to them should often be re-routed to the governments of the MS. For example, while it would both reduce the complexity of the application procedures and be highly beneficial to many of the most needy groups and areas if matching funding was not required, it is not in the Commission's power to make such a radical alteration in the system. Similarly, although recent reforms have attempt to prevent governments from substituting EU funding for their own outlays, national expenditure accounting is notoriously opaque and it is not easy for the Commission to detect all the ways in which the MS may 'massage' their accounts.[25]

---

[23] Teague and Grahl, op. cit., p. 136.

[24] Giandomenico Majone, 'The European Community Between Social Policy and Social Regulation', *Journal of Common Market Studies*, 31, 2, June 1993.

[25] For a critique of the operation of the funds, see 'Report of the Committee on

The funds are now designed to combat both *regional* problems (those areas with a per capita GDP of less than 75% of the EU average and areas of industrial decline) and to target particular groups (for example, women, young people, and people with disabilities) wherever they live. There has also been an attempt to by-pass the governments of MS and work more directly with the sub-state governments, regions, and voluntary groups concerned. Naturally, the approach is beset with difficulties, but the results have often compared favourably with MS's own initiatives.

'Tidying up' regulations and facilitating exchanges.   The EU is normally able to make an impact where differing regulations already exist within MS, and where there is a clear need for compatibility if other policy aims are to succeed. For example, the evident requirement that social security benefits be made available to migrants from one EU country to another if the free movement provisions were to have any reality, led to the gradual simplification of the procedures throughout the 1960s. Similarly, the EU may make progress in relatively non-controversial areas even when regulations do not yet exist in some of the MS. For example, there was no opposition when the Commission presented proposals to ensure that all workers had the right to receive a document from their employers informing them to the nature of the work they were required to perform, the duration of the contract, and other basic rights and duties. This was seen to constitute a minimum obligation on companies, and the Directive was accepted in October 1991. Nevertheless, it meant that new labour legislation was necessary in Denmark, Greece, Spain, Belgium and Portugal.[26]

While each individual change of this kind may be non-contentious, the cumulative impact may be considerable. When considered in relation to initiatives in areas such as the ERASMUS student exchanges, progress towards mutual recognition of qualifications, and town-twinning schemes, some sense of 'Europeanisation' in relatively 'low profile' matters is no doubt developing.

Social Affairs, Employment and the Working Environment on the European Parliament's approach to the revision of the European Social Fund', *European Parliament Session Documents*, A3-0057/93, 18 Feb. 1993.
[26] Teague and Grahl, op. cit., p. 128.

ACTION ON GENDER INEQUALITY: A PARTIAL SUCCESS

Since gender inequality has been the 'high profile' area in which the EU has been the most active, its successes and failures are of great significance in evaluating its overall record as a social policy actor.

As already noted, Art. 119 provided the Community with a more concrete legal basis for action than was the case in most other areas of social policy. Nevertheless, it was only activated during the 1970s, as a result of a series of judgments by the ECJ in the Defrenne case, which was initiated when an air stewardess took action against Sabena Airlines, on the grounds of sexual discrimination.[27] The most important judgment was in 1976 when the Court ruled that equal pay was directly applicable and that the Belgian government could not therefore evade the obligations of Art. 119 by arguing that no such domestic law existed. These judgments coincided with the incorporation of the goal of gender equality in the 1974 Social Action Programme, which led to three Equality Directives (on Equal Pay, Equal Treatment, and Social Security) being adopted by the Council in 1975, 1976 and 1978 respectively (although the last only came into effect in 1984). However, the Commission was also soon persuaded that the fundamental causes of gender inequality were deeply embedded in the social, economic, cultural and political structures and that the formal equality legislation would have only a limited impact. The Council agreed to fund the New Community Action Programme on the Promotion of Equal Opportunities for Men and Women in 1982, and the women's networks which have been established since then have played an important role in maintaining the impetus. But how successful has the EU been in this respect?

Positive aspects.   First, the legislation itself led to important changes in the domestic law of several MS, with a new law in Belgium and reforms in Germany, Italy and Luxembourg.[28] It also led to a series of amendments in British legislation and it is notable that, even when the Labour Party was pledged to withdrawal from the Community

---

[27] For a detailed analysis, see Sonia Mazey, 'European Community Action on Behalf of Women: The Limits of Legislation', *Journal of Common Market Studies*, 27, 1, Sept. 1988.

[28] Ibid., p. 69.

in 1983, it recognised that it would need a firm commitment to maintain the standards set by the EC.[29]

Secondly, it seems clear that, once women's campaigning groups had raised the level of consciousness on the subject, the EU – primarily through the Commission and the EP – has subsequently played an important role in maintaining it as a high priority in its social policy. Action on gender inequality has been incorporated into the anti-poverty and vocational training programmes, and the EU has become increasingly sophisticated and informed in its analysis of the multi-dimensional causes of gender inequality. Thus, for example, the chapter on 'Equality of Opportunity between Women and Men' in the 1994 White Paper on Social Policy was probably the most impressive part of the document (see further below).

Thirdly, and more generally, the EU role has had a catalytic effect upon MS, perhaps particularly in some of the countries where the women's movement was less well-developed. The very fact that there has been EU involvement has facilitated the growth of campaigning groups where they hardly existed, and has probably helped to maintain pressure elsewhere. For example, although the British Conservative government's refusal to accept various EU Directives has had a negative impact on the position of women, the EU dimension has certainly constrained it to some extent. Not only has it complied with ECJ judgments, but anxiety to avoid further politically damaging publicity may sometimes have led it to compromise. It has, for example, been argued that it finally agreed to accept (an admittedly diluted) Directive on maternity leave in November 1991 for fear of precipitating an outcry shortly before a general election.[30]

---

[29] This was not mentioned in the NEC's statement presented to the 1981 Conference, 'Withdrawal from the EEC'. However, a research paper prepared by the Labour Party Research and International Departments, stated in relation to the 1978 Equality Directive: '. . . it is a step in the direction of promoting full equality between men and women and it is true to say that it is a step that has only been taken because of our membership of the EEC. Measures to promote equality would otherwise have been low on the agenda. It is important, therefore, that with withdrawal from the EEC, the issue is not allowed to slip back on the list of priorities and the steps taken under EEC pressure must be maintained and built upon'. 'Withdrawal from the EEC', Research Paper 5, pp. 25-6.

[30] Wise and Gibb, p. 196. For a full discussion of the Conservative government's policy on EU action on gender equality, see Clarke, op. cit.

Overall, the EU has therefore directly benefited some women and has had some positive, though less tangible effects, on the wider issues.

Limitations. As was noted earlier, the EU itself recognised – through its various action programmes – that the inequalities were deeply embedded. But recognition is, of course, insufficient to ensure success. The depressing conclusion is thus that even after twenty years of action at EU level, and within the MS, the extent of gender inequality remains immense. Thus although there has been a significant improvement in the educational attainments of women in the EU countries, this has not been reflected by equal progress in the labour market.[31] In 1991 the wage differentials between men and women were as shown in Table 4.1. At the same time,

Table 4.1. WAGE DIFFERENTIALS (WOMEN/MEN, %) OF GROSS MONTHLY EARNINGS OF NON-MANUAL WORKERS AND GROSS HOURLY EARNINGS OF MANUAL WORKERS, 1991

	Bel	Den	Ger	Gr	Sp	Fr	Irl	It	Lux	NL	P	UK
MANUFACTURING												
Manual	−26.2	−15.5	−26.5	−20.8	−22.6	−21.4	−30.2		−39.0	−24.4	−29.5	−32.0
Non-manual	−35.5		−32.6	−31.5	−36.2	−32.6			−44.1	−34.2	−30.8	−41.3
RETAIL												
Non-manual	−26.8		−30.0	−19.8	−36.2	−31.7			−38.0	−32.5	−19.7	−36.2

Source: Women in the European Community, EUROSTAT, 1993.

the percentage of women working part-time, in which job security, social protection and career prospects are generally worse is shown in Table 4.2. Such inequalities are reflected in the power structure of the MS, with massive under-representation of women in senior positions in the professions, management, and the civil service. The involvement of women in senior government positions is also extremely low, as indicated in Table 4.3.

---

[31] Between 1985 and 1990 the number of women in higher education as a percentage of total student population rose from 47% to 48%. In Ireland, Spain, Denmark and Portugal the number of female students increased by 30-40%. Only in (West) Germany was there a decline. 'Women in the European Community: Rapid Reports', Population and Social Conditions, no. 10, EUROSTAT.

Table 4.2. PART-TIME WORKING AS %
OF WOMEN IN EMPLOYMENT

EU12	Bel	Den	Ger	Gr	Sp	Fr	Ire	It	Lux	NL	P	UK
27.9	27.4	37.8	30.1	7.2	11.2	23.5	17.9	10.4	18.2	59.9	11.0	43.7

Source: 'Women in the European Community', EUROSTAT 1993.

Table 4.3. WOMEN IN NATIONAL GOVERNMENTS[32]

	Government formed	Total members of govt.	No. of women	% of women
Be	1992	16	2	12.5
Den	1990	19	4	21.1
Ger	1992	53	9	17.0
Gr	1992	37	3	8.1
Sp	1991	18	2	11.1
Fr	1992	42	7	16.7
Irl	1992	30	5	16.7
It	1993	62	8	12.9
Lux	1989	12	1	8.3
NL	1989	25	6	24.0
P	1991	71	7	9.9
UK	1992	99	7	7.0
EU12		484	61	12.6

Source: 'Women in the European Community', EUROSTAT, 1993.

Because the sources of gender inequality are so deep-rooted, it is perhaps not surprising that the EU has been relatively unsuccessful in eradicating them. Moreover, because the operation of the labour market is of fundamental importance, economic changes may easily negate the effectiveness of policies specifically designed to improve the position of women. In particular, the move towards more part-time and temporary employment throughout the EU has reinforced many of the problems, particularly as Britain has blocked the extension of employment rights in this sphere.

EU policy on gender inequality will be discussed further below. But the above points suggest that its achievements are 'mixed', rather than 'outstanding'.

[32] It is notable that the Delors Commission had a worse record than any of the governments: 1 woman out of 17 commissioners (5.9%).

HARMONISATION POLICIES ON SENSITIVE ISSUES

It was noted above that the implied minimum wage commitment of the Social Charter was withdrawn because of objections from Ireland and Portugal, and Britain has resisted a whole range of policies which would limit its freedom to deregulate the labour market. The Commission has also failed almost entirely when it has sought the harmonisation of policies on the basis of 'best practice' in highly sensitive areas. The two outstanding examples are in fields of social security and industrial relations.

During the 1970s the Commission appeared to believe that it was insufficient to facilitate movement by making it easier for workers to secure benefits in another country, and thought that social security needed to be harmonised completely. But, as Brewster and Teague suggest, this would be a massive – and perhaps impossible – task. First, there are very significant differences in the rationales for provision in the various MS. For example, French family benefits are still designed to encourage larger families, while the British system means that families will be relatively better off with one or two children. Secondly, specific aspects of policy, such as pension arrangements, differ so radically between MS that harmonisation may not be a feasible option. Thirdly, if alignment were to take place at the highest level there would be a vast burden on the poorer MS – probably meaning that the richer countries would need to transfer resources to them to subsidise their social security expenditure.[33] A further factor would be resistance from populations in countries which were asked to make the most extensive changes in their systems so as to achieve the harmonisation. For example, even if health expenditure *per capita* is higher in other countries than in Britain, there would no doubt be very considerable opposition to any suggestion that an alternative procedure (of initial payment, and then partial state rebate) should be introduced. Difficulties of this kind led the Commission to move away from the harmonisation principle and to adopt a less ambitious approach, involving more limited agreements. However, in the industrial relations area, this conclusion was drawn only after long and damaging conflicts.

As noted earlier, the Treaty of Rome had mentioned various aspects of industrial relations as fields in which the Commission should encourage close co-operation among MS (Art. 118). Little

[33] Brewster and Teague, op. cit., pp. 270-1.

was done on this until the early 1970s, when the attempt to secure stronger Trade Union and working-class support for the Community became an important element in the attempt to create a 'social Europe'. The general basis for this was through the development of the so-called Social Dialogue, on the assumption that close consultation between employers and workers (the 'social partners') was necessary if the Community, and its social policy, were to advance. This was not controversial but the Commission also sought to advance a more specific initiative, which had originally been proposed in 1972, as part of the Social Dialogue. This was the Draft Fifth Directive, which proposed that all limited liability companies with at least 500 workers should establish a two-tier board structure, with significant workers' representation. This triggered opposition, not only from predictable quarters, such as the European Union of Employers' Confederations (UNICE) and from MS which did not have this system, but even from West German companies which already operated it. A succession of drafts was put forward, causing considerable conflict between the 'social partners' within the Social Dialogue, and between the Commission and the Council of Ministers. In 1980 the Commission made a second proposal on a similar subject – the so-called Vredeling Directive. This required companies and subsidiaries employing at least 100 people to give the workforce information every six months on such issues as structure and manning, the economic and financial situation, business prospects, production and investment programmes, rationalisation plans, envisaged changes in working methods, and indeed anything likely to have a substantial effect on the employees' interests.[34] The proposals which, like the Fifth Directive, had been influenced by the German model, unleashed a storm of protest, not only from employers' groups and many MS, but even from Japanese and American multinational corporations, which threatened the Commission with reduced investment if the Directive were introduced.[35] As a result of all the pressure, it was substantially diluted, but Britain still vetoed the revised draft in 1983 and threatened to do so again in 1986. A far weaker version was finally introduced in June 1994 under the Social Agreement (that is, excluding Britain).[36]

[34] Ibid., p. 76.

[35] Wise and Gibb, op. cit., p. 172.

[36] The Directive, agreed on 22 June 1994, was that European works councils should

Should the Commission have ever introduced the more ambitious abortive proposals, which led to a breakdown in the 'Social Dialogue' in the early 1980s? The answers of employers' organisations and their supporters in governments are predictable, but it is also clear that some trade unions campaigned in favour of the proposals solely for tactical reasons, and without really favouring workers' representation on company boards.[37] Thus even analysts, who are very sympathetic to the development of a more progressive European industrial relations regime, have been extremely critical of the Commission for seeking to introduce these Directives.[38] Labour lawyers have suggested that it is difficult to transplant industrial relations systems from one environment to another since they are embedded in the social, economic and political structures of the countries in which they are based.[39] The Commission was therefore probably naive in believing that it could harmonise systems of labour relations on the basis of 'best practice', *both* because it was confronting issues at the heart of the labour-capital relationship, and *because* each MS had some specific traditions which were resistant to harmonisation.

In summary, it therefore seems that the overall record of Community social policy has been as follows. It has made progress in relatively 'low profile' areas, which nevertheless have a cumulative impact; it has facilitated networking and campaigns on particular issues; the ESF and ERDF have funded some useful projects; and it has maintained equal opportunities as a high priority with an important legislative effect in this sphere. But it has not made significant inroads into deep rooted inequalities, and attempts at

---

be established in transnational companies with at least 1,000 employees in the EU outside Britain. The law was designed to ensure that workers were consulted about strategic corporate decisions which would affect their livelihoods, such as changing technology, shifts in production from one country to another, or large-scale redundancies. The Directive was designed to encourage managements to agree arrangements with their trade unions, with a fall-back procedure imposing works council machinery if such negotiations failed. No compulsory machinery could be established before the year 2000. *The Guardian*, 23 June 1994.

[37] Mazey, 'EC Social Policy', op. cit., p. 120.

[38] For an extensive argument of this kind, see Teague and Grahl, *Industrial Relations*, op. cit.

[39] R. Blainpain (ed.), *Comparative Labour Law and Industrial Relations*, Deventer: Kluwer, 1985, p. 14, quoted in Brewster and Teague, op. cit., pp. 93-4.

harmonisation in sensitive policy areas have generally failed. What lessons may be drawn from this record?

Democracy and EU social policy: prospects and possibilities

EU social policy is almost inevitably the victim of a paradox. Because welfare issues affect the lives of ordinary people in obvious ways, those who seek greater popular support for the Community have naturally wanted it to become involved in social policy as a means of enhancing its legitimacy. But this creates the danger that the very involvement may then rebound upon the EU and actually *diminish* its popular appeal. There is an obvious reason for this. EU involvement in social policy will have a legitimising function only if the problems which it seeks to address are already salient. However, their salience stems from the failure of the MS to resolve them and therefore may also make them intractable at EU level. It may therefore prove counter-productive to have raised expectations that could not be realised. This has relevance for the two occasions on which social policy has become a particularly 'high profile' affair. Thus the 1974 Action Programme was announced when the economic recession, following the oil crisis, was at its height and when governments were cutting budgets and unwilling to transfer major resources or policy-making powers for social policy to the Community. It was therefore unrealistic to expect it to have any dramatic impact upon the problems. Yet its failure to do so contributed to the 'Eurosclerosis' of the late 1970s. The current situation is similar.

In the late 1980s Delors, backed by the European Parliament, played a particularly active role in fostering the belief in the 'social dimension' to counterbalance the negative effects of the single market, and to ensure 'social cohesion' and social justice. This raised hopes amongst many, particularly in Social Democratic parties and the trade union movement, that the EU could act as a kind of supranational welfare state and resolve the massive problems of poverty, unemployment, inequality, and social exclusion that now existed in Europe. It was certainly important to have raised the demand for an active social policy to provide protection against the rigours of the open market. But expectations may have been raised too high, and this may have been a factor in causing the alienation from the EU, which was manifested in the post-Maastricht crisis.

Such attitudes are also evident in rather pessimistic recent academic analyses of the prospects for EU social policy.[40]

There are certainly some good reasons for such pessimism. First, the actions of the British government in refusing to accept the Social Charter in 1989, in blocking a whole series of Directives, and in opting out of the Social Chapter at Maastricht, have certainly played a role in undermining the EU's role in this area of policy. Indeed, as noted in Chapter 2, the legal status for social policy-making is now highly obscure and the current situation is perhaps being treated as an inter-regnum in the hope that a new British government will 'opt-in' so that normal procedures may be applied. Secondly, there are some signs that the advocates of 'neo-liberalism' have made advances at EU level and are now having an impact on its social policy.[41] And thirdly, as noted in the previous chapter, poverty, inequality, and social exclusion have become desperately serious problems throughout the EU. The situation is therefore certainly very serious. Yet pessimism may also have been the consequence of unrealistic aspirations. Some of the grounds for caution about exaggerating the possible role of the EU have already been dealt with in previous chapters. First, the decision-making system obviously enables a recalcitrant state – such as Britain – to block social policy initiatives. Secondly, the divisions in the Commission – and the comparatively low position of the Social Affairs Commissioner in the hierarchy – mean that it has not always been a united force in favour of active social policy intervention. Thirdly, the limited budget is also obviously a major constraint. However, all these weaknesses are also reflections of more fundamental issues, which

---

[40] Wolfgang Streeck and Philippe Schmitter, 'From National Corporation to Transnational Pluralism: Organised Interests in the Single European Market', *Politics and Society*, 19, 2, June 1991; Robert Geyer, 'Socialism and the EC' in Cafruny and Rosenthal, op. cit.; Paul Teague, 'Co-ordination or Decentralisation? EC Social Policy and Industrial Relations' in Lodge, *European Community and the Challenge of the Future* (2nd edn), op. cit.; M. Rhodes, 'The future of the "Social Dimension": Labour Market Regulation in Post-1992 Europe', *Journal of Common Market Studies*, 30, 3, March 1992.

[41] For example, the July 1994 White Paper certainly placed some emphasis on shifting social security benefits 'from the objective of assistance to the objective of employment generation' (Introduction: paras 13 and 14), and also expressed anxiety about the problem of rising social protection expenditure (chapter 6, para. 7).

are related to the role of social policy within the domestic systems of the MS.

On average in 1992 the governments of the EU12 spent 25.9% of GDP on social protection benefits.[42] States are involved in almost all spheres of society, particularly through their health, education and social security policies. While most governments would be keen to reduce their own expenditure in these areas, they would not wish to lose the credit for their positive aspects. For the claim that the 'nation-state' has become a 'welfare' state has been a crucially significant aspect of its legitimacy. The post-war liberal-democratic system as a *whole* justified itself on the basis of this claim, and rival political forces within the states have often used social policy arguments as the major elements in their electoral contests. Because the welfare systems have been so deeply embedded in the societies, they have also become important in influencing the development of 'national' – and nationalist – consciousness.[43] Thus while those who have wished to enhance the legitimacy of the EU have naturally turned to social policy as a key element in their strategy, many MS have been just as adamant in resisting this attempt. Since the mid 1980s this battle has obviously been fought the most keenly by Britain. This is not surprising since the British Conservatives were simultaneously going the furthest towards neo-liberalism domestically and were the keenest to restrict the development of the EU in most areas. Because the other governments were less ideologically opposed to the post-war 'consensus', and less hostile to the expansion of EU competences, they did not view the comparatively mild Social Charter as a threat. But this does not mean that other MS would accept EU *primacy* in the social policy area, or that they would be prepared to accept harmonisation of welfare systems, if this involved any significant loss of their autonomy in this area. This was the main element in the original dispute over social policy between the Commission and the Council in the 1960s and it is still evident. Certainly, EU competence in the area has developed very consid-

---

[42] 'Facts through figures: A Statistical Portrait of the European Union', EUROSTAT, 1994. The figure includes expenditure on old age, sickness, invalidity/ disability, survivors, maternity, unemployment, housing, occupational accidents and diseases, vocational guidance, and the family. It *excludes* expenditure on education.
[43] Michael Mann, 'The Autonomous Power of the State' in Hall, *States in History*, op. cit.; Puchala, op. cit.

erably since then, but this does not mean that the governments would be prepared to grant it an unlimited role.

Yet it is also clear that the EU could not act as a 'supranational welfare state' – equivalent to the MS – even if the most obvious obstacles were removed. For it has none of the attributes that a public authority requires if it is to limit the growth of class inequalities and to effect transfers between different groups. It thus lacks the coherence, unity of purpose, and solid state structure which enabled Sweden to establish a welfare system before the Second World War, and Britain to do so immediately after it.[44] Its policy networks do not penetrate very deeply into the societies of the MS, while reforming administrations require the co-operation of many links in a chain of interactions if their strategies are to succeed.[45] And, above all, it lacks the legitimacy which would be necessary to secure support for extensive redistribution. It therefore seems that the EU is ill-suited to act as the *primary* agent in the establishment of a new 'European social model'.[46] Indeed it would probably be counter-productive for it to take the lead in this, for it would be far too easy for those adversely affected by any redistributive measures to precipitate a nationalist backlash against it. So if it is unrealistic to expect the EU to 'save' the post-war welfare system or to establish a new 'European social model', what kind of social policy role might it play?

It has been suggested that there is not only a difference in *degree* but also a difference in *kind* between social policy within the MS and that of the EU. The MS, it is argued, are involved in a highly complex network of social interactions and may implement welfare policies for redistributive reasons or for other ends which are non-economic. However, social policy within the EU is derived from welfare economics. This means that intervention (through

---

[44] Margaret Weir and Theda Skocpol, 'State Structures and Possibilities for "Keynesian" Responses to the Great Depression in Sweden, Britain and the United States' in Evans, Rueschemeyer, Skocpol, op. cit.

[45] P. Katzenstein (ed.), *Between Power and Plenty: Foreign Economic Policies of Advanced Industrial States*, Madison: University of Wisconsin Press, cited in Theda Skocpol, 'Bringing the State Back in: Strategies of Analysis in Current Research' in Evans, Rueschemeyer, Skocpol, op. cit., pp. 19-20; R. Rhodes, *Beyond Westminster and Whitehall: The Sub-Central Government of Britain*, London: Unwin Hyman, 1988.

[46] Geyer, op. cit.; Streeck and Schmitter, op. cit.; David Miller, 'The Nation-State: A Modest Defence' in C. Brown (ed.), *Political Restructuring in Europe: Ethical Perspectives*, London: Routledge, 1994.

regulation) is justified as a result of 'market failures' – effectively negative consequences of economic processes – but not for specifically redistributive reasons.[47] This implies that the EU should build on its developing regulatory role in 'quality of life' issues in Health and Safety and Environment and leave the MS to follow their own inclinations in the wider social policy realm.

This may be a more 'realistic' view than the notion of the EU as a universal welfare provider, but it is hardly satisfactory. First, it could be used to narrow the scope of the EU in social policy matters to relatively non-sensitive issues; secondly, it would remove its role as a catalyst and focus for campaigns; thirdly, it suggests that the EU should have no rights in relation to domestic welfare systems; and finally, it implies that areas of social policy may be isolated from wider democratic involvement.

A second view, reflecting a Christian Democratic perspective, is a little more satisfactory, in the sense that it at least suggests political intervention to secure goals based on moral values. This holds that the role of the state since World War Two has been as a 'corrector' of the detrimental social effects of unconstrained market relationships. If the single market produces negative consequences, which the MS themselves can no longer resolve, it is argued that the Christian Democratic response will be to upgrade elements of 'social policy' to the EU level. Thus Wilfried Martens claimed in 1991 that Christian Democrats had helped to build, and would continue to work for, a West European model of society based on free enterprise and extensive forms of social protection.[48] This position has some support in the Commission and appears to underlie some of the assumptions behind the 1994 White Paper on Social Policy. But it is not based upon redistributive aims or egalitarian principles. It also implies a restricted view of democracy in which reform will come about when political elites are convinced of its necessity. This has little to do with conceptions of social policy based on empowerment and notions of rights.

Despite the extreme difficulties in the current situation, there are some positive aspects, which provide a basis for the belief that the

---

[47] Majone, op. cit.

[48] Kees van Kersbergen and Bertjan Verbeek, 'The Politics of Subsidiarity in the European Union', *Journal of Common Market Studies*, 32, 2, June 1994, p. 233.

EU may play a fuller, and more democratic, role in social policy than either of the above views suggest. Furthermore, the Green Paper *European Social Policy: Options for the Union,* published in November 1993, and the White Paper of the same name published the following July indicate that the Commission may have absorbed some lessons from the past.

The process of policy-making.   The first encouraging element concerns the *process* through which social policy ideas are currently being fed into the EU decision-making system. One of the negative aspects of the harmonisation initiatives of the 1970s and '80s (particularly the Fifth Directive and the Vredeiing Directive) was that they were taken with minimal consultation. Subsequently Delors' intention was to try to build a consensus, but this was thwarted by a number of factors: the total opposition of the British government, the economic situation, a rather traditional notion of 'consensus-building' through the peak organisations of labour and capital, and perhaps his own temperament. However, perhaps because of the general crisis over integration after Maastricht, the Commission's more recent approach has been one of far wider consultation. Thus the Green Paper called for responses from any organisations or individuals to the fundamental question 'what sort of society do the Europeans want?' And the paper was 'user friendly', with each section presenting an analysis of the problems, followed by key questions. 65 multiple questions of this type were asked, making discussion and response by a wide range of groups comparatively straightforward. Over 500 submissions were received by the closing date in March 1994 and a large European Conference on 'The Future of European Social Policy' was then held in Brussels on 26-28 May 1994. Following this, the Commission published its White Paper on 27 July 1994, with an accompanying volume, containing an analysis of the responses. Of course, there was no guarantee that those submitted by non-governmental organisations would have a major impact on the policy ultimately adopted by the EU, but the process was certainly a refreshing exercise in open government, which could have an important effect in stimulating debate and raising 'consciousness'.

Open recognition of conflict.   Secondly, and closely related, the publication of the responses made the divisions over policy quite transparent. Some of these were already predictable: for example, as would be expected, the British government submitted easily the most responses and disputed the basis of the Green Paper more fundamentally than any of the other governments. Similarly, it was hardly surprising that there were differences between trade unions and non-governmental organisations on the one hand and employers on the other about the *levels* at which minimum standards should be set on workers' rights, the *range* of organisations that should be covered, and the *pace* at which the EU should move.[49] However, there were also some less predictable responses – for example, the fact that both the Spanish and Portuguese governments supported the call for a fourth Action Programme for the Equal Treatment between men and women. But the main point is that this publication of opinions on fairly specific policy issues enables the formation of alliances and pressure to build up towards the 1996 intergovernmental conference.

Gender equality and networks. The White Paper has obviously benefited from the input from the various women's networks. Gender equality issues have been 'mainstreamed' into the whole body of recommendations, and the chapter on 'Equality of Opportunity between Women and Men' is the most forceful of the whole document, with a number of commitments by the Commission, including:

– the introduction of codes of practice on equal pay for work of equal value, on training and on desegregation of the labour market;
– measures to encourage the development of the professional qualifications and skills of women, including measures designed to help women set up their own businesses;
– proposals for the removal of discriminatory fiscal and social protection policies and for the individualisation of rights i.e. rather (than being based on overall family income);
– the establishment of a new Action Programme to come into force in 1996 (the current programme finishes in 1995);
– continuation of attempts to secure the adoption of the proposed Directive on parental leave (subsequently vetoed by Britain in September 1994);

[49] Part B, chapter 2, 'The Political Scene: Defining a European Social Policy' in European Social Policy White Paper, op. cit.

– encouragement of the adoption of the outstanding proposal for a directive on the burden of proof, or alternative proposals if this was not adopted by the end of 1994 (i.e. placing the burden on employers to prove *non-discrimination* when an action is taken against them); and

– examination of ways of building monitoring by gender into all relevant Union policies and making it a requirement in their evaluation.[50]

In addition, it included various other measures to enhance monitoring of action by the MS in such fields as childcare, and training and proposals for action on the increased participation of women in decision-making in both the private and public sectors. It also made a long overdue statement about its own record:

> Closer examination is required of the entrenched institutional and cultural barriers that inhibit or prevent the proportional representation of women in public and political bodies, including organisations of the social partners. The European Union should exercise leadership by taking concrete steps to enhance the role of women in its own institutions, and should assist the Member States and other European institutions to make progress in the same direction.[51]

This may also be advanced by the presence of five women in the Commission established in January 1995 and the creation within it of a new Equal Opportunities committee chaired by Jacques Santer.[52]

Of course, none of these measures will *ensure* that any further progress is made in tackling the entrenched barriers to gender equality, and this point will be discussed further below. But the

---

[50] White Paper, op. cit., chapter 5. Note: the above are summaries of parts of the relevant paragraphs.

[51] Chapter 5, para. 13.

[52] The women Commissioners are Ritt Bjerregaerd (Denmark), Emma Bonino (Italy), Edith Cresson (France), Monika Wulf-Mathies (Germany) and Anita Gradin (Sweden). All of them are from Social Democrat/Socialist parties, except Emma Bonino who is from the Radical Party. Their presence raises the percentage of women in the Commission to 25%. (Jacques Santer became Chair of the new committee after MEPs objected to Padraig Flynn taking this position in view of his past record on gender equality issues in Ireland. *The Guardian*, 10 and 17 Jan. 1995.)

programme shows that the issue remains a high priority for action by the EU.

Anti-racist action. The White Paper proposed some positive steps to facilitate the integration of migrant workers from non EU countries into the Community and to combat racism. Furthermore, it announced its intention to press for specific powers to combat racial discrimination to be incorporated into the Treaty, when revised after the 1996 inter-governmental conference. From a democratic perspective, this would be a crucially important step forward by the EU, and it will be discussed in the next chapter.

Democratisation. The Commission itself stressed the value of democratisation and 'bottom up' approaches and, as already noted, there is internal evidence from the document that this went beyond rhetoric. When discussing the operation of the ESF, it emphasised the need for a broader partnership involving NGOs, community bodies, local authorities, the social and economic partners, and the private and public sectors, and continued:

> Experience has shown the growing importance of the local level and of decentralised management. The development of implementation mechanisms which facilitate a bottom-up approach is especially relevant for the two new themes of the ESF: combating exclusion and promoting adaptation to industrial change, where much experience lies outside the public domain.[53]

Similarly, while continuing to emphasise the importance of agreements between the traditional social partners (employers and trade unions), it recognised that 'in relation to problems, such as exclusion, racism, demographic trends and ageing, the Union needs to develop partnerships with a wider range of institutions' and proposed to institute a forum for discussion and debate on social policy issues every 18 months, involving the widest possible range of interested bodies.[54] This would offer an opportunity to maintain some form of campaigning momentum by concerned groups, although its success in this respect will depend on whether it has any discernible impact on policy.

[53] White Paper, op. cit., chapter 2, para. 22.
[54] Ibid., chapter 8, paras 12 and 14.

Social rights.   The White Paper drew attention to the fact that many
responses to the Green Paper called for a further step forward
through the 'establishment of the fundamental social rights of citizens
as a constitutional element of the European Union'. The Commission did not explicitly endorse this demand – suggesting that it was
an issue to be considered in the context of future revisions of the
Treaties – but it asserted the necessity to 'ensure that all people in
Europe are aware of, and are able to exercise, their fundamental social
rights'.[55] Obviously, there would be enormous barriers in securing
agreement to any such statement, or in *defining* any such rights.
Nevertheless, the attempts at definition could involve wide debate
and participation, leading to increasing pressure on governments.

There are two final features of the White Paper, which may
warrant cautious optimism. First, the current approach to social
policy is *not* designed to raise unduly high expectations. It is a rather
judicious analysis of the EU's past record and future prospects, which
frankly recognises the contradictory pressures. Thus, for example,
on the pivotal issue of protecting labour standards, the White Paper
simply acknowledges the unresolved tension between the different
views represented in the MS.[56] Some might take this recognition of
conflict, and inability to suggest a clear way out of it, as further
grounds for pessimism. But an understanding of the alignment of
forces on both sides may also encourage those seeking change to
work for it *at all levels.* Secondly, although the concept of subsidiarity
is highly ambiguous, it does not necessarily indicate a victory for
those forces – like the British government – which simply want to
deregulate without external intervention. On the contrary, it may
suggest that the Commission has learned some valuable lessons from
past experience.

It was argued earlier that the attempt, in the seventies and early
eighties, to harmonise industrial relations systems failed because of
employers' resistance and because the systems within the MS were
both divergent and integrated into the specific state–society traditions.[57] Similarly, Jill Rubery has argued that gender inequality has
complex interactions with other forces, and particularly labour

[55] Ibid., p. 53.
[56] Ibid., chapter 3, paras 11 and 12.
[57] See also K. Doogan, 'The Social Charter and the Europeanisation of Employment
and Social Policy', *Policy and Politics*, 20, no. 3, July 1993.

market conditions, which are embedded in *specific* circumstances which differ from country to country.[58] Thus, for example, while increased rights for part-timers might be highly beneficial for women in Britain, it cannot be assumed that similar policies would have equally positive effects in Italy or France where women are less likely to take career breaks when they have children. Rubery's general conclusion is therefore that standardised gender equality policies may not work. The EU should therefore set targets, monitor results, and continue to play the 'catalyst' role, but should not be too prescriptive in dictating exactly *how* the particular MS should attain the goals. This needs to be determined at a more local level, taking into account the specific 'culture' and system of organisation in the labour market.[59] It could no doubt also be argued that the education and socialisation systems also have specificities which need to be recognised.

The current thinking on social policy suggests that the Commission has learned such lessons. The White Paper thus argues:

> The future development of the Union needs to build on the richness of its diversity, which adds to the quality of life and to the vigour of socio-economic systems in the face of new and unforeseen challenges. This diversity means that total harmonisation of social policies is not an objective of the Union. However, the convergence of goals and policies over a period of time by fixing common objectives is vital, since it will permit the co-existence of different national systems and enable them to progress in harmony towards the fundamental objectives of the Union. . . .
>
> . . . Minimum standards are needed to preserve the cohesion of the Union, having regard to differing national systems and needs, and to the relative economic strengths of the different Member States. They should not over-stretch the economically weaker Member States, and they should not prevent the more developed Member States from implementing higher standards.

---

[58] Jill Rubery, 'Women and Men in the European Labour Market' in Brouwer, Lintner and Newman, op. cit.

[59] However, there is some anxiety that some of the specific programmes to support women are being phased out because of the emphasis on 'mainstreaming'. 'Draft Opinion of the Committee on Women's Rights for the Committee on Social Affairs, Employment and the Working Environment: Reform of the Social Fund and the Position of Women', European Parliament Session Documents, A3-0057/93 18 Feb. 1993, annex 2.

... The continuing aim should be to develop and improve standards for *all* the Members of the Union.[60]

Similarly, the stress on promoting 'a framework in order to allow for the diverse national systems to determine detailed methods of implementation' is the appropriate lesson to draw from previous failures, and could be constructive in encouraging democratic debate and action at more local levels.

Such arguments are not designed to disguise the fact that the current situation is, in many respects, very depressing and that the dual pressures of external competition, and internal 'beggar-my-neighbour' policies could result in further downward pressures on welfare systems.[61] If these forces prevail *within* the MS, the Commission (and the European Parliament) will be able to do relatively little to counter them. But if the neo-liberal approach is defeated within the MS, the EU can play a very positive role in the establishment of a new 'European social model'.

In any case, the EU has now established itself as a social policy actor. I would suggest that its most crucial functions are as follows:

− providing data and analysis of the situation in the EU as a whole, and within each MS;
− facilitating cross national networks and campaigns on issues which have been accepted as EU priorities;
− establishing minimum standards, norms and targets;
− monitoring results;
− exerting pressure and, where necessary and possible, passing legislation to ensure compliance with minimum standards;
− demonstrating a willingness to learn from 'below' and helping to empower local groups;
− distributing targeted funds to support local activities on agreed priorities;
− establishing equalities policies for particular groups (in particular to counter inequalities based on gender, ethnicity or disability)
− helping to define an overall conception of social rights.

None of these activities is a substitute for existing welfare systems at state or sub-state levels, but they may enable the EU to maintain a critically important presence as a catalyst for change.

[60] White Paper, op. cit., Introduction, paras. 18 and 19.
[61] M. Rhodes, op. cit.

5

EUROPE OF THE REGIONS?

In recent years there has been increasing enthusiasm for the idea of the region as a location for political, economic and cultural activity. This has involved both specific demands for self-determination or decentralisation in particular regions, and an ideology favouring a 'Europe of the regions'. Such developments have obvious relevance for the issues discussed in this book. If power were to be concentrated at regional level, the state-centred tradition in political thought and practice would be called into question. If this were accompanied by a simultaneous movement in the other direction – towards supranationalism – the whole notion of the territorial state as a location for democracy would be rendered anachronistic. The 'region' therefore raises issues of crucial importance, which are considered in this chapter.

The first major section examines some of the arguments in favour of a regional dimension, both within states and the EU as a whole, and discusses the progress that has been made. The second section then analyses some of the theoretical and practical difficulties involved in decentralisation. Finally, a brief conclusion summarises the factors which need to be balanced when considering regions in relation to democracy, the state and the EU.

Towards a Europe of the regions?

Democracy and decentralisation. There are powerful democratic arguments in favour of decentralised political systems. While there is no firm correlation between the *size* of the polity and the *extent* of citizen participation, it is no doubt true that the majority of the people feel powerless in relation to their central governments, which are responsible for populations of several million in extensive geographical areas.[1] Given the extent of territorial interdependence

---

[1] There is recent empirical evidence that larger cities may elicit more involvement

in the modern world, it may not be possible to recreate the local power of the Greek city-state, but there are, in principle, over-whelming democratic arguments for ensuring that large states also contain sub-central governments which are closer to the people, and more susceptible to their influence, than central government.

It is also clear that there are pragmatic arguments for decentralisa-tion. Given the diversity of conditions which exist, particularly in large countries, or those with strong regional or linguistic differen-ces, central government lacks the information for effective policy-making or implementation throughout the territory. It therefore needs expertise and personnel with more local 'roots' to enhance its effectiveness. However, this does not necessarily lead to an increase in local democracy, for governments may seek to achieve such goals by a Napoleonic system: that is, by creating a *Préfecture* as the agency for central government in the regions. In reality, as happened in France, the result is likely to be one of much negotiation and bargaining between the centre and local political elites, rather than one of *diktat* by the state.[2] However, sub-central *democracy* implies more than this, for it suggests that aspects of policy and policy-implementation, should be locally or regionally determined, with appropriate systems of election and accountability at this level.

There is naturally also a crucially important economic dimension to the subject, for many regions will inevitably feel – often with good reason – that central government is relatively indifferent to their needs and either bases its policies on a uniform, and crude, assessment of the overall territorial interest or upon the needs of particular regions which it favours. Moreover, there is a further significant factor which has fuelled the demand for local or regional determination of economic policies: the process of globalisation. If *national* economic management has become less effective because of the increasing internationalisation of the economy, this may mean that some regions may be able to exploit their relative advantages

---

than smaller towns because they provide more organisational outlets for political participation. G. Parry, G. Moyser and M. Day, *Political Participation and Democracy in Britain*, Cambridge University Press, 1992.

2 Sonia Mazey, 'Power outside Paris' in Peter A. Hall, Jack Hayward and Howard Machin, *Developments in French Politics*, London: Macmillan, 1990. More general-ly, it has been argued that, however centralising the state may be, social, economic and political life will always remain local for the majority of people. Andrew Kirby, 'State, Local State, Context and Spatiality' in Caporaso, op. cit.

more effectively than central government. Thus the success of
Emilia Romagna, the centre of the so-called 'Third Italy', in
jumping from forty-fifth to tenth place among the regions of the
EU in GDP *per capita* between 1970 and 1991 has been taken by
many as an example of the potential for regional development.[3]
While this dramatic performance, based upon 'flexible specialisation'
and local networks, probably rests on specific features of the
economy and society in central Italy, which cannot be generalised,
there are certainly a whole range of other economic strategies which
regions may pursue if granted the opportunity to do so. They may,
for example, attempt to 'embed' industries within the area through
various forms of partnership and training and seek to attract the
subsidiaries of transnationals by providing the infrastructural support
that they require. Certainly some analysts believe that their success
is likely to exceed that of central governments, which necessarily
have blunter policy instruments and less local expertise.[4]

Of course, it may often be the case that there is no contradiction
between the pragmatic aims of a central government and local or
regional democracy. For example, the centre might believe that
sub-national democracy in some spheres could diminish damaging
political alienation or reduce some costs currently borne by central
government. Similarly, it might also accept that the locality or region
was better able to determine its own strategy in securing inward
investment or EU funding. There could therefore be both democratic
and pragmatic arguments for sub-central democracy.

In any case, whatever the theoretical case for decentralisation, it
is clear that there has recently been considerable development in this
direction in practice. Up till 1970 the Federal Republic of Germany
was the only major West European state with any substantial
regional tier of government. Moreover, even there the federal

---

[3] R.D. Putnam, *Making Democracy Work: Civic Traditions in Modern Italy*, Princeton
University Press, 1993, p. 154; *Competitiveness and Cohesion: Trends in the Regions*,
5th Periodic Report on the Social and Economic Situation and Development of
the Regions in the Community, Commission of the European Communities,
Luxembourg: Office for Official Publications of the European Communities,
1994.

[4] A. Amin and N. Thrift, *Globalization, Institutions and Regional Development in
Europe*, Oxford University Press, 1994; Robin Murray , *Local Space: Europe and
the New Regionalism*, Stevenage/Manchester: SEEDS/CLES, 1991; Soete, op.
cit.

system was generally seen to be moving in a more unitary direction as central government increased its powers at the expense of the *Länder*. Indeed commentators were asking whether the system should be regarded as a Federal one at all.[5] Elsewhere the dominant West European pattern was of unitary states with varying degrees of administrative decentralisation. However, this situation then changed rapidly. First, in 1970, Italy finally began the process of implementing the system of regional devolution which had been a dormant part of the constitution for almost twenty-five years.[6] Secondly, in 1975 Franco died and it became an urgent task for the post-Franco state to establish a system of regional autonomy which would encourage the Basque country and Catalonia to prefer remaining within Spain than seeking total separation. The result has been the creation of seventeen autonomous communities, enjoying varied amounts of political, economic, and legal rights.[7] Thirdly, the Socialist government in France introduced a major set of decentralisa-tion measures in 1982, counteracting its previous (though probably unjustified) reputation as the most centralised state in Western Europe.[8] Fourthly, the endemic tensions between the Dutch and French-speaking communities in Belgium erupted and led, from 1970 to 1993, to an ongoing process of constitutional reform, which has now made it the most decentralised country in the EU.[9] Finally, the German *Länder*, having long seen a dilution in the powers originally guaranteed to them under the Basic Law, have 'struck back' since 1987.[10] Exploiting their power in the Bundesrat they

[5] Simon Bulmer, 'Territorial Government' in G. Smith, W. Paterson and P. Merkl (eds), *Developments in West German Politics*, London: Macmillan, 1989, pp. 40-1.

[6] David Hine, *Governing Italy: The Politics of Bargained Pluralism*, Oxford University Press, 1993, chapter 9; Putnam, op. cit.

[7] Peter J. Doughty and Michael T. Newton, *Spain: A Guide to Political and Economic Institutions*, Cambridge University Press, 1989.

[8] Sonia Mazey, 'Decentralisation: La Grande Affaire du Septennat?' in Sonia Mazey and Michael Newman (eds), *Mitterrand's France*, Beckenham: Croom Helm, 1987.

[9] E. Witte, 'Belgian Federalism: Towards Complexity and Asymmetry', *West European Politics*, 15, no. 4, October 1992; J. van Ginderachter, 'The Belgian Federal Model', paper presented at the Eighth Lothian Conference, 'Subsidiarity and Federalism within the European Union', Royal Holloway and Bedford New College, 17-18 Dec. 1993.

[10] Charlie Jeffery, 'The *Länder* Strike Back: Structures and Procedures of European Integration Policy-Making in the German Federal System', paper presented at

thus ensured that, in return for agreeing to the Maastricht Treaty they recovered lost rights and gained strong constitutional guarantees to maintain them.[11]

Certainly, the *extent* and *nature* of decentralisation vary considerably among the MS, but only Britain and Ireland remain undeniably centralised systems. Of the two, the British position is far more significant for two reasons. First, it is one of the 'big four' states and, in terms of the size of both its population and territory, regional tiers of government might now be expected. Secondly, it has been the location for one prolonged violent national conflict (Northern Ireland) and includes two other territorial nations (Scotland and Wales) in which there have been strong demands for democratic decentralisation. Yet while the tendency elsewhere in the EU has been towards concessions when faced with such pressures, the British Conservative government moved in the opposite direction. It refused to entertain any notion of democratic decentralisation, and weakened local government by abolishing the metropolitan counties in large cities by new legislation in 1985, and by removing very substantial powers from the remaining local authorities. This has placed Britain in a unique position within the EU, and both the Labour and Liberal Democratic Parties (as well as the nationalist parties) now support constitutional reform in which democratic decentralisation is a major element.

The EU and the regions: the economic dimension.   The preamble to the Treaty of Rome proclaimed the intention 'to ensure. . . harmonious development by reducing the differences existing between the various regions and the backwardness of the less favoured regions', but failed to elaborate any specific policies to achieve these laudable aims. Until 1973 regional policy was primarily seen as a derogation from the competition policy which permitted the MS to grant 'aid to promote the economic development of areas where

---

the ESRC Research Seminar on State Autonomy in the European Community, Christ Church, Oxford, June 1994.

[11] The new article 23 of the Basic Law stipulates that the central government may only transfer either Federal or *Länder* powers to the EU if it secures a two-thirds majority in both the Bundesrat and the Bundestag. Any transfers which amend or supplement the content of the Basic Law are also subject to article 79/3 which prohibits any amendments which would alter Germany's Federal structure. For full details, see Jeffery, op. cit.

the standard of living is abnormally low or where there is serious under-employment'.[12] Only the Mezzogiorno and south-western France were recognised as regions with longer term problems but, again, this was seen as a problem for the governments rather than the Community. However, the entry of Britain and Ireland led to the establishment of a far stronger conception of regional policy, with the argument that the Community had a responsibility to help improve economic conditions in regions suffering from problems that were endemic, rather than temporary. As a result, new regions were recognised as deserving support – much of the north and west of Britain, the north-west of France and the whole of Ireland.[13] The ERDF funding was limited, but there was an implicit recognition of the case that was normally applied *within* states: that is, that the Community had an obligation to attempt to equalise conditions throughout the territory it comprised. As has already been noted in earlier chapters, the enlargement to the South (through the accession of Greece, Spain and Portugal) and the SEA and Maastricht agreements, have all precipitated further demands (and agreements) to channel funds to disadvantaged regions. Increases in the structural funds in 1988, and the establishment of the Cohesion fund at the Edinburgh summit in December 1992 (with effect from 1993), have thus been based on acceptance of the argument that the Community has an obligation to tackle regional disparities. The allocation of funds has become increasingly sophisticated in its targeting. Thus in 1992 EU assistance to two of the poorest states – Greece and Ireland – accounted for 6% of their GDPs and, from 1994, the four poorest MS are expected to receive 70% of the available funds (compared with 63.5% in the period 1989-93). By the end of the decade EU regional policies are likely to finance approximately 5% of investment in Objective 1 regions (the poorest in the EU) and this could rise to between 7% and 13% in the four poorest MS, which are beneficiaries of the new Cohesion Fund.[14] The significance and success of such policies will be considered in the second section.

An allied development, encouraged by the Commission, has been inter-regional co-operation, building on the 'town-twinning' in-

[12] Article 92.3(a), Treaty of Rome.

[13] Christopher Harvie, *The Rise of Regional Europe*, London: Routledge, 1994, p. 2.

[14] *Competitiveness and Cohesion: Trends in the Regions*, op. cit., p.13.

itiatives. In general, transregional networking is based upon agreements between regional authorities, and often covers a variety of different activities. These are of two broad types: *cross-regional European area* agreements, linking geographically adjoined regions, and *cross-regional Motors of Development* agreements, which link regions which have common interests or future prospects.[15] Examples of the first include the Atlantic arc, linking twenty-two coastal regions in the EU, and the Saarland-Lorraine-Luxembourg-Trier/Westphalia Euro-district. These typically involve thematic conferences, and attempts to develop closer co-operation through the development of organic links. In the case of the Saarland Euro-district, co-operation has also led to extensive research activities and agreements on higher education and research and technology transfer. The most developed example of the second type is the so-called Four Motors agreement, between Rhône-Alpes, Lombardy, Catalonia and Baden-Württemberg (to which Wales later affiliated). The idea here is to create a market for transborder R & D co-operation between firms and research institutes, and more than seventy cross-regional co-operative agreements in such fields as investment, exhibitions, information and events, student exchanges, partnerships between educational institutions, universities and public and private research institutions have taken place.[16]

It is difficult to evaluate the importance of these agreements: some attach considerable significance to them as a new dimension in 'European economic and social space', while others imply that they are largely artificial means of attracting funding and promulgating propaganda.[17] In any case, it is clear that these limited forms of co-operation feed into the wider political debate about a 'Europe of the Regions'.

The EU and the regions: the political dimension. During the 1980s there was an increasing tendency to celebrate regions as the basis of a vibrant Europe. As the President of the European Parliament, Egon Klepsch, put it in a lecture in July 1993:

Europe should not be about anonymous bureaucracies and

---

[15] For this distinction, and further details, see Holland, op. cit., part 4, chapter 4.

[16] Holland, op. cit., p. 216.

[17] For the two views, see respectively Holland, op. cit., p. 209, and Harvie, op. cit., chapter 5.

supranational power games. It is above all about the quality of life and aspirations of the individuals who live in our regions, cities, towns and villages.

Without its citizens, the Europe we desire would not, and cannot, exist. The achievement of European Union depends on their trust, support and direct involvement. The regions have a crucial role to play in bringing that about. Life must be breathed into the concept of a 'Europe of the Regions'. The future of the European Community depends on it.[18]

Sometimes the emphasis has been on regional diversity as a positive value. Thus, for example, Oskar Lafontaine, the SPD Minister President of Saarland in 1989, stated:

> *Rapprochement* and communication, the magic formulae of glo-
> balisation, don't mean . . . that we should surrender before the
> economic tendencies towards unification, standardisation and
> levelling-out. Our political will should aim at variety. We don't
> want, parallel to the development of world-wide compatible
> systems, an anonymous 'Mao-look'; we want the coexistence of
> local, regional, inter-regional and national sub-cultures, some-
> thing which, in the case of the United States, has helped create
> wealth through the power and dynamism of cultural interac-
> tion.[19]

But at times it has also been seen as a more potent political force, which may be capable of resolving hitherto intractable political problems. For example, in the late 1980s the SDLP in Northern Ireland argued that the dual erosion of the 'nation-state' from above and below meant that 'state sovereignty' might be transformed into a 'Europe of the Regions' which would remove the whole basis for the conflict in Ireland.[20] Similarly, while both the Basques and the Scots would normally dispute any suggestion that their ter-ritories should be regarded as regions rather than countries, many

[18] Dr. Egon A. Klepsch, 'A Europe of the Regions', Inaugural Sunderland Lecture, 9 July 1993, London: UK Office of European Parliament, 1993.
[19] Oskar Lafontaine, 'Mehr Macht für Europas Regionen', *Geo*, 4 (April 1989), pp. 210-11, quoted in C. Harvie, op. cit., p. 3.
[20] R. Kearney, *Across the Frontiers: Ireland in the 1990s*, Dublin: Wolfhound, 1988.

nationalists in both areas have seen a decentralised 'Europe of the Regions' as a potential political solution to a long-term conflict.[21] Yet the notion is inherently ambiguous. In its most radical form it implies the dissolution of the 'nation-state', with the majority of current central government functions being carried out either by a European Union tier or by regional and local authorities. This is a fully Federalist vision which would seem to be based on an unrealistic assessment of the state and its continuing power.[22] A second and more tenable view is that the regions should *supplement* the existing states within the EU decision-making process rather than replace them. This is sometimes termed 'co-operative regionalism', and one recent study justifies it as follows:

> When common actions are necessary, efficiency gains can be realised if policies are implemented through actions coordinated within new institutions which facilitate exchange between subnational governments. Many 'higher level' goals agreed between national representatives may be implemented more efficiently by subnational authorities than by a single, higher level in the governmental structure. However, to ensure the effective and uniform implementation of broad EC policy objectives, subnational authorities often need to consult one another and formulate common implementation strategies, particularly for policies which have cross-border implications . . . . Even in areas such as regional development or vocational training, where a pan-regional approach may be less vital, 'networking' between subnational authorities encourages them to learn from one another and discover 'best practice' behaviour.
>
> Co-operative regionalism has the potential to provide EC citizens with more effective input into EC policy-making while still securing the benefits of enhanced efficiency in policy implementation. It can help to reconcile the rise of 'territorial politics' with the creation of a European Union.[23]

How far has the EU advanced towards this kind of 'co-operative

---

[21] Dave Edye and Valerio Lintner, *Contemporary Europe*, Brighton: Harvester Wheatsheaf, 1996.

[22] See chapters 1 and 8.

[23] A. Scott, J. Peterson and D. Millar, 'Subsidiarity: A "Europe of the Regions" v. the British Constitution?', *Journal of Common Market Studies*, 32, 1, March 1994, p. 59.

regionalism'? This may be considered in three ways: first, through the impact of new forms of regional policy; secondly, by examining the political changes established in the Maastricht Treaty; and thirdly, by exploring the doctrine of subsidiarity.

In terms of the 'Europeanisation' of the regional issue the 1989 reform was extremely important in two respects. First, because of frustration – particularly with the British government – for substituting Community funding for expenditure which would otherwise have been borne by the Exchequer, a new system was established which involved direct links between the Commission and the potential recipients of the funding. This meant that, at least to a limited extent, the Commission was by-passing the Central governments of the MS and dealing with sub-central government or others within the MS. Secondly, and a related point, the new system provided the Commission with some opportunity to encourage the development of regional groupings within the MS. In particular, in the partnership arrangements for structural funds, Article 4 (1) called for:

> ... close consultation between the Commission, the Member State concerned and the competent authorities designated by the latter at national, regional, local or other level, with each party acting as a partner in pursuit of a common goal.[24]

This inevitably generated pressures within MS to develop the kinds of collaboration between the private sector and public authorities which would have the greatest potential to secure funding. These included greater regional co-ordination – often directly encouraged by the Commission – even where there was no preexisting structure.[25] In the case of Britain this was certainly an influence over the opposition parties, which were soon arguing that Britain needed democratic regional structures to ensure that it secured its share of EU funding. Such changes even influenced the government itself, which in November 1993, introduced integrated regional offices, bringing together the regional offices of the Departments of Employ-

---

[24] *Official Journal*, L185/9, 15 July 1988, quoted in I. Bache, S. George and R. Rhodes, 'The European Union and Subnational Authorities in the United Kingdom', paper presented to the ESRC Research Seminar, 'State Autonomy in the European Community: National Administrative Styles and the EC Tier of National Policy Making', Christ Church, Oxford, 22 June 1994, p. 21.
[25] Ibid.

ment, Environment, Trade and Industry and Transport under a single Regional Director.

It has therefore been argued that the changes in structural polices are having a major impact upon decision-making within the EU as a whole. As one author has expressed it,

> I believe we are witnessing the emergence of *multilevel governance* in the European Community, characterised by co-decisionmaking across several nested tiers of government, ill-defined and shifting spheres of competence (creating a consequent potential for conflicts about competencies), and an ongoing search for principles of decisional distribution that might be applied to this emerging polity [. . .] The experience of structural policy suggests that it might be fruitful to describe the process of decisional reallocation to European Community institutions merely as one aspect of a centrifugal process in which some decisional powers are shifted down to municipal, local, and regional governments, some are transferred from states to the EC, and (as in the case of structural policy) some are shifted in both directions simultaneously.[26]

No doubt this impact is discernible in countries which are already Federal in structure, and perhaps also in some of the poorer states which are very heavily dependent upon EU funding. But it would be unrealistic to suggest that this effect is uniform throughout the MS. In particular, given the determination of the British Conservative government to maintain the unitary political system and to centralise power, these shifts in structural policy would be very unlikely to force it to yield to pressures for democratic decentralisation. Instead its strategy is to ensure the maintenance of its leadership role within the structures established to secure EU funding.[27] However, the economic impact of the structural policy cannot be isolated from political developments – particularly, the changes arising from the Maastricht treaty and the doctrine of subsidiarity.

There were many factors which led to the Maastricht reforms: as already noted, many of the MS now had regional tiers of government which were affected by EU policies and which sought an input

---

[26] Gary Marks, 'Structural Policy and Multilevel Governance in the EC' in Cafruny and Rosenthal, op. cit., p. 405.

[27] Bache, George, Rhodes, op. cit., pp. 40-1.

into them, there was the movement of opinion in favour of 'Europe of the Regions', and the Commission was keen to establish direct links within the MS rather than always being dependent upon central governments. However, there is a strong argument for suggesting that the most important factor was the campaign by the German *Länder*.

One of the reasons for the steady loss of power by the *Länder* in relation to the Federal Government from the 1950s had been the EC.[28] The Preamble of the Basic Law (the 1949 Constitution) had been highly unusual in that it had explicitly called upon the German people 'to serve the peace of the world as an equal partner in a united Europe', and the Constitution itself had granted the Federal Government exclusive competence in the realm of foreign policy.[29] West European integration had then been dealt with under the general heading of 'foreign policy', but this resulted in an incipient constitutional tension within Germany, for it enabled the Federal government to transfer powers to the EC which, according to the Basic Law, were to have been exercised exclusively or co-operatively by the *Länder*. From the late 1950s until the 1980s this was tolerated with little difficulty because the *Länder* also favoured the European policy and because the general encroachment on the powers of the *Länder* was accepted, particularly because of the economic benefits that appeared to follow from the process of greater centralisation. In addition, *Länder* consent (through the Bundesrat) was needed for a far greater proportion of legislation than had originally been envisaged (more than 50% as against an expectation of around 10%).[30] Furthermore, most centrally determined policies were still implemented by the *Länder*, and nearly two-thirds of public expenditure, and 80% of public investment was carried out at *Länder* level. There had therefore been considerable compensations for the reductions in autonomy that had been experienced. However, by the 1980s the tensions were growing and, despite divisions on other issues, the *Länder* were united in regarding the Single European Act as a threat to their position. For this involved some EC competence in areas such as culture, education and training, broadcasting, health, research, and environment, which had been exclusive responsibilities

---

[28] Bulmer, op. cit.

[29] Quoted in Rudolf Steiert, 'Germany' in Church and Keogh, op. cit., p. 83.

[30] Bulmer, op. cit., p. 44.

for the *Länder*. Nor were the latter granted any role in the determination of those policies at Community level. Since Bundesrat agreement was necessary for the ratification of the SEA, they were able to secure some concessions, but they remained dissatisfied, as they had failed to exert any influence over the original treaty, to bind the Federal government to their views, or to ensure that the same situation could not recur.[31] The wider significance of this is that they remained united and sought allies in other EU countries. They began to discuss future strategy before the Maastricht negotiations started, and were thus able to play a formal role in voicing their demands within Germany and to promote opinion and facilitate networks in favour of regions throughout the EU.[32] They had four fundamental goals:

– the entrenchment of the principle of subsidiarity in any treaty amendment;
– the opening up of the Council of Ministers in matters of exclusive sub-national responsibility to ministers from the 'third level' (i.e. a level beneath the nation-state);
– the establishment of a 'regional organ' at European level; and
– the establishment of a right of appeal of the 'third level' to the European Court of Justice against measures of the Council or the Commission which infringe 'third level' powers.[33]

The first three of these aims were realised in the Maastricht Treaty, and the *Länder* may be expected to return to the fourth (on which they received a compromise from the Federal government) at the time of the next major discussions over the future shape of the EU in 1996.[34] They also secured very extensive internal concessions from the Federal government, which have done much to restore their position within Germany and to safeguard their rights with regard to any future developments in the EU, and to ensure them a role in negotiating such developments. The principle of Subsidiarity (the first aim) will be considered separately below. What is the significance of the other two changes?

The Treaty of Rome had stipulated (under article 146) that only

[31] Rudolf Steiert, op. cit., pp. 91–101.
[32] For a detailed account, see Jeffery, op. cit.
[33] Ibid., p. 7.
[34] Ibid., p. 10.

central government members could represent each state in the Council of Ministers. However, an amendment at Maastricht means that any central government can now authorise a Minister from a sub-central tier to represent it. Both Belgium and Germany have subsequently allowed sub-central governments to take part in Council discussions on issues which have specific relevance for them, thereby facilitating direct regional input into EU decision-making. The second reform was the establishment (under article 198a of the Treaty of the Committee of the Regions (COR). Representation was based on population size, with twelve from each of the biggest MS, down to 6 for Luxembourg. COR's status is only advisory, but the Commission is required to consult it on the following:

– the framework of EU policy on education;
– EU policy on culture;
– EU policy on public health;
– when defining guidelines concerning the establishment and development of trans-European networks;
– in the case of specific action within the framework of the policy on economic and social cohesion; and
– on the regulations which provide the framework and coordination of the structural funds and on the regulations concerning the implementation of the European Regional Development Fund.[35]

In the five sessions held in 1994 the new committee discussed a wide range of issues but was not able to establish a clear function for itself.[36] In particular there were problems in the rapporteur system – with criticisms that this gave rise to conflicts when the rapporteur had a particular stake in the subject under discussion – there was a tendency to become too involved in specific local issues, and the relations with some members of the European Parliament, which also has a regional committee, were sometimes strained.[37] Such difficulties are hardly surprising in a new institution, which has widely diverse and rather arbitrary representation, and which has

---

[35] Charles Gray, 'The Committee of the Regions' in Brouwer, Lintner and Newman, op. cit., p. 104.

[36] *Official Journal*, c217, 6 Aug. 1994; European Information Service (EIS), no. 155, Dec. 1994, LGIB.

[37] Report of seminar on 'The Committee of the Regions – The First Year', 21 Nov. 1994 at the School of Advanced Urban Studies, Bristol University, in EIS no. 155, Dec. 1994.

only advisory status. However, it would, at present, be optimistic to view this as an organ for co-operative federalism. Much depends upon the evolution of the doctrine of subsidiarity.

Discussion of subsidiarity oscillates between two extremes. On the one hand, there are esoteric discussions about its derivation from Catholic (and sometimes Dutch Protestant) doctrines, through 'Personalism' and into Christian Democracy, combined in Delors' case, with a form of Christian Socialism.[38] Sometimes this is combined with interpretations of its essence, and distinctions are made between 'positive' and 'negative' subsidiarity, and its territorial and non-territorial forms.[39] On the other hand, it may be treated – as it was by the British Conservative government in relation to the Maastricht Treaty – simply as a vindication of the principle of state supremacy. Rather than following either of these approaches here, the intention is to examine the relationship between the principle and the issue of regional government. It is helpful to begin with the Treaty, and the subsequent clarification, and then consider their significance.

The definition in Article 3b of the Treaty is very brief:

> The Community shall act within the limits of the powers conferred upon it by this Treaty and of the objectives assigned to it therein.

> In areas which do not fall within its exclusive competence, the Community shall take action, in accordance with the principle of subsidiarity, only if and in so far as the objectives of the proposed action cannot be sufficiently achieved by the Member States and can therefore, by reason of the scale or effects of the proposed action, be better achieved by the Community.

> Any action by the Community shall not go beyond what is necessary to achieve the objectives of this Treaty.

At the same time Article A of the Treaty pledged that decisions would be taken as closely as possible to the citizen; and Article B

---

[38] Paul Spicker, 'Concepts of Subsidiarity in the European Community', paper presented at the Conference on 'Democracy and Subsidiarity', 12 Nov. 1993, University of Manchester; Ken Endo, 'The Principle of Subsidiarity: From Johannes Althusius to Jacques Delors', *Hokkaido Law Review*, 44, 6, 1994; Van Kersbergen and Verbeek, op. cit.

[39] Endo, op. cit.

stipulated that the objectives of the Union would be achieved 'while respecting the principle of subsidiarity as defined in Article 3b'.

Many commentators have pointed out the ambiguities in these formulations, but the relevant point here is that there was no explicit reference to sub-Central government.[40] It is often assumed that the establishment of the Committee of Regions and acceptance of sub-central government representation on the Council of Ministers were based on the principle, but this was not stated in the Treaty.

The reason is fairly clear. Both the use of the term 'subsidiarity' and its definition had involved compromise between three particular interests: the German *Länder*, which had sought a constitutional clarification of the powers of each level, the British government, which had wanted to *preclude* references to sub-central government and to restrict the competencies of the EU, and Delors, who had wanted to maintain the initiative of the Commission, while acknow-ledging that the various policy areas required solutions at different levels.[41] Moreover, the 'clarifications' of subsidiarity following the post-Maastricht ratification crisis, retained references to only two tiers – the Community and the Member States.[42] Why then has the principle of subsidiarity been used to promote the demand for democratic decentralisation?

First, the very attempt to define and limit powers between MS and the EU institutions implies that both of them are part of a single system. As one analyst has put it, 'Once the EC countries have adopted the subsidiarity principle, these countries have tacitly ac-cepted a hierarchy vertically organised among the several polities, each of which has its own competencies.'[43] In other words, even though the British government was vehemently attempting to roll back the Commission by invoking the doctrine of subsidiarity, it was implicitly recognising the EU as an entity within which power was distributed amongst various organs. Yet once it was acknow-ledged that the EU could be viewed in this way, there was no logical

---

[40] Church and Phinnemore, op. cit., p. 71.

[41] Endo, op. cit., van Kersbergen and Verbeek, op. cit.

[42] The only exception was one reference to 'local authorities' in para. 3 (ii) in the Edinburgh Declaration of December 1992. The Declaration (officially entitled 'Overall Approach to the Application by the Council of the Subsidiarity Principle and Article 3b of the Treaty on European Union') is reproduced in Church and Phinnemore, op. cit.

[43] Endo, op. cit., p. 1979.

reason to stop at the two-tier system – the same principles could apply within the Member States (as, of course, they already did in many of them). Secondly, the requirement that decisions should be 'taken as closely as possible to the citizen', and 'without excessive centralisation' could obviously also be used to justify a case for democratic sub-central government.[44] Finally, while the extensive document produced at the 1992 Edinburgh summit to clarify the 'overall approach to the application by the Council of the subsidiarity principle', gave no direct justification for the introduction of sub-central government, it was again clear that many of the criteria for action that it stipulated as between the EU and the MS could equally well apply to the demarcation between Central and sub-Central government: for example, the notions that the higher body should only take an action where an objective could better be attained than at the lower level, or that the methods employed should be proportional to the goals in question and at the appropriate intensity.[45] These ideas may be nebulous, and the ECJ will be placed in an unenviable position when called upon to adjudicate on contested applications of the principles, but they could obviously be used to regulate the relations between sub-state tiers of government.

It is therefore easy to appreciate the way in which such principles may be used to justify demands for the introduction of new sub central governments. Thus, for example, the Committee of the Regions submitted a *Resolution on Subsidiarity* to the Essen European Council in December 1994 recommending that the Committee of the Regions be given the right of recourse to the Court of Justice concerning breaches of subsidiarity which affected the specific powers of regional and local authorities, and it also called on the 1996 IGC to Amend article 3b of the Treaty to ensure that it contained a specific reference to the role of regions and local authorities in the implementation of subsidiarity.[46] Such interpretations of subsidiarity have also received support from academic theorists.[47]

---

[44] Article A of the Maastricht Treaty and Birmingham Declaration of October 1992, para. 5. (The Birmingham Declaration is reproduced in Church and Phinnemore, op. cit.)

[45] Edinburgh statement: Basic principles, paras 1 and 2.

[46] EIS, no. 155, Dec. 1994, p. 10.

[47] Scott, Peterson, and Millar, op. cit.

Yet in the final analysis, victory in the battle over subsidiarity will be determined by power relations rather than by theoretical exegesis. When combined with the changes in EU regional policy, and the institutionalisation of regional government in many EU states, there is clearly pressure upon the unitary system in Britain, particularly given the strength of domestic regional or nationalist movements. It is therefore highly probable that, if the Conservative government remains in power, there will be clashes between Britain and some of the other EU countries about the role of the 'third tier' in EU institutions and – at least implicitly – about Britain's domestic political structure. However, it must also be emphasised that Britain is not the sole unitary state, and that even some of those – such as France – which have moved towards decentralisation are in no way comparable to Belgium, Germany or Spain. It is therefore not at all clear that there would be any general agreement to strengthen regional representation or to grant powers to the Committee of the Regions. Belgium, Spain and now Italy are driven by their internal dynamics to support stronger 'third level' representation in the EU. Thus, for example, it is notable that it was Belgium, rather than Germany, which actually made the formal proposal for the third level representation in the Council of Ministers. Given the fact that the federalisation of Belgium is now far more extensive (and complex) than that of Germany, this is hardly surprising, and the regions and communities within Belgium would clearly have an interest in strengthening their position within the EU.[48] Similarly, pressures from the Northern League in Italy and from the Basque country and Catalonia in Spain may also be expected to mean support for a greater entrenchment of regional power at EU level. However, given their role in influencing the Maastricht reforms, it is probable that, once again the role of the *Länder* will be of pivotal importance. Certainly, the German Christian Democrats have continued to promote the notion of a Federal Europe.[49] On the other

[48] The 1993 constitution divides the state into three communities and three regions, with asymmetrical powers exercised within each of them and considerable overlaps between them. There is an additional complex structure for Brussels. The Federal level retains competence for monetary and fiscal affairs, the judiciary, defence, social security, public debt, the co-ordination of foreign relations, and civil, commercial and penal law. Van Ginderachter, op. cit.

[49] The controversial foreign policy paper of the CDU/CSU published on 1 Sept. 1994 proclaimed that: 'The goal must be to strengthen the EU's capacity to act

hand, if the *Länder* are now satisfied that they have secured sufficient concessions to safeguard their interests *within* Germany, they might be less concerned to strengthen the role of other regions within the EU.

The notion of the 'Europe of the Regions' – even in the weaker sense of 'co-operative regionalism' – therefore remains highly questionable for the foreseeable future. However, there are, in any case, more theoretical problems in the idea than is sometimes implied.

Problematic issues

The definition of a region. There is no adequate definition of a 'region' within the EU. Thus, for example, some politically-defined regions are larger in various respects than other MS. To take the most extreme example, North Rhine-Westphalia has a population of 17.5 million, which means that more than one in five Germans, and one in twenty-one EU citizens, live there. It has a surface area of 34,000 square km. and an economy which accounts for approximately 25% of Germany's GDP. In world terms this means that, as an export economy, North Rhine-Westphalia alone would rank tenth.[50] At the other extreme Denmark accounts for less than 1.4% of total EU population, Ireland for less than 1% and Luxembourg less than 0.1%. This diversity is not only a problem for academic theory, but also for practical economic and political planning. The Commission, for example, is forced to make extremely complex calculations in an attempt to ensure some comparability between regions which are defined quite differently in each MS.[51] Obviously, no region is economically autonomous, and those which are defined politically may not even have economic distinct-

---

and to make its structures and procedures more democratic and federal.' It called for a quasi-constitutional document describing the division of powers between the EU, the nation-states and the regions, which would be 'oriented to the model of a "federal state" and to the principle of subsidiarity'. *The Guardian*, 7 Sep. 1994.

[50] Reimut Jochimsen, 'The Regionalisation of Structural Policy: North Rhine-Westphalia in the Europe of the Regions' in Charlie Jeffery and Roland Sturm, *Federalism, Unification and European Integration*, London: Cass, 1993, pp. 81-4.

[51] *Nomenclature of Territorial Units for Statistics*, Luxembourg: Office for Official Publications of the European Communities, EUROSTAT, March 1992.

iveness. There are also often problems in defining the separate status of cities and their relationship with regions.[52]

It is also evident that there is little correlation between the notion of a 'regional identity' and constitutional recognition. For example, regional identities, culturally and linguistically, are far stronger in Italy than in Germany. Whereas Italy has never developed a strong sense of national unity, so that regional government is a partial response to deep-rooted traditions, this was not the case with the *Länder*, which were unpopular in the early years.[53] However, Scotland, which has not possessed its own government for several centuries, has nevertheless retained a strong sense of cultural separateness. Nor is there any consistency in the extent of power exercised even by regions which have been granted a degree of self-government. Thus while the French and Italian regional reforms have certainly opened up scope for greater political and economic autonomy than previously existed, these have not led to a situation which is in any way comparable to that of the German *Länder*. Yet even the *Länder* are not so strong – at least in constitutional terms – as the newly established regions and communities in Belgium, which have assumed many of the functions which would normally be exercised by a central government. Moreover, the status of the Spanish autonomous communities is still in a process of flux, but is characterised by differential degrees of power between the different republics. This could therefore ultimately lead to a situation in which Catalonia and the Basque country exercised a very strong element of autonomy, while other regions remained highly dependent on Madrid.

It is not at all surprising that there is no consistent pattern of decentralisation, since each constitution has reflected particular circumstances within the country in question. In Germany the establishment of the *Länder* was as a result of *external* decisions, with the specific aim of weakening central government; in Italy and France decentralisation was an attempt to reform previously centralised systems; but in Belgium and Spain the measures were responses to crises which threatened the disintegration of the state.

Such differences between the size and power of regions do not

[52] For problems arising in the German case, see Bulmer, op. cit., pp. 55-6.

[53] Elisabeth Noelle and Erich Peter Neumann, *Jahrbuch der Öffentlichen Meinung*, Allensbach: Institut für Demoskopie, 1967, p. 458, and Elisabeth Noelle, *The Germans: Public Opinion Polls, 1967-1980*, Westport: Greenwood Press, 1981, p. 175, cited in Putnam, op. cit., p. 58.

constitute a serious problem for the EU in current circumstances. While the COR is purely advisory the arbitrary nature of its representation can be tolerated. Similarly, other governments can accept Belgian or German regional representatives in the Council of Ministers as long as these simply act as substitutes for ministers from central government. However, if the Committee of Regions were to allocate resources, or if regional governments secured decision-making powers within the EU that were *additional* to those exercised by central government, the definition of a region would become a very significant problem.

Regions and uneven development. 'Uneven development' results in inequalities that are spatially distributed (as well as existing between social groups within any particular space). Of all the countries within the EU, Italy provides the most dramatic example of this, with *per capita* income approximately 80% higher in the North than in the South, but the same phenomenon exists in each country and across the EU as a whole.[54] It has thus been calculated on a 'synthesis index' (measuring high unemployment, low GDP and rapid change in the labour force) that, in the Southern member states in the late 1980s Spain had seventeen regions ranked more than one standard deviation below the EU average, Greece had nine, Southern Italy had seven, and Portugal had all its regions. In the Northern periphery the most intensive problems were in Northern Ireland and the Irish Republic.[55] However, while Germany includes some of the richest areas in the EU, it also now includes, in the former East Germany, the three poorest regions.[56] The UK also exhibits very uneven development. Of the eleven standard regions, three – East Anglia, the South-East, and the South-West – are relatively prosperous (though with areas of deprivation), the East Midlands is further down the scale, and there are seven regions lagging behind, with Northern Ireland in the worst situation.[57] While Britain has the fourth highest region in the EU Twelve in terms of GDP per head (Greater London), its lowest unemployment region (Grampian)

[54] Putnam, op. cit., p. 158.

[55] F. Gaffikin and M. Morrissey, 'In Pursuit of the Holy Grail: Combating Local Poverty in an Unequal Society', *Local Economy*, 9, 2, Aug. 1994.

[56] *Competitiveness and Cohesion*, op. cit., table A.25.

[57] Gaffikin and Morrissey, op. cit.

ranks only thirty-sixth out of the 181 regions considered.[58] Uneven
development naturally raises a whole range of difficult issues for
public authorities. These will be considered initially in relation to
the individual state, and then with reference to the EU dimension.

In the case of a unitary central government, there will obviously
be considerable pressure from the disadvantaged regions to bring
about greater equalisation. On the other hand, in some cases – as,
for example, that of Scotland – the argument that the centre is
deriving a disproportionate amount of its wealth *from* a particular
region without providing equivalent benefits to it will fuel demands
for independence or democratic decentralisation. However, even if
a particular state seriously intended to equalise standards across the
territory, it could not do so unless it redistributed some of the
revenues and capital derived from richer regions to poorer ones. Yet
this is often resisted in the regions which are relatively advantaged
and in some circumstances such redistributive policies generate
separatist pressures from these areas. This, for example, has certainly
been the case with the Northern Leagues in Italy, and was also a
factor in stimulating Flemish nationalism within Belgium.

Yet if distributive policies are often a factor in the rise of territorial
movements, decentralisation does not necessarily resolve the problems.
Decentralised systems normally make the system of budgetary transfers more transparent and open, but this does not always satisfy the
demands of either the advantaged or disadvantaged regions. Indeed
there have been very sharp conflicts within Germany, Spain and
Italy over this very issue and, in the latter case, demands for total
separation by the Northern League.[59] It is also apparent that some
of the German *Länder*, which have been the most active in supporting the idea of 'Europe of the Regions' have been the wealthiest,
and this is also true in Spain and France. It has thus been suggested
that, at least in some cases, richer areas have been keen to 'Europeanise'
the issue of regions so as to avoid the budgetary transfers which they
have hitherto been forced to pay to central government.[60]

---

[58] *Competitiveness and Cohesion*, op. cit., table A.26.

[59] Bulmer, op. cit., pp. 52-5; Hine, op. cit., pp. 269-70; Doughty and Newton, op.
cit., p. 118.

[60] Thomas O. Hueglin, 'Federalism, Subsidiarity and the European Tradition: Some
Contextual and Critical Clarifications', paper presented at the ECSA-World
Conference, 'Federalism, Subsidiarity and Democracy in the European Union'
Brussels, 5-6 May 1994; Harvie, op. cit. pp. 4-5, 65-6.

A further notable tendency has been the shift in the regional policies of the richer, Northern states during the 1980s. With the exception of Italy, where it may be presumed that the major motive was the attempt to maintain Christian Democratic support in the South, regional policies became less oriented towards redistributing income and employment to poorer regions, and more designed to bring about structural change in order to enhance overall economic growth and competitiveness. The general tendency in the richer countries was to lower expenditure and to adopt a more selective approach to regional development, with Germany concentrating upon its new Eastern regions.[61]

There is no doubt that reducing regional disparities is an extremely difficult task – even when public authorities have serious intent. Many traditional models of development have been shown to be unsuccessful, and budgetary transfers and grants are often relatively ineffective.[62] There is now much more emphasis on training, networking, public-private partnerships, and local initiatives than was previously the case. It has also become clear that the large-scale companies have their own locational preferences which may counteract governmental policies and influence the regional economic hierarchy. It is therefore, possible that one reason for the shift in policy by the North European states has been a recognition that previous strategies were only partially successful. However, although it is generally recognised that uneven development cannot be overcome simply by budgetary transfers, there can be little doubt that *redistributive policies of some kind* are necessary to help break a cycle of cumulative disadvantage. If the richer governments appear to be reducing their support for regional development within their own countries, how does the situation appear in the EU as a whole?

Once the EU is introduced into the analysis of spatial uneven development there are two aspects to consider. First, there is the inequality *between* the MS and secondly, there is the inequality throughout the EU area. These may be considered in turn. As Table 5.1 below shows, Greece is the only poor country which shows a serious negative trend, with a more encouraging situation in Ireland, and to lesser extent, in Portugal. Of the richer countries Finland shows the most dramatic deterioration, largely

[61] *Competitiveness and Cohesion*, op. cit., pp. 135-45.
[62] Holland, op. cit., pp. 192-200.

because of the loss of the Soviet market. But the overall picture shows a slight reduction in disparities over the period 1982-1993.

Table 5.1. GDP PER HEAD OF THOSE EMPLOYED, 1982-1993
(EU15 + Norway = 100)

	1982	1988	1993
Bel	107	103	106
Den	108	109	106
Ger	117	116	117
Ger (+ new *Länder*)			104
Gr	52	49	49
Sp	71	73	76
Fr	116	110	109
Irl	65	64	78
It	103	104	104
Lux	117	122	132
NL	104	100	101
P	54	54	60
UK	98	105	99
Aus	108	105	107
Swe	113	112	98
Fin	101	104	86
Disparity (EU 12)	18.6	17.9	16.8

Source: Adapted from Table A.5 in *Competitiveness and Cohesion: Trends in the Regions*, 5th Periodic Report on the Social and Economic Situation and Development of the Regions in the Community, Commission of the European Communities, 1994.

However, it is worth noting that one study of the EU12, based on sectoral analysis of the economies, has argued that, over time, the impact of the Single European Market, will reinforce the disparities between the MS, with Germany benefiting the most, followed by the other five original EC members. Ireland, Denmark and Britain might not 'lose' but were less well positioned, Spain was the best placed of the Southern states, while Portugal and, still more, Greece were the most vulnerable.

The overall conclusion was that the relative gains were likely to accrue to the more advanced states, while the less developed members were likely to experience relative, if not absolute, losses.[63]

[63] Dale L. Smith and Jürgen Wanke, '1992: Who Wins? Who Loses?', Cafruny and Rosenthal, op. cit.

This remains speculative at present, but tallies with some of the evidence about regional disparities, which will now be considered. As table 5.2 shows, there was a consistently high disparity in GDP per head of employed population from 1980 to 1991 between the richest and poorest regions in the EU. However, this already bleak

Table 5.2. DISPARITIES IN GDP PER HEAD IN THE COMMUNITY
(EU 12 = 100)

	Average 10 Weakest regions	*Average 10 Strongest regions*
1980	44.0	145.8
1984	42.6	150.6
1988	41.0	152.4
1991	41.8	151.6
1991 (incl. new *Länder*)	33.4	151.6

Source: Table A.4 *Competitiveness and Cohesion: Trends in the Regions*, 5th Periodic Report on the Social and Economic Situation and Development of the Regions in the Community, Commission of the European Communities, 1994.

picture has become considerably worse since 1991, with the new recession. Thus in 1993 unemployment in the ten worst affected regions averaged 25.3% compared with 3.6% in the ten least affected. Certainly, the situation is not entirely gloomy – for example unemployment fell by nearly 3 percentage points between 1986 and 1993 in regions of industrial decline (objective 2 regions) whereas it remained virtually static elsewhere in the EU.[64] Nevertheless, the situation of the poorer regions is generally depressing. Not only do the areas of highest unemployment in the South European countries and the island of Ireland tend to have the fastest growing populations, but they also have the least adequate infrastructure and skills levels.[65]

Yet it is surely clear that the EU will play only a modest role in counteracting uneven development. As noted in earlier chapters, the budget is relatively small, and the net contributors have opposed increases in structural funds. Moreover, if there has been limited solidarity between regions within 'nation-states' – for example, between Lombardy and Calabria or Catalonia and Andalusia – it is surely likely that there will be even less between advantaged and

[64] *Competitiveness and Cohesion*, op. cit., pp 9-13.
[65] Ibid.

disadvantaged regions across countries which are not even geographically contiguous? It also seems that the wealthier regions have
derived the most benefits from inter-regional co-operation. Baden-
Württemberg has been able to create its own intra-European con-
federation of regions specialising in high technology, and regions
such as Rhône-Alpes and Lombardy are also well-represented in
ventures of this kind. But Stuart Holland concludes:

> A major message of the map of . . . interregional cooperation is
> that the Centre and South-Centre of the Community is net-
> worked but the Deep South still is mainly excluded from such
> networking. The same also is true for some of the northern
> regions of the UK, and northern Ireland.[66]

The cumulative disadvantages of poorer regions are even demonstrated
by the Italian experiment in regional decentralisation, which suggests that stronger regions may benefit disproportionately from
constitutional reform of this kind. Thus it has been convincingly
argued that, because relations of civic solidarity had developed over
centuries in the north and centre of Italy, while the tradition in the
south had been feudal and hierarchical, regional government in the
former areas has been far more successful. Indeed it seems that the
regional reform may be exacerbating, rather than mitigating, the
historical disparities, freeing 'the more advanced regions from the
stultifying grasp of Rome, while allowing the problems of the more
backward regions to fester'.[67] And, more generally, the authors
conclude:

> *Social context and history profoundly condition the effectiveness of
> institutions.* Where the regional soil is fertile, the regions draw
> sustenance from regional traditions, but where the soil is poor,
> the new institutions are stunted.[68]

This is *not* an argument against regional government. The evidence
suggests that the south of Italy has also benefited from the reform
and that even there the institutions are, at least, viewed more
positively than those of central government (though this is not very
strong praise!). Nor is uneven development the only relevant issue.

[66] Holland, op. cit., 209.
[67] Putnam, op. cit., 61.
[68] Ibid., p. 182.

It may, for example, be argued that democratic considerations should prevail even if the new institutions were to have no impact on the economic problems. However, tackling the problem of spatial inequality must be an important consideration, and institutional reform is unlikely to be more than one element in a possible solution.[69]

Political fragmentation.   One of the features of a unitary system is that, in theory at least, once policies have been agreed by the central government, they may be implemented throughout the territory. In Britain this has sometimes been acclaimed as a positive democratic virtue, but has also been denounced as 'elective dictatorship'. Neither major party has taken a consistent stance on the issue over time, but the Left increasingly called for constitutional reform in response to Conservative ascendancy, and centralising policies, after 1979. The recent dramatic changes in the relationships between central and sub-central government in Britain have also led to some sophisticated analyses of their underlying features. An important conclusion has been that there have been two major phases since the Second World War. The first, which existed during the 'consensus politics' era, was one of a 'dual polity', in which central government concentrated mainly on 'high politics' and overall macroeconomic management, while local government was left relatively autonomous within its own sphere. The second involved a virtual destruction of that autonomy, after the Conservative government found that the 'dual polity' meant that its policy networks with sub-central government were too weak to implement its programme by a process of bargaining and negotiation.[70] There is therefore a strong case for arguing that a system of open inter-dependencies between tiers of government, permitting bargaining relationships, may be more satisfactory on both democratic and efficiency criteria. Indeed democratic decentralisation may be beneficial in all large unitary states, particularly when there are significant political, cultural, or economic disparities between the regions.

Yet there are obviously also *some* political costs involved. Indeed, these were foreseen by one of the founders of the American federal

[69] For an argument that regional decentralisation is *always* economically disadvantageous for poorer regions, see P.J.D. Wiles, 'The Economics of Regional Centralization and Decentralization' in M. Hebbert and H. Machin, *Regionalisation in France, Italy and Spain*, London School of Economics, 1984.
[70] In particular, see Rhodes, *Beyond Westminister and Whitehall*, op. cit.

system, James Madison, who pointed out that shared powers meant permanent controversy.[71] For decentralised political systems inevitably involve divisions of powers and bargaining relationships, both horizontally – between the regional tiers – and vertically – between the regional tiers and the centre. This may be viewed as a positive feature of the system, with the argument that the 'general good' is likely to emerge from a relatively open process of negotiation between different tiers of democratic government. But it may also make policy co-ordination more problematic.

Even if there is no dramatic advance towards a 'Europe of the Regions', it is likely that the EU as a whole will be affected by the distribution of powers between central and sub-central government with each MS. It is, for example, already evident that the power of the *Länder* within Germany is an important factor in reducing internal policy co-ordination, particularly with reference to the EU.[72] Because the Federal Republic is (with the partial exception of the eastern *Länder*) so united a country in most ways, this has not generally affected its ability to secure its most important policy goals within the EU. However, it seems that some of the other MS find it difficult to interpret German policy within EU negotiations because of the complexities of its domestic policy-making processes, and this problem is likely to intensify with the recent entrenchment of the position of the *Länder*. Belgium, Spain and even Italy are relatively fragmented and, over time, their policy-making on EU issues could reflect these pressures.

Again it must be stressed that this is not an argument against democratic decentralisation, which may be beneficial both for particular regions and for the EU as a whole. However, as was argued in chapter 2, the EU is already an extremely fragmented policy-making system. Each phase of enlargement will inevitably make decision-making still more complex, as a greater number of states, with ever greater diversities, need to be accommodated. If each MS decentralises internally and regional representation becomes more fully reflected in EU policy-making, the challenge will be to prevent fragmentation or paralysis.

[71] Putnam, op. cit., p. 47.
[72] S. Bulmer and W. Paterson, *The Federal Republic of Germany and the European Community*, London: Allen and Unwin, 1987; Jeffery, op. cit.

Robert Dahl, the most famous contemporary American theorist of democracy, once stated:

> The smaller the unit the greater the opportunity for citizens to participate in the decisions of their government, yet the less the environment they can control. Thus for most citizens, participation in very large units becomes minimal and in very small units it becomes trivial.[73]

Although the relationship between size and participation is less direct and constant than this implies, there is little doubt that Dahl identifies a genuine democratic dilemma. The establishment of sub-central tiers of government with genuine powers and responsibilities provides a partial solution to the problem. When, as in Britain, there are not only sharp regional disparities politically and economically, but also separate nations in Scotland and Wales, the case for regional government is, in my view, now unarguable. However, I have also sought to show that democratic decentralisation is no panacea.

Regional government and the quest for 'co-operative regionalism' could be highly positive goals, which could help regenerate democracy within the EU. But they are not necessarily positive *per se*. Democracy, in this respect, as in others, should not be identified with a single aim. The increased freedom to make decisions at regional level, needs to be balanced against issues of equality and effective policy-making and implementation at all levels and in all regions. This may be very difficult to attain in practice, but such considerations cannot be ignored if democratisation is the goal.

[73] Quoted in K. Newton, *Is Small Really so Beautiful? Is Big Really so Ugly?* Glasgow: University of Strathclyde Centre for the Study of Public Policy, no. 18, 1978.

6

CITIZENSHIP

In recent years there has been a striking increase in interest in the ancient concept of 'citizenship'. Both academic theorists and practical politicians have argued that it is a vital component of democracy, and the debate has been extended beyond the individual state, with the category of 'EU citizenship' conferred by the Maastricht Treaty. But because the term has positive connotations, it has been appropriated by contending ideological movements and parties to justify their general preferences and programmes. Its meaning is therefore contested and controversial and some have doubted whether it has any value at all. One political philosopher has thus become so exasperated with the lack of clarity of the term as to proclaim:

> Goering reached for his revolver when he heard the world 'culture'. Now it is tempting to do the same when people talk about 'citizenship': the great, but wholly indistinct, thing that parties and voters agree we should have more of . . . but is there anything concrete hidden in the clouds of rhetoric, or has the idea of citizenship reached a stage of vacuity?[1]

Yet the ultimate test of the usefulness of a political concept is whether it conveys an important idea or set of ideas which cannot easily be conveyed by other terms. I believe that 'citizenship' does succeed in this sense. Moreover, whatever the *theoretical* difficulties in the idea, its *practical* applications have extremely serious implications.

This chapter considers citizenship as follows. The first section seeks to explain the revival of interest in the concept and explores its meaning; the second section examines the theoretical possibilities for EU citizenship; the third analyses concrete developments, with particular reference to the Maastricht Treaty; and the fourth deals

---

[1] Alan Ryan, *The Times*, 12 Sept. 1990, quoted in Geoff Andrews (ed.), *Citizenship*, London: Lawrence and Wishart, 1991, p. 17.

with the position of those who are denied full citizenship rights in the EU. This is followed by a brief conclusion which evaluates the overall implications of the current position.

The concept of citizenship

Like the allied concept of democracy, 'citizenship' has undergone theoretical and practical transmutations over the centuries since its original development in ancient Greece. However, the author of a recent thorough history of its ancient and modern uses explains its essential continuity as follows:

> From very early in its history the term already contained a cluster of meanings related to a defined legal or social status, a means of political identity, a focus for loyalty, a requirement of duties, an expectation of rights and a yardstick of good social behaviour. . . No subsequent discussion of the topic has required any more components nor would have been complete with any fewer.[2]

But why has there been a renewed emphasis upon the importance of such ideas, particularly since the late 1980s? Three concerns have probably been particularly important. First, the growth of a massive 'power gap' between individuals and those who control their lives has raised the question of 'rights' in an acute way. In Britain, this has taken a particular form because the Conservative government used its power to re-structure institutions and society in a far more fundamental way than any of its predecessors this century. This led a broad coalition of opponents to question the whole nature of the British political system and to claim that extensive constitutional reform is vital. Organisations such as Charter 88 have therefore argued that only this will enable 'subjects' to become 'citizens'.[3] Yet

[2] Derek Heater, *Citizenship: The Civic Ideal in World History, Politics and Education*, Harlow: Longman, 1990, p. 163, quoted in Elizabeth Meehan, *Citizenship and the European Community*, London: Sage, 1993, p. 4.

[3] 'We have had less freedom than we believed. That which we have enjoyed has been too dependent on the benevolence of our rulers. Our freedoms have remained their possession, rationed out to us as subjects rather than being our own inalienable possession as citizens. To make real the freedoms we once took for granted means for the first time to take them for ourselves. The time has come to demand political, civil and human rights in the United Kingdom.' Charter 88, quoted in Andrews, op. cit., pp. 208-9.

this is only a part of a far wider set of concerns about the 'rights' of citizens in the face of the overwhelming power of the contemporary state and private corporations. Many of those emphasising the importance of citizenship are raising such questions as: what 'rights' are there to privacy in relation to the massive accumulation of data about individuals? and what 'rights' are there to employment when whole sectors of the economy can be threatened by rapid movements of currency or capital? In other words, issues about 'citizen rights' have been raised by the very nature of power and modernity.

A second fundamental cause of the revived interest in 'citizenship' has been the relative failure of many traditional forms of socialism. Thus long before the collapse of the regimes in Eastern Europe and the former Soviet Union, it had become increasingly clear that no real 'citizenship' was possible in one-party systems with rigid control over information sources and political life. This led to considerable interest in the notion of 'civil society' in which citizenship could be exercised. As David Held put it:

> A socialist democracy would only be fully worth its name if citizens had the actual power to be active as citizens, to enjoy a bundle of rights which allowed them to command democratic participation and to treat it as an entitlement.[4]

Thirdly, the 'rediscovery' of citizenship was promoted by the rise of 'new social movements'. The rise of feminism, and the development of previously marginalised groups, such as gay rights movements, and ethnic minorities, raised urgent questions about identity and rights which confront traditional political forces. Once again, Held expresses this idea particularly clearly:

> If citizenship involves the struggle for membership and participation in the community, then its analysis involves examining the way in which different groups, classes and movements struggle to gain degrees of autonomy and control over their lives in the face of various forms of stratification, hierarchy and political oppression. The . . . debate needs to extend the analysis of citizenship to take account of issues posed by, for instance, feminism, the black movement, ecology . . . and those who have advocated the rights of children. Different social movements have

---

[4] David Held, 'Between State and Civil Society' in Andrews, op. cit., p. 24.

raised different questions about the nature and dimensions of citizenship.[5]

But what does it mean to be a citizen?

The possession of 'citizenship' implies that a person is recognised as a full member of a community by a legally instituted authority. But while citizenship may be legally conferred and partly legally defined, its resonance is political. From the eighteenth century onwards – and typified in the French revolutionary Declaration of the Rights of Man and of Citizens (1789) – citizenship has been closely bound up with the demands for 'rights' by oppressed groups within society.[6] The argument has been that only a privileged sector has possessed full citizenship: those denied such benefits have therefore demanded the recognition of their *rights* so that they too may become full citizens. Of course, the nature of those rights has varied in different historical eras, and with different groups. At times they have been expressed primarily in political and civil terms – the right to vote, the right to free expression, the right to form political associations; at other times the emphasis has been economic and social – the right to a minimum wage, to affordable housing, to education and health care. More recently, some movements and groups have called into question the existing definition of 'citizenship'. In particular, feminists have argued that prevailing notions have been 'gendered' and have therefore demanded rights to equal citizenship which also entail acknowledging 'difference'. Similarly, minority ethnic groups have demanded the ending of conceptions of citizenship which actually prescribe conformity with a dominant cultural conception and have insisted on full recognition of multi-ethnicity as an aspect of citizenship. But even when the demands are on the basis of 'difference', the campaign is still for equality in the name of citizenship rights. This again points to the inadequacy of a purely legal approach. For example, possession of British citizenship provides the holder with a passport which confers legal rights throughout the EU. However, in practice, a black British citizen may find it much more difficult to secure recognition of these rights than a white

[5] 'Citizenship and Autonomy' in David Held, *Political Theory and the Modern State*, Oxford: Polity Press and Blackwell, 1989, p. 199.
[6] The Declaration of the Rights of Man and of Citizens is reproduced in Merryn Williams (ed.), *Revolutions, 1775-1830*, Harmondsworth: Penguin/Open University Press, 1971, pp. 96-9.

citizen. Legal citizenship cannot therefore, in itself, always confer even the rights that it purportedly provides, even though these may often be regarded as a minimum entitlement. Thus the legal title might be viewed as a necessary, but not a sufficient, condition of citizenship. For citizenship also involves this notion of the recognition of rights. In this case, therefore, black British citizens expect not only the equal entitlement which the legal rights already theoretically provide, but equal recognition of that entitlement by all EU customs officials and police. But this raises a further fundamental problem: what are the rights which confer genuine citizenship? Is it possible to define them?

In general, modern European thought has rejected the natural law tradition (which held that certain rights were God-given and only needed codification in civil law) in favour of the notion that rights are created and constituted by human society. But as society changes so will its conceptions of rights.[7] Yet even a constant flow of demands for *rights* is not the same as the demands for total *equality*. If, therefore, equality is a fundamental goal, is the demand for full citizenship helpful? Or is it, as Marx argued, a diversion, which offered abstract, atomised rights which masked the real nature of the capitalist system?[8]

One of the most influential answers to Marx's line of argument was provided – a century later – by the British sociologist T.H. Marshall in *Citizenship and Social Class* (1950). Here he argued that citizenship comprised three fundamental elements which had

[7] '[Rights] are not historical in the sense that they have at some time won their recognition . They are not natural, in the sense that a permanent and unchanging catalogue of them can be compiled. They are historical in the sense that, at some given period and place, they are demanded by the character of its civilisation; and they are natural in the sense that, under those same limitations, the facts demand their recognition.' Harold Laski, *A Grammar of Politics*, London: Allen and Unwin, 4th edn, 1938, p. 91.

[8] 'None of the so-called rights of man goes beyond egoistic man, man as he is in civil society, namely an individual withdrawn behind his private interests and whims and separated from the community. Far from the rights of man conceiving of man as a species-being, species-life itself, society, appears as a framework exterior to individuals, a limitation of their original self-sufficiency. The only bond that holds them together is natural necessity, need and private interest, the conservation of their property and egoistic person.' 'On the Jewish Question' in David McLellan (ed.), *Karl Marx: Selected Writings*, Oxford University Press, 1977, p. 54.

developed in historical phases. The first, or *civil element*, was composed of the rights necessary for individual freedom – liberty of the
person, freedom of speech, thought and faith, the right to own
property and to conclude valid contracts, and the right to justice.
This conception, he suggested, had developed in the eighteenth
century, as a condition for the development of capitalism and led to
new forms of class inequality. The second, or *political element*, was
the right to participate in the exercise of political power, as a member
of a body invested with political authority (such as parliament or
local government), or as an elector of the members of such a body.
This, he claimed, was the battle which had been fought in the
nineteenth century and had provided a basis for further advances.
The third, or *social element*, included:

> The whole range from the right to a modicum of economic
> welfare and security to the right to share to the full in the social
> heritage and to live the life of a civilised being according to the
> standards prevailing in the society. The institutions most closely
> connected with it are the education system and the social ser-
> vices.[9]

This, he argued, had been the battle of the twentieth century and,
while it had not established equality, it had at least brought about a
greater equality of status and had 'civilised' capitalism.

Marshall's work has been criticised on various grounds. It has
been seen as complacent, as based on an inaccurate one-dimensional,
evolutionary view of history, as gender-biased, as ethnocentric, as
paternalistic, and as too narrow.[10] There is, no doubt, some validity
in all these points. However, his general approach has two features
which are of great importance (and which are acknowledged by
most of his critics). First, it suggests a connection between the
various forms of rights: civil rights provided a basis for the development of political rights, which also provided conditions in which
social rights could be advanced. He was discussing the historical
evolution of different kinds of rights, but the same inter-connections

---

[9] T.H. Marshall, *Citizenship and Social Class*, Cambridge University Press, 1950, p. 10.
[10] See, for example, Anthony Giddens, *The Nation-State and Violence*, Berkeley:
University of California Press, 1985; Maurice Roche, *Rethinking Citizenship:
Welfare, Ideology and Change in Modern Society*, Oxford/Cambridge: Polity Press,
1992; Sylvia Walby, 'Is Citizenship Gendered?' *Society*, 28, no. 2, May 1994;
David Held, 'Citizenship and Autonomy', op. cit.

exist between them within a single period. For example, it is almost impossible to campaign effectively for social and economic rights in a dictatorship which denies political rights. But it is equally difficult for the socially excluded to exercise their political rights. Secondly, even if Marshall may have exaggerated the impact of social policy on inequality, most critics would agree that the 'welfare state' enabled far more people to become 'citizens'. For example, Bryan S. Turner, who takes a neo-Marxist position, nevertheless argues that it meant that the citizenship rights in 'welfare states' could no longer be regarded simply as abstract rights which reinforced capitalism by masking its oppressive nature, as Marx had suggested.[11] Similarly Sylvia Walby, who criticises Marshall's notion of citizenship from a feminist perspective, acknowledges:

> The welfare state has socialised some forms of previously privatised domestic labour, through schools, nurseries, hospitals, and other forms of publicly provided care, albeit at levels which do not satisfy women's demands. It is the socialised provision as much as the welfare transfers, which is crucial in socialising women's domestic role. . . . The development of social citizenship is con-stituted at least as much by changing gender relations as it is by changing class relations.[12]

If this suggests that 'citizenship' needs to be understood in terms of a constant redefinition of rights, are any *duties* involved? The original sense of 'civic-republication' stressed the notion of 'duty'. Because one was a citizen, with the privileges that this confers, one had the obligation to defend and promote the well-being of the polity. Thus in the Greek city-state those who failed to participate in political decision-making could forfeit their rights of citizenship.[13] As Adrian Oldfield has recently shown, this tradition of civic republicanism was maintained by such thinkers as Machiavelli, Hegel, Rousseau and Tocqueville.[14] However, this emphasis on citizenship carrying *duties* has generally been less emphasised in recent usage and is

[11] Bryan S. Turner, *Citizenship and Capitalism*, London: Allen and Unwin, 1986, pp. 135-6.
[12] Walby, op. cit., pp. 391-1.
[13] Cynthia Farrar, 'Ancient Greek Political Theory as a Response to Democracy' in Dunn, *Democracy*, op. cit.
[14] Adrian Oldfield, *Citizenship and Community*, London: Routledge, 1990.

virtually ignored by many of the contemporary advocates of the concept.[15] One reason for this is probably that many of those who do proclaim such 'duties' do so with a clear intention, and from a very right-wing point of view. For example, the argument that those who receive social security benefits have a *duty* to work so as to 'pay back' society is surely designed to stigmatise the poor? Another, similarly weighted use of 'duty' is to suggest that people should be 'active citizens' by work in charities or by supporting the victims of crime. As Tony Wright argues, this is really to 'privatize citizenship' so that it will 'not interfere with the business of "real" politics'.[16] More fundamentally, there are obviously difficulties in suggesting that, in a massively unequal society, the disadvantaged have any obligations at all even when they theoretically possess at least the legal rights of citizenship. Indeed Danilo Zolo argues that the whole notion of duties or moral responsibilities should be avoided as it simply strengthens subordination to the authorities.[17] And yet the idea of 'duty' is deeply embedded in the original notion of 'citizenship'. If it is simply jettisoned, it might be argued that the term is now being used in a propagandist way to reinforce the demand for rights. I therefore believe that the idea of 'duty' should still be maintained.

The original notion of 'duty', as already noted, stemmed from the idea that the citizen should be actively engaged in promoting the well-being of the republic. But what kind of activity is required in our vastly complex contemporary society? Laski was clear that one fundamental duty was vigilance about the policies implemented by political authorities:

> You and I are part of the leverage by which that policy is ultimately enacted. It therefore becomes a moral duty on our part to examine the foundations of state-action. The last sin in politics is unthinking acquiescence in important decisions.[18]

[15] However, 'duty' is certainly emphasised in the works of Oldfield, op. cit., and Roche, op. cit.

[16] Tony Wright, *Citizens and Subjects*, London: Routledge, 1994, p. 127.

[17] Danilo Zolo, 'Citizenship in a Post-Communist Era' in David Held (ed.), *Prospects for Democracy*, op. cit., p. 266.

[18] 'The Pluralistic State' (originally in *Philosophical Review*, November 1919) in Harold Laski, *The Foundations of Sovereignty*, London: Allen and Unwin, 1922, p. 245.

This is as relevant as ever but raises the question of what citizens can do, even when they disagree with the basis of policy. We do not live in city-states and our political rulers may take little notice of our views. Yet it is surely even more certain that they will ignore us if they believe that we do not even care what they are doing? But even if people succeed in understanding the implications of political decisions, how is it possible to *act* as a citizen? Adrian Oldfield is surely right in arguing that motivation is the fundamental issue and that there are ample opportunities for action in a plethora of formal and informal organisations.[19] Yet there is one problem in this suggestion, for it may imply a sense of ultimate harmony. As Anne Phillips puts it:

> Citizenship often propels us towards an ideal of transcendence, a greater collectivity in which we get beyond our local identities and concerns. When we are called upon to act as *citizens*, we are by implication not acting simply as women or men, black or white, manual worker or professional, homeowner or council tenant, however powerful these affiliations are that bind us to a particular social definition or location.[20]

But, of course, we are not all in harmony, for there are bitter conflicts between groups in society. Yet the notion of the duties of citizenship does not need to imply that the republic – or its modern equivalent – is harmonious or just. It can also be based on the assumption that such participation is necessary to improve it. The alternative, after all, is inaction on the basis of isolated individualism. All this suggests that the concept of 'citizenship' is important, for it connects the ideas of legal status, identity, rights and duties. Moreover it suggests that democracy could never be defined in terms of a final goal, for 'citizenship' would constantly involve a re-definition of 'rights' and new forms of participation which various groups saw as 'duties'. The notion of 'citizenship' is therefore bound up with that of 'democratisation' – both suggest constant change. But what is the relevance of citizenship for the EU?

[19] Oldfield, op. cit., pp. 173– 4.
[20] 'Citizenship and Feminist Theory' in Andrews, op. cit., p. 81.

Citizenship and the EU: theoretical considerations

As already noted, the Maastricht Treaty conferred the title of 'Citizenship of the Union' on the legal citizens of all MS. However, it has been argued that, long before this, EU citizenship rights existed, even if they were not labelled as such, and that these are being constantly enlarged as the EU develops. This is the essence of the argument of an extremely stimulating book by Elizabeth Meehan, *Citizenship and the European Community*.[21] Her arguments merit close examination, and it is not possible to do full justice to them here.

She elaborates her positive case by refuting a view proposed by Raymond Aron that European citizenship was not possible.[22] Aron had claimed that it was not possible to conceive of European citizenship, and the principal relevant elements in his case were as follows:

(*a*) National and EC authorities provided sets of rights which were of a different order from one another;

(*b*) European citizenship would have to involve a transfer of legal and political powers from the national to the EC level (in a similar way to the transfer of Scottish and English citizenship to British citizenship with the Act of Union);

(*c*) Citizens can insist that the nation-state respects their rights because the state can demand that citizens fulfil their duties to defend it (but no multi-national polity has such authority).

(*d*) There was no popular demand for a European federation to have responsibility for legal-political rights and economic regulation and which could command duties by citizens.

(*e*) It was very unlikely that nationalities with grievances within current states would believe that their problems could be regulated at a European level.[23]

Clearly Aron's view was dominated by the modern development of 'nation-states' and the realist theory of international relations. Heater's historical approach is endorsed by Meehan to discredit the relative parochialism of 'nation-statism':

[21] Meehan, op. cit. A brief version of the main conclusions are also in Elizabeth Meehan, 'Citizenship and the European Community' in *Political Quarterly*, 62, 2, April-June 1993. (All subsequent references are to the book.)

[22] Raymond Aron, 'Is Multinational Citizenship Possible?', *Social Research*, 4, 1974.

[23] This summary of Aron is based on that by Meehan, op. cit., p. 3.

The early history of citizenship may. . . lead us to question the *modern* assumption that the status necessarily adheres to the sovereign nation-state. [It] can be associated with any geographical unit from a small town to the whole globe.[24]

However, Meehan is not arguing that EU citizenship has, or will, *replace* citizenship based on the MS. Rather she is developing three major propositions: First, that the EU has developed over time so that many of Aron's apparently categorical statements no longer apply, or have been partially invalidated. Secondly, that citizenship is in the process of being detached from a single focus and may become more equivalent to that which existed in the Roman empire, where citizens were able to appeal to more than one set of enforceable standards when claiming their rights. Thirdly, she is suggesting that, because the nation-state and the EU developed in different historical eras, their concepts of citizenship also differed. The states tended to emphasise legal and political rights, but:

The creation and development of the EC took place at a time when it was accepted in a substantial body of political theory, by citizens and even by governments . . . that there was a connection . . . amongst civil, political and social rights.[25]

Thus the process of integration has involved regulation of such matters as social security, social assistance, and sex equality. And, whatever the wishes of the governments, these forms of intervention have provided a dimension of EU citizenship, as people have acquired social rights enacted and guaranteed at this level. Moreover, there have also been campaigns and 'networks' across the EU for the enhancement of those rights. All this means that a 'reconceptualization is taking place in which . . . the citizen's legal status and the content of his or her rights are not determined by nationality alone'.[26]

Meehan substantiates her argument with constant reference to theories, but also through detailed examination of EU directives and ECJ judgments in social policy areas, with particular reference to sex equality. She also pays attention to the development, both through networks, and through general public realisation of com-

[24] Heater, op. cit., p. 163, quoted in Ibid., p. 4.
[25] Ibid., p. 6.
[26] Ibid., p. 8.

mon problems, of changes in consciousness. She thus argues that there is evidence that integration is making the sense of identity more 'fluid' and giving rise to the notion of 'multiple identity'.[27] This then leads to her conclusions that, despite its admitted short-comings:

> The Community can still be regarded as a potential arena for the realization of democratic citizenship. This is because it already offers us the opportunity to act on the fact that we have more identities than our nationality; the framework of the Community makes it possible to recognize people who share such identities, but who are of other nationalities; and it means that we can understand that our interests are best articulated by an appropriate combination of vertical channels through governments and of horizontal routes through common institutions. . . . We have a range of identities and interests . . . which have been furthered as a result of Community membership. . . . As such, we have acquired some secondary rights of political participation in transnational associations and it is precisely the experience of those avenues that encourages people to think that primary, as well as secondary, political rights are needed.[28]

In effect, then, Meehan has dealt with Aron's main objections to European citizenship. She has shown that national and EU authorities provide overlapping sets of rights, rather than rights of a different order; she has shown that relevant powers have indeed been trans-ferred from the MS to the EU; she has argued that citizens can insist that the EU respects their rights and compels the MS to do so; and she has suggested that there is a demand for it to develop politically. Finally, as against Aron, she insists that, with the development of regional networks, the wish of Scottish and other national move-ments to secure independence within Europe, and the general move towards regionalism, there are indeed signs that nationalities within existing states are now looking towards the EU for a solution. Her overall conclusion is thus that:

> There is a new framework – a complex, multi-dimensional con-figuration that is both difficult to cope with and provides oppor-tunities. Our political actions are now having to be carried out

[27] Ibid., pp. 152-3.
[28] Ibid., p. 155.

through a web of common institutions, states, regional and local authorities and voluntary associations on the domestic front and simultaneously, in national and/or transnational alliances at the common level. . . . While the complexity of this framework is intimidating in the demands it makes in finding our way around the European public space, it can provide many openings for challenging authority, for expressing our various loyalties associated with our various identities, and for expressing our rights and duties in more than one arena.[29]

In my view, Meehan's refutation of the theoretical assumptions implied by Aron's argument is successful and she argues convincingly that there are important 'rights' which are now guaranteed at least as much by the EU as by the MS. As noted in Chapter 4, it is apparent, for example, that much health and safety legislation is effectively 'supranational' and that sexual equality policies have often been advanced more effectively by the EU than by individual states. Meehan is therefore no doubt correct in suggesting that some of the rights on which people depend have been partially detached from the MS. She is also on strong ground in arguing that there are some people in each EU country who *perceive* the situation in this way, and there are also many who share her commitment to 'multiple identities' as a positive goal. Similarly, there are people in particular regions, or of a particular nationality, who would prefer to regard themselves as EU citizens than as 'nationals' of an existing state. The same is true of those who have a strong commitment to the 'European idea'. However, while Meehan's general argument is very persuasive, I believe there are some problems which it does not address sufficiently.

First, it is debatable how many people genuinely regard themselves as 'European' or 'EU' in their citizenship? It is extremely difficult to know the answer, but she tends to take an optimistic view.[30] Others are far more pessimistic about this point, emphasising the limited development of subjective identification with the EU or Europe.[31] Secondly, it is also notable that Meehan actually says very little about the 'duties' of citizenship in relation to the EU. Again,

[29] Ibid., p. 159.
[30] Ibid., pp. 150-6.
[31] Ibid., see, for example, Church and Phinnemore, op. cit., p. 82. This point is discussed extensively, with further references in chapter 8.

I have no doubt that those who have already become involved in horizontal networking – for example in anti-poverty groups – may regard their obligations to support communities which are geographically remote as at least as important as those 'at home'. But one suspects that this kind of consciousness is not general. Indeed there is surely little doubt that old-fashioned appeals to 'patriotic duties' still have considerable potency and that many people believe that they have primary obligations to the 'nation-state'. This is not to suggest that there is no sense of international solidarity, but people are perhaps at least as likely to identify with suffering in other parts of the world as with that elsewhere in the EU. This latter point would not detract from Meehan's argument about 'multiple identities', but it may raise questions about the extent to which an EU consciousness has any particular priority in the general constellation of identities.

The purpose of raising these questions is not to argue that Meehan is necessarily wrong in suggesting that the development of integration is giving rise to new subjective identities and perceptions of citizenship. Still less is it to suggest that there is some 'natural' and unbreakable bond between people and either the nation or the state, which precludes other identities. Meehan's stress on 'multiple identities' offers a far more positive outlook. However, it seems probable that the majority of the population in the majority of MS retain a far stronger sense of common citizenship within the 'nation-state' than with the EU as a whole. If this is so, it is hardly surprising since states have far greater power over people's lives than the EU.

In one sense, such power is tangible and material. As already noted in earlier chapters, MS expenditure vastly outweighs that of the EU and there are therefore good reasons for people to believe that their livelihood is dependent upon the MS (even if interdependence and integration make this a far more complex issue than it might appear). But, whatever the reality, people are likely to *believe* in the importance of the MS because states have a preeminent role in inculcating such beliefs through education systems, the media, language, the political process, tradition and so on. In other words, the means by which states mould 'national consciousness' are likely to impede the development of a European consciousness which could provide the basis for 'multiple identities'. Naturally, the extent to which this is so depends upon both the success of the particular MS in promoting a specific kind of identity, and the extent to which that identity is antagonistic towards, or harmonious with, the EU. For example, neither Belgium nor Italy has been particularly successful in promoting 'national' integration and this may provide some potential for the development of European consciousness. On the other hand, British governments have sought to heighten domestic solidarity by presenting a generally negative attitude towards the EU, and this obviously inhibits the development of the kind of outlook which could facilitate the development of 'multiple identities'. Yet even Luxembourg, the smallest MS, has been keen to sustain its own sense of 'national' identity and to resist being 'submerged' within the EU.[32] Of course, Meehan is definitely not suggesting the replacement of 'national' identity by an EU identity. However, a European identity, based on multiple identities, cannot really come to fruition unless it is nurtured by our environment.

In the final analysis, the implication of Meehan's argument is that, by a process of constant incremental development, a qualitatively new situation is arising: the establishment of a European citizenship alongside the citizenship which exists within the MS. However, there is little sense of *power* in this theory – and, in particular, the power of some states to block developments which they do not welcome. This becomes clear if the concrete developments in EU citizenship are now considered.

The Maastricht Treaty and citizenship of the Union

For most of its history, the EU has not talked of 'citizens' but of 'workers'. However, when discussion intensified about the creation of a political union during the 1980s, the emphasis shifted from the category of 'workers' to the category of 'citizen'. In 1984 the Council of Ministers established an ad hoc committee, chaired by Pietro Adonnino, which reported the next year. Its main recommendations were for the creation of symbols of identity – flags, passports and so on. However, it also asked the Council to invite the EC institutions to bring into existence 'the citizen as a participant in the political process in the Community'.[33] As a halfway stage

---

[32] Bruno De Witte, 'Cultural Legitimation: Back to the Language Question' in Soledad García (ed.), *European Identity and the Search for Legitimacy*, London: Pinter, 1993, p. 155.

between 'worker' and 'citizen' the Single European Act used the word 'person' and between 1989 and 1991 both the Commission and the EP tried to ensure that the rights of 'union citizenship' could be given substance. Meanwhile, some of the governments were taking up the idea. In June 1990 Mitterrand made a statement on the subject and three months later the Spanish government submitted a plea for a declaration of the rights, freedoms and obligations of citizens to be incorporated into the Treaty.[34] The result, after much discussion in the inter-governmental conference, was the establishment of a new part in the Treaty, establishing 'Citizenship of the Union'. It is worth summarising the relevant articles before commenting on them.

Art. 8 states that 'citizenship of the union' is established, and that every person holding the nationality of a MS shall be a citizen, and 'shall enjoy the rights conferred by this Treaty and shall be subject to the duties imposed thereby'.

Art. 8a: Citizens shall have the right to free movement and residence within the Union, subject to any limitations or conditions in the Treaty; the Council may adopt provisions to facilitate this, acting by unanimity and after obtaining the assent of the EP.

Art. 8b: Every citizen has the right to vote and stand as a candidate in municipal elections in any MS on the same conditions as nationals of that state, and also has the right to vote and stand as a candidate to elections to the EP under the same conditions as nationals of that state. Detailed arrangements on both were to be adopted by the Council, acting unanimously after consultation with the EP and, in both cases, the arrangements could provide for derogations where warranted by problems specific to a particular MS.

Art. 8c: Every citizen living in a third country in which the MS of which s/he is a national is not represented becomes entitled to protection by the diplomatic or consular authorities of any MS, on the same conditions as nationals of that state.

Art. 8d: (and Arts 138d and 138e): Every citizen has the right to

---

[33] Quoted in Meehan op. cit., p. 147.

[34] For a discussion of these developments, see Carlos Closa, 'The Concept of Citizenship in the Treaty on European Union', *Common Market Law Review*, 29, 6, Dec. 1992.

petition the EP, individually or in association with others, on a
matter which comes within the Community's fields of activity and
which affects her/him directly. This right also applied to non-
citizens legally residing or having a registered office in a MS.

Every citizen (and every non-citizen legally residing or having a
registered office in an MS) has the right to apply to the Ombudsman
(a new office also to be established by the EP under Art 138e of the
Maastricht Treaty). The Ombudsman is empowered to receive
complaints concerning instances of maladministration in the activities of Community institutions (except the courts acting in their
judicial capacity).

Art. 8e: The Commission would report by 31 December 1993 and
then every three years (to the EP, the Council and the Economic
and Social Committee) on the application of the provisions on
citizenship. The Council, acting unanimously, and after consulting
the EP, may adopt provisions to strengthen or to add to the rights
laid down, which it will recommend to the MS for adoption.[35]

Many of the above articles constitute a codification of the existing
Treaty position on citizen rights, rather than conferring significant
additions, although the encouragement to free movement is no
longer specifically attached to employment, but has become more
general.[36] Some of the new elements which have been introduced
– notably the creation of the office of Ombudsman and the possibility of petitioning the EP – extend the rights irrespective of
citizenship. This is quite legitimate – indeed I will argue below that
the principle of non-citizens sharing citizenship rights should be
extended – but it makes it difficult to argue that the rights are
specifically those of citizenship.

The most controversial issues concerned the extension of voting
and candidacy rights (Art. 8b). Since approximately 4.9 million
citizens of one MS now live elsewhere in the EU, the right to vote
and stand in local and European elections involved acceptance of an
important new principle (although some MS already allowed this).[37]

---

[35] This summary does not quote the Articles in full or always use the original
wording.
[36] It is notable that, although duties are mentioned in the Treaty's definition of
citizenship, these are not specified. The implication is that compliance with EU
law is a duty.
[37] Denmark, Ireland and the Netherlands already granted such rights. For a very full

However, it also raises the obvious question of why such rights were not extended to 'national' elections. A possible rationale might be that EU citizens resident in a MS other than their own are affected by the locality in which they are living, and by the EU as a whole, but that the nature of the central government is not their concern. Yet there is little logic in this, as voting in both EU and local elections has always been dominated by national concerns and, in any case sub-central government depends to a greater or lesser degree on central government in all states. The real reason is that the governments of the MS accord far lower importance to both local and European elections than to 'national' ones and were therefore prepared to agree to allow EU citizens to exercise democratic rights at these levels, but were not willing to allow the same logic to apply at state level. However, even the limited electoral rights agreed at Maastricht have proved highly controversial. The issue was a factor in the Danish 'no' vote in the first referendum, and in France it caused a major political dispute.[38] For example, the then RPR General Secretary, Alain Juppé (Prime Minister at the time of writing) stated that the party would oppose changing the constitution to give those without French citizenship the vote and, in the ratification debate, Charles Pasqua (Interior Minister from 1993 to 1995) described any such constitutional revision as 'treason'. Although the RPR amendment was defeated, the UDF 'compromise', which was accepted, only allowed the *possibility* of permitting non-French citizens the vote (rather than granting them the right to do so) and stipulated that EU citizens 'cannot exercise the function of mayor or deputy mayor, nor take part in the appointment of senatorial electors or the elections of senators'.[39] The idea that 'foreigners' could become mayors was projected as a threat to the 'national' character of the French state. Such controversies, which also occurred elsewhere arise from a more fundamental question: that of 'national' citizenship.[40]

analysis of the issues, see Ray Koslowski, 'Intra-EU Migration, Citizenship and Political Union', *Journal of Common Market Studies*, 32, 3, Sept. 1994.

[38] The Danish objections were not to the practice, which was already operated, but to the principle that it should be implemented as an externally imposed legal obligation. Church and Phinnemore, op. cit., p. 78.

[39] Ibid., pp. 378-9.

[40] The most complex situation was in Luxembourg where 27.9% of the population is composed of EU nationals from other countries (10.5% from Portugal). Certain

The second Declaration, annexed to the Final Act of the Maastricht Treaty, explained the fundamental principle the governments were applying to Union citizenship:

> Wherever in the Treaty establishing the European Community reference is made to nationals of the Member States, the question whether an individual possesses the nationality of a Member State shall be settled solely by reference to the national law of the Member State concerned. . .[41]

In other words, the determination of Union citizenship is solely a question for decision by MS, following whatever internal systems they have for determining national citizenship. But in many cases these are highly illiberal.

Nationality laws based primarily on birthplace (*jus soli*) are generally far less restrictive than those based on ancestral lineage (*jus sanguinis*) since they make naturalisation and the acquiring of citizenship rights much more straightforward. Germany has traditionally been one of the most restrictive countries, with *jus sanguinis* the fundamental principle, while France had been far more liberal. (Britain had maintained *jus soli* as its fundamental principle but has become increasingly restrictive since the 1961 Commonwealth Immigration Act and, following the 1981 British Nationality Act has moved towards *jus sanguinis*).[42] Since 1991 Germany has made some tentative steps towards making its naturalisation laws a little more liberal and in November 1994 Kohl proposed offering limited citizenship rights to third generation immigrants, provided that their parents had lived in Germany for more than ten years and one of them had been born there.[43] However, France has been moving in the opposite direction, with a bill in May 1993 constituting a significant step in the direction of *jus sanguinis*. And several other EU states also base citizenship on the *jus sanguinis* principle. Thus while a general move towards *jus soli* would have facilitated the development of EU citizenship, the Maastricht formula may actually lead to its trunca-

---

concessions were included in the treaty requirements to accommodate Luxembourg. Koslowski, op. cit., p. 389.

[41] Declaration on Nationality of a Member State.

[42] For a full discussion of both the principles and practice, and an extensive bibliography on the subject, see Koslowski, op. cit.,

[43] *The Guardian*, 15 Nov. 1994.

tion. However, it was regarded as far too sensitive to attempt to influence the ways in which each MS ascribed legal citizenship, for such issues go to the core of the whole notion of the 'nation-state'. In principle, the idea of 'union citizenship' could threaten to 'denationalise' citizenship completely, and this was certainly a step that the MS were not prepared to take. But even the *theoretical* breach from ascription solely by states implied by the notion of 'union citizenship' was regarded as threatening by opponents of the EU – or was so exploited by nationalist forces.

There is a further important issue about the Maastricht conception of citizenship: the limitation of the rights that are specified. Many organisations, including the EP, had wanted Union citizenship to be defined on the basis of clear principles established in some form of constitutional statement, incorporating the European Convention of Human Rights.[44] However, the Maastricht treaty did not do this because those states (including Britain) which have not themselves incorporated the Convention into their legal systems, did not want it to be brought in 'through the back door' via the EU. It is true that there was a somewhat ambiguous reference to the Convention in the Maastricht Treaty.[45] But, once again, there was a tacit understanding that primary citizenship rights were guaranteed by the MS, and that the EU had added to these mainly by the body of law that it had *already* passed, rather than by creating or defining a particular set of EU principles. However, this is obviously regarded as inadequate by all those who believe that citizen rights are insufficiently safeguarded in some or all of the MS.

I have not considered the conventional minimal democratic right of electing and dismissing a 'government', or the powers of the EP in relation to the Council of Ministers, in relation to 'citizenship'. These issues will be examined in the next chapter. But the limitations in the Maastricht conception discussed so far seem to provide

[44] Church and Phinnemore, op. cit., p. 76.
[45] Article F of Title 1 reads: '1. The Union shall respect the national identities of its Member States, whose systems of government are founded on the principles of democracy. 2. The Union shall respect fundamental rights, as guaranteed by the European Convention for the Protection of Human Rights and Fundamental Freedoms. . . and as they result from the constitutional traditions common to the Member States, as general principles of Community law. 3. The Union shall provide itself with the means necessary to attain its objectives and carry through its policies.'

additional grounds for the argument developed above about the power of the MS to impede the emergence of citizenship based on 'multiple-identities', as suggested by Elizabeth Meehan. Some of them are certainly attempting the opposite: they are trying to ensure the dominance of 'national' identity, with EU identity as a residual element. However, there is an even more serious issue to consider: the position of 'second-class' and 'non-citizens' in the EU.

'Second-class citizens', 'non-citizens' and the EU

As discussed earlier, the legal ascription of 'citizenship' confers some advantages on an individual, which are normally denied to those who do not possess legal citizenship. Similarly, those who are not recognised as 'full citizens' either legally or in social, economic, cultural or political terms, may suffer a deterioration in their relative positions in comparison with those who are so regarded. Who are the 'second-class' and 'non-citizens' who are suffering in this way in the EU?

A case may be made for suggesting that all victims of inequality are denied full citizenship. In this sense, all the 'socially excluded' may be regarded as having their full rights denied and it has, for example, been argued that EU citizenship should include the 'right to work' or at least a positive employment and welfare strategy.[46] Similarly John Grahl and Paul Teague have developed the concept of 'economic citizenship' and have argued that this requires action by the EU on labour market regulation, training and professional qualifications, regional policy and employment generation at macro-economic level.[47] These are powerful points but, as suggested in earlier chapters, it is at least debatable how far the remedies lie at EU level. The extent to which the EU itself should be held responsible for creating 'second-class citizens' through the phenomena of 'social exclusion' and economic insecurity is therefore also unclear.

Women also suffer from multiple inequalities and, as already noted, there are good arguments for suggesting that citizenship has

---

[46] Peter Leisink and Harry Coenen (eds), *Work and Citizenship in the New Europe*, Aldershot: Edward Elgar, 1993.

[47] John Grahl and Paul Teague, 'Economic Citizenship in the New Europe', *Political Quarterly*, 4, Oct. 1994.

been 'gendered' in each MS. It therefore follows that EU citizenship incorporates the inequalities which exist within each MS. Nevertheless, there is perhaps an even stronger case for suggesting that, rather than *denying* full citizenship to women, the EU's equality policies have provided benefits in women's campaigns to secure full citizenship.[48]

Are there arguments for suggesting that the EU denies full citizenship to such victims of inequality as people with disabilities, and the elderly? The Social Policy initiatives have included programmes to facilitate opportunities for both these groups.[49] Moreover, in the Social Policy White Paper of 1994, the Commission suggested that specific references to combating discrimination on the grounds of disability or age should be included in the treaty.[50] In fact, the current position for both the elderly and people with disabilities is entirely dependent upon MS legislation and provision. They are 'second class' citizens within the EU because free movement, which is supposedly guaranteed to all those with citizenship, is impeded by the unevenness of treatment in the different MS. For example, in May 1989 the Commission recommended that elderly people should be granted reduced-rate travel passes within each EU country, but this has not yet been adopted because of the reluctance of some MS, including Britain.[51] However, once again it is not the EU itself that has created this inequality and both the Commission and the EP have attempted to press the MS into action.

Gays and lesbians also have a strong case for arguing that they are treated as 'second class' citizens within the EU, and a more persuasive argument that the EU itself has done nothing to improve

[48] Meehan, op. cit., particularly chapter 6.

[49] In December 1994 the Social Affairs Council of Minister agreed a revised programme for the continued development of the so-called Handynet system to support and promote the training of people with disabilities, although the original text had been diluted to secure support from the governments, particularly Britain. The EU has implemented one Action Programme on behalf of the Elderly, but a second programme is now likely to be delayed until the summer of 1995 at the earliest. However 5.5 million ECU have been earmarked for activities related to older people. *European Information Service*, 155, 19 Dec. 1994, Local Government International Bureau.

[50] *European Social Policy: A Way forward for the Union*, op. cit. p. 40.

[51] Belgium, Ireland and Portugal favoured the proposal. *Eurolink Age Bulletin*, Nov. 1990.

their position. While there are some social stigmas attached to
homosexuality throughout the EU, there is enormous variety in the
legal position, with Britain having the most laws discriminating
explicitly, or in practice, against homosexuals – reaffirmed in 1994
with the continuation of a differential age of consent for homosexuals
and heterosexuals.[52] Apart from the general human rights issue, there
is direct EU involvement because the inequality of treatment
between MS may again negate the free movement provisions. For
example, in some MS gay or lesbian couples have the same rights as
heterosexual couples.[53] However, their ability to move to another
EU country which offers less favourable treatment may be regarded
as a form of discrimination. Yet the EU has failed to tackle these
issues at all. The EP approved a report from its Committee on Social
Affairs, Employment and the Working Environment urging equality
for gays and lesbians in 1984 and in 1989 recommended that the
Social Charter should ensure the right of all workers to equal
protection regardless of their sexual preferences.[54] In February 1994
it reiterated this when urging an amendment of the Maastricht treaty
to outlaw various forms of discrimination.[55] But the Commission
did not suggest legislating against discrimination on the grounds of
sexuality in its 1994 White Paper on Social Policy. While, once
again, it would be difficult to argue that the EU itself has actually
caused 'second-class' citizenship for gays and lesbians, the failure of
the Commission and Council even to recognise the issue certainly
reinforces the barriers against equality.

While all the above cases of inequality are serious, the EU itself
has not been directly responsible for the situation. However, there
are very strong arguments for suggesting that it – or rather the
European Council – does have direct responsibility for discriminating against non-EU citizens, particularly from Asia and Africa, and

[52] See Michael Spencer, *1992 and All That: Civil Liberties in the Balance*, London:
Civil Liberties Trust, 1990, pp. 122-3. For a detailed analysis, see Paul Crick, 'All
Men are Created Equal..? A Study of UK law in relation to the rights of gay men
and lesbians, and its position and possible contribution to European Law', unpubl.
dissertation for the Postgraduate Diploma in Modern European Studies, University of North London, 1994.
[53] Denmark and the Netherlands were the most advanced of the EU Twelve. For
a detailed discussion, see Crick, op. cit.
[54] Spencer, op. cit., p. 122.
[55] *The Guardian*, 9 Feb. 1994.

for knowingly creating a situation which will exacerbate discrimination against black people, whether or not they are citizens. To sustain this argument, it is necessary first to summarise the increasingly discriminatory climate and then to explain why there is a direct EU responsibility for the situation.

Racist discrimination. First, there is abundant evidence that in most EU states migrants from developing countries have been regarded as temporary workers, who have been expected to do unskilled jobs at a time of labour shortage and to return home when no longer needed.[56] In Germany, for example, it has been extremely difficult for Turkish workers to acquire citizenship even when they have lived there for two or more generations. And even where it was easier to acquire citizenship – as in Britain – black and Asian people have been the victims of multiple forms of discrimination. It is estimated that there are now some 10 million people, who are legally resident in the EU without having citizenship, and although there has been greater migration within Europe since 1989, over 6,500,000 of these are from Africa, Asia and Turkey.[57] Secondly, since the late 1970s there has been a marked increase in racism throughout Europe, reinforced by the effects of the economic recession. In many countries there has been a rise of neo-fascist and Far Right parties, and some mainstream politicians have pandered to racism. Furthermore, media and press coverage have reinforced negative stereotypes, associating non-white people with crime, drugs, terrorism and fundamentalism.[58]

---

[56] See, for example, Z. Layton-Henry (ed.), *The Political Rights of Migrant Workers in Western Europe*, London: Sage 1989; Dave Edye, *Immigrant Labour and Government Policy*, Aldershot: Gower, 1987; S. Collinson, *Beyond Borders: West European Migration Policy towards the 21st Century*. London: Royal Institute of International Affairs, 1993.

[57] The estimate of 10 million is given in: European Commission: Background Report, Immigration and Asylum Policies, ISEC/B14, 9 Aug. 1994. A Commission estimate of the origins of legally resident non-EU citizens on 1 Jan. 1991 gives the following figures: 4,128, 544 from non-EU Europe, 2,698,224 from Africa, 799,064 from America, and 1,525,089 from Asia. The figures from non-EU Europe includes those from Turkey (estimated at 2,347,234 on 1 Jan. 1992). Communication from the Commission on Immigration and Asylum Policies, COM (94) 23 final, 23 Feb. 1994.

[58] *European Parliament Report drawn up on behalf of the Committee of Inquiry into Racism and Xenophobia on the findings of the Committee of Inquiry* (Rapporteur: Glyn Ford),

Thirdly, since the 1970s European immigration policies have become increasingly restrictive. In effect, apart from highly skilled workers, students, and visitors, the only new legal immigrants have been the families of those who were already resident and those granted asylum. However, the rights for family reunification have also become increasingly restrictive, as have policies on admission for employment.[59] Nevertheless, the attempt to control immigration has been complicated by the fact that famine, economic crises and civil war have led to a vast increase in refugees seeking asylum. In 1980 65% of asylum-seekers were accepted as refugees in Europe.[60] As a result asylum policies have become ever more stringent: indeed there has been a tendency to treat asylum seekers in the same way as illegal immigrants.[61] Yet the predictions of massive migratory flows to the EU proved unfounded. For example, while the world refugee population in 1989 was between 13 and 15 million, between then and 1991 the number of asylum seekers and refugees to the EU totalled around 1.5 million – a figure which included ethnic Germans settling in Germany.[62] It is true that the number of people seeking asylum in EU countries rose from 447,275 in 1991 to 571,718 in 1992, but the 1993 figures indicate a significant drop to 420,718.[63] In any case, the average acceptance rate had only been 9%.[64] Moreover, Germany's amendment to its previously liberal asylum policies in May 1993 removed the main haven for refugees in the EU.[65]

Luxembourg: Office for Official Publications of the European Communities, 1991 (hereafter *Ford Report*).

[59] European Commission: Immigration and Asylum Policies, 9 Aug. 1994, op. cit.

[60] Frances Webber, 'The New Europe: Immigration and Asylum' in Tony Bunyan (ed.), *Statewatching the new Europe: A Handbook on the European State*, London: Statewatch, 1993.

[61] Danièle Joly et al., *Refugees: Asylum in Europe*, London: Minority Rights Group, 1992.

[62] Dave Edye, 'Migration, Race, Asylum, Refugees', *Labour Focus on Eastern Europe*, 44, 1, January 1993. As Edye points out this was a ratio of refugee to indigenous population of 1:400, which was far lower than in many other parts of the world.

[63] Com (94) 23 final, 23 Feb. 1994, op. cit., table 5.

[64] John Benyon, 'Policing the European Union: The Changing Basis of Co-operation on Law Enforcement', *International Affairs*, 70, 3, July 1994, p. 502.

[65] From 1983 until 1992 Germany accounted for 44% of applications, France for 16%, the Netherlands for 5% and Britain for only 2%. Edye, 'Migration, race,

Fourthly, specific anti-racist legislation exists in Belgium, France, the Netherlands and Britain, but many of the other EU countries have argued that there is no need for such laws as long as all citizens are treated equally. It is, of course, true that specific legislation is no guarantee that prosecutions will be made, and there are serious weaknesses in existing laws. Britain, for example, has the longest-standing and most comprehensive codes against racism and discrimination, but it relies mainly on civil law, whereas other countries have made greater use of criminal law. Similarly, while France has been unique in actually defining racism, its assimilationist political culture has legitimised forms of racism by effectively denying the existence of ethnic and national minorities.[66] Nevertheless, as the Commission has argued, it is preferable to adopt comprehensive anti-discrimination laws, for these offer 'an integrated and more coherent approach to combating racism, racial discrimination and xenophobia'.[67] This may apply particularly to Germany, which denies that it is a country of immigration, while housing 6 million immigrants, and denies the existence of widespread discrimination or xenophobia.[68]

EU responsibility.   The EU's responsibility is, I believe, of two kinds. First, it created a situation which had predictably negative results for the victims of racism. Secondly, it constructed an elaborate non-accountable machinery to introduce policies which would contribute to the discrimination. These points may be considered in turn.

Some negative results of the free movement provisions in the Single European Act were entirely predictable. The distinction between EC 'nationals' and 'non-nationals' would mean that the former would be able to move from one EC country to another, while the latter would have no such guaranteed rights. The EP had already recognised this discrimination in a resolution of 14 February

---

asylum, refugees', op. cit., p. 23.
[66] M. Silverman, *Deconstructing the Nation: Immigration, Racism and Citizenship in Modern France*, London: Routledge, 1992.
[67] *Commission of the European Communities: Legal Instruments to Combat Racism and Xenophobia*, Luxembourg: office for Official Publications of the European Communities, 1993, p. 75.
[68] Ibid., p. 16.

1989 which called for freedom of movement on the same terms for all legally resident workers living in an EU country, irrespective of their nationality. But this was not adopted.[69] Secondly, because internal movement was being facilitated in an atmosphere of growing racism and of a 'fortress Europe' mentality *vis-à-vis* new immigration, it also followed that visible ethnic minorities were likely to be subjected to more controls, which might also be carried out in inhumane ways. The EP also recognised this in its 1989 resolution, and in 1990 Michael Spencer summarised the position as follows:

> Black and ethnic minority groups . . . are justifiably apprehensive that even those who are citizens of an EC state will suffer after 1992, particularly if the abolition of internal border controls is accompanied by more stringent internal checks (by the police and others) on citizenship and immigration status. Raids on homes and workplaces, and identity checks in public places on non-white people, could all increase as a result.
>
> In the absence of Community-wide anti-discrimination measures, black EC nationals who exercise their right to work in another EC state may find not only that their immigration status is repeatedly checked by over-zealous officials; they may also find it impossible (say) to rent accommodation or to obtain insurance, because of unchecked discrimination in the country to which they have moved.[70]

The governments involved were clearly aware of these probable effects but were unwilling to counteract them by any EU anti-discrimination law (see below). The EU's direct responsibility becomes apparent if the apparatus that the governments have constructed to make policy in these areas is now considered.

The first stage was the establishment in 1975 of the so-called TREVI group of Justice and Home Affairs Ministers meeting in secret twice a year. This was followed by the Schengen Agreement in 1985 to abolish internal frontiers between the signatories in advance of the general abolition of frontiers by all EU states. Ratification was constantly delayed and it was only on 22 December 1994 that Portugal, Spain, France, Germany and the Benelux

---

[69] Official Journal C69, 20 March 1989, substantially quoted in Spencer, op. cit., p. 47.
[70] Spencer, op. cit., p. 50.

countries all agreed to eliminate internal border controls on 26 March 1995 (with Italy and Greece joining later).[71] But it was always understood that abolition of such controls would mean stronger internal security measures and the initial agreement led to further moves on the exchange of information about immigrants, including the establishment of the computerised Schengen Information Service (SIS), which could be shared with all MS. In October 1986 the Ad Hoc Group on Immigration, comprised of EU Interior ministers, was established to 'end abuses of the asylum process'.[72] Subsequently, this group agreed a series of restrictive measures and collaboration on asylum and immigration.[73] A further key stage was the establishment of the so-called Coordinators' Group which was set up following the December 1988 Rhodes summit, and included a member of the Commission along with the governments. This produced the 'Palma Document' submitted to the 1989 Madrid summit, which outlined all areas of co-operation relating to free movement.[74] It also defined which inter-governmental discussion groups were to be involved and what actions needed to be taken to harmonise policies.

All this constituted the construction of a policy-making apparatus to institute an increasingly restrictive set of measures, the impact of which would overwhelmingly be felt by non-EU citizens, visible ethnic minorities, and asylum-seekers. Moreover, this was all happening without any effective democratic control. For example, the British Home Secretary said of the TREVI group:

---

[71] *The Guardian*, 23 Dec. 1994. The original Schengen group members were France, Germany, Belgium, Luxembourg and the Netherlands.

[72] Frances Webber, 'European Conventions on Immigration and Asylum', in Bunyan, op. cit., p. 144.

[73] In April 1987 it proposed sanctions on airlines bringing in undocumented asylum-seekers and those with false documents; in 1990 it produced the so-called Dublin convention to prevent asylum-seekers making more than one application in the EU; in 1991 it put forward proposals for fingerprinting asylum-seekers, and set up a 'rapid consultation centre' on immigration problems; and in 1992 it produced draft resolutions for dealing with 'manifestly unfounded' asylum claims. Ibid.

[74] Action at external frontiers, action at internal frontiers and inside the territory, drug trafficking, terrorism, visa policy, refugees, deportation, judicial co-operation, and articles carried by travellers. For further details, see Spencer, op. cit., Appendix 1.

It does not need any safeguards. . . Trevi is merely a gathering together of the Ministers of the Interior of the EC countries to give, hopefully, political impetus to various plans of closer policing co-operation. . . . It is not an executive body. Therefore, accountability is from the individual Ministers of the Interior to their own governments, and there is no need for the body as a whole to be thought of as responsible to any organisation.[75]

But in practice there is very little possibility of any national control over this form of European co-operation. At the same time, however, there was no accountability at Community level either. For several years the Commission itself was excluded but, following the appointment of the coordinators group in 1988, it secured some involvement – and also advocated restrictive measures.[76] But the EP was totally excluded and, in 1990, threatened to take the Council of Ministers to the ECJ on the issue.[77] As the Joint Council for the Welfare of Immigrants put it in 1989:

> Without a clear lead from Community institutions or national parliaments, what appears to be happening is that individual countries' increasingly restrictive and reactive policies, targeted at people from Third World and Mediterranean countries, are being translated into a system of supranational control which is not directly accountable to any central or elected body.[78]

The Maastricht treaty has hardly improved the situation. In one sense, it has formalised the position by establishing a whole 'pillar' devoted to 'Justice and Home Affairs' as Title VI. However, this remains outside the normal legal processes of the Community, with minimal democratic accountability. At the same time the inter-

[75] 'Practical Police Co-operation in the European Community', Home Affairs Select Committee, 1989-90, HC 363 – II, pp. 162-3, quoted in Tony Bunyan, 'Trevi, Europol and the New European State' in Bunyan, op. cit., p. 23.
[76] See, for example, the Commission's 'Communications' on immigration and asylum of October 1991, summarised in Webber, 'European conventions on immigration and asylum' in Bunyan, op. cit., pp. 143-4.
[77] Ford Report, op. cit., Recommendations 10 and 40.
[78] Memorandum by JCWI to House of Lords, Select Committee on the European Communities, '1992: Border Control of People', House of Lords Paper 90, 7 Nov. 1989, quoted in Dave Edye, *1992 and the Free Movement of Labour*, London: University of North London Press, 1990.

governmental structure of co-ordination has become still more sophisticated. Article K.1. of the Treaty thus lists the following as matters of common interest:

(1) asylum policy;
(2) rules governing the crossing by persons of the external borders of the Member States and the exercise of controls thereon;
(3) Immigration policy and policy regarding nationals of third countries:
   (a) conditions of entry and movement by nationals of third countries on the territory of Member States;
   (b) conditions of residence by nationals of third countries on the territory of Member States, including family reunion and access to employment;
   (c) combating unauthorised immigration, residence and work by nationals of third countries on the territory of Member States;
(4) combating drug addiction in so far as this is not covered by (7) to (9);
(5) combating fraud on an international scale in so far as this is not covered by 7 to 9;
(6) judicial cooperation in civil matters;
(7) judicial cooperation in criminal matters;
(8) customs cooperation;
(9) police cooperation for the purposes of preventing and combating terrorism, unlawful drug trafficking and other serious forms of international crime, including if necessary certain aspects of customs cooperation, in connection with organization of a Union-wide system for exchanging information within a European Police Office (Europol).

Given the fact that racist propaganda frequently associates immigration with drug dealing, terrorism and crime, even the conjunction of these policy areas within a single treaty article was offensive. Similarly, the association of asylum with illegal immigration was an affront to refugees. There is a partial balance to this in that the first part of article K.2 stipulates that the above matters 'shall be dealt with in compliance with the European Convention for the Protection of Human Rights and Freedom of 4 November 1950 and the Convention relating to the Status of Refugees of 28 July 1951. . . .' However, as already noted, it did not incorporate the Convention into the Treaty. Overall, the complexities of Article K mean that there is a confusing mixture of 'Europeanisation' and state autonomy in the treaty provisions.[79]

One of the most controversial aspects of the 'Justice and Home Affairs' Title is that Article K.4 formalises and strengthens all the networks of officials that had been developing since the establishment of the TREVI group, and particularly since the Rhodes Council meeting in December 1988. It thus states that the Commission 'shall be fully associated' with the policy areas outlined in K.1 and establishes a Committee to coordinate activities and give opinions either at the Council's request or on its own initiative. The committee – subsequently known as the K.4 Committee – now consists of one representative from each EU country and an observer from the Commission and normally meets on a monthly basis. It has subsumed all the working groups which already existed in the areas covered by the 'Justice and Home Affairs' Title, has a secretariat in Brussels, and feeds its reports through COREPER to the Council of Ministers.[80] An overwhelming preoccupation in all this activity has been to prevent new immigration and to counter clandestine immigrants, and some senior police officers themselves believe that fighting clandestine immigration has been the principal reason for their increased co-operation.[81]

Democratic control – or even information – remains minimal at EU level. It is true that, for the first time, the EP has been granted an opportunity to ask questions, make recommendations, and hold

[79] Article K.5 allows for the Council, on the initiative of either a MS or the Commission, to adopt joint positions or joint action to draw up conventions in any of the areas referred to in Article K.1. However, the Commission may only put forward proposals in policy areas K1 (1)-(6). Although all measures covered by Title VI are to be adopted on the basis of unanimity, the Council may decide that measures to implement joint action may be adopted by Qualified Majority Voting (QMV). Procedural matters are also to be adopted by QMV and measures implementing a convention by a two-thirds majority. (K.3(2) and K.4(3)). However, each MS retains the right to veto any initiative put before the Council. The joint positions are not legally binding on the MS, but they are expected to defend them internationally (Article K.5).

[80] It has three steering groups: steering group 1 on Immigration and Asylum; steering group 2 on Police and Customs cooperation, and Steering Group III on Judicial Cooperation. Each of these has a number of working groups. Benyon, op. cit. pp. 509-10.

[81] Ibid., pp. 501-2.

a debate on progress on the areas covered by the Justice and Home Affairs 'pillar'. But this certainly does not provide a sufficient basis for effective scrutiny.[82] The legal basis for ECJ involvement is also inadequate.[83] As already noted, it is also extremely difficult for domestic parliaments or organisations to control matters which are effectively being carried out at EU level in virtual secrecy.

Visa policy is the only area in the whole pillar of 'Justice and Home Affairs' which has been brought under normal EC procedures by an amendment to the Treaty of Rome.[84] The development of a common visa policy has been in train for some years as a further element in sealing the external frontiers of the EU. When the draft list was finally announced in January 1994, it contradicted the EP resolution of February 1989 by formally breaking the historic links between countries. For example, visa restrictions were to be imposed on thirty-one Commonwealth countries which were currently exempt from British visa requirements.[85]

It is difficult to come to any conclusion other than that the EU governments, with some Commission involvement, have *deliberately* acted in an increasingly restrictive and intolerant way with regard to external (and mainly non-white) would-be migrants or refugees, and have implemented measures which will inevitably exacerbate the difficulties already experienced by non-white residents. The individual liberality of the governments varies considerably, but *collectively* they have acted repressively and with minimal democratic

---

[82] Article K.6 stipulates: 'The Presidency and the Commission shall regularly inform the European Parliament of discussions in the areas covered. . . . The Presidency shall consult the European Parliament on the principal aspects of activities. . . and shall ensure that the views of the European Parliament are duly taken into consideration. The European Parliament may ask questions of the Council or make recommendations to it. Each year, it shall hold a debate on the progress made in implementation of the areas referred to in this Title.'

[83] It is thus entirely a matter for the governments to decide unanimously whether to secure European Court of Justice interpretations of the provisions contained in any conventions it may draw up, and even then this would apply only to formal conventions and not to joint action or joint positions the governments might adopt. (Art. K.3.2c).

[84] Article 100c specified that the Council, acting unanimously on a proposal from the Commission and after consulting the EP, shall determine the third countries whose nationals must possess a visa to enter the EU. After 1 Jan. 1996 the Council will act on a qualified majority.

[85] *The Guardian*, 8 Jan. 1994.

control. Since the Maastricht Treaty has formally established the European Council as the highest political body in the Union (Article D) it is legitimate to suggest that the EU itself shares responsibility, even though most of the policy in the Justice and Home Affairs pillar lies outside its normal legal procedures. However, there may be some signs that limited steps are being taken to redress this bleak record.

The EU and anti-racism.   The European Parliament has taken an active anti-racist stance for several years. In 1985 its *Report of the Committee of Inquiry into the Rise of Fascism and Racism in Europe* (the Evrigenis Report) documented the extent of the problem and effectively led the Commission and the Council to acknowledge it. This led, in June 1986, to a joint Declaration Against Racism and Xenophobia by the EP, the Council, the Representatives of Member States meeting with the Council, and the Commission.[86] Despite the apparently firm commitments made in this Declaration, however, the situation was frustrating for those committed to action in the EP. The governments, as has been shown, continued to develop their uncontrolled collaboration on restrictive measures, while the Commission insisted that it had no competence in the area – a point which the EP disputed.[87] Finally, in 1988 the Commission proposed a non-binding Resolution on racism and xenophobia with an action programme to promote inter-cultural understanding.[88] However, when the Council eventually adopted the Resolution two years later (in May 1990) it had been so diluted that the Commission refused to associate itself with it and withdrew. The EP's view was that the resolution signified 'a step backward' and went 'against not only the spirit but also the contents of the June 1986 Joint Declaration against Racism and Xenophobia'. In the same year the EP accepted a new report of its Committee of Inquiry on Racism and Xenophobia (the Ford Report) which made seventy-seven detailed and reasoned recommendations, including the threat of legal action against the Council (recommendation 11). It also called for a 'draft Directive to be prepared by 31 March 1991 to provide a Community

[86] The Declaration is reproduced as appendix II in Spencer, op. cit.
[87] For this and the information in the rest of the paragraph, see the Ford report, op. cit., pp. 105-7 and 153-68.
[88] Ibid., pp. 105-7.

framework of legislation against any discrimination connected with belonging or not belonging to an ethnic group, nation, religion, race or religion, covering all Community residents' (Recommendation 31). In its accompanying commentary it also proposed the establishment of a watchdog body similar to the Commission for Racial Equality in Britain.

The encouraging point is that, following Maastricht, the EU has taken up these policy aims. The Corfu European Council meeting in June 1994 established a Consultative Commission (the Kahn Commission) to work towards a global strategy against racism.[89] This included Glyn Ford, who had been rapporteur for the EP's second Committee of Inquiry into Racism and Xenophobia, and the Commission appointed Kamlesh Bhal, Chair of the British Equal Opportunities Commission, as its representative on the committee.[90] In the Social Policy White Paper of July 1994 the Commission stated its intention to 'press for specific powers to combat racial discrimination to be included in the Treaty' and Padraig Flynn, the Commissioner responsible, followed this up with a speech in Bonn in September highlighting 'racism and xenophobia as potent and dangerous enemies', reinforcing the determination of the Commission to press ahead with measures to outlaw discrimination, and maintaining a 'multi-cultural and multi-ethnic' society as a positive goal.[91] Finally, at its meeting in Essen in December 1994, the European Council approved the (unpublished) guidelines of the interim report of the Kahn commission and called upon it to 'step up its discussions in particular in the various areas of education and training, information and media, and in the areas of police and justice'.[92]

None of this guarantees that action will be taken, particularly given the reluctance of some governments – including the British – to allow the EU to legislate in this area. Nor, if action is taken, will it compensate for the restrictive policies implemented thus far. But there are signs that some forces in the Commission are now taking an opportunity to use its limited role in 'Justice and Home Affairs'

[89] Jean Kahn is head of the European Section of the World Jewish Congress.
[90] *Agence Europe*, 14 Sept. 1994.
[91] Ibid.
[92] *Agence Europe*, 11 Dec. 1994. For a more detailed summary of the probable recommendations, see *The Guardian*, 17 Nov. 1994.

to promote more liberal policies, and the Maastricht Treaty contains a provision (Article K.9) for more elements to be incorporated in the Treaty of Rome – and hence in normal Community procedures – if the governments so wish.[93]

There is, therefore, at least a possibility that the EU will take some steps to turn the 'second class' and 'non-citizens' it has created into full citizens. But, as France Webber warns:

> The danger of the Maastricht process is that, once the transitional period of intergovernmental cooperation comes to an end, [the] extremely illiberal conventions and resolutions, drafted solely from the perspective of policing and with no regard to the rights of immigrants and refugees, will be incorporated into EC law.[94]

'Citizenship' is a crucially important concept, and its practical applications have vast implications in the legal, political, and social realms. It can confer positive advantages for those to whom it is granted, which may also be used to expand the definition of rights and to provide new opportunities for participation. But it can also entail enormous disadvantages for those who are excluded, or partially excluded. As Elizabeth Meehan has argued, the 'rights' that have been established by ECJ judgments, and by campaigning and networking activities, make the EU a potential arena for the realization of democratic citizenship' based on multiple identities.[95] But, as has also been argued, there are powerful forces which are seeking to ensure that citizenship is defined by the 'nation-state' and is intolerant of 'outsiders'. One duty of EU citizens is therefore to try to ensure that such forces do not prevail and that the EU does not follow a typical pattern of 'nation-state' construction in which rights for citizens 'lead to a diminution or abolition of rights for minority groups where these groups fall outside an exclusionary political definition of membership'.[96]

---

[93] In December 1994, the governments made a slight concession by agreeing that non-EU school children resident in one of the MS would no longer need visas to participate in organised school trips to other EU states. European Information Service (LGIB) 155, 19 Dec. 1994.

[94] 'European Conventions on Immigration and Asylum' in Bunyan, op. cit., p. 153.

[95] Meehan, op. cit., p. 155.

[96] Turner, op. cit., p. 140.

7

DEMOCRATIC DEFICITS

It is a basic axiom of democracy that non-governmental opinion needs to be able to influence outcomes, expose injustice and incompetence, and offer alternative policies based on information about current policy failures. Yet it is also evident that such notions are exceedingly difficult to implement in *practice* in most political systems, and that there are particular problems involved in applying them within the EU. Indeed there is widespread agreement between supporters and opponents of the EU that the current system is deeply unsatisfactory in terms of democratic control and accountability. However, the *primary* location for the 'deficit' is perceived to lie in different places according to the overall conceptual framework through which the EU is interpreted.

One position effectively views the EU as comparable to a 'polity', even if it is of a unique kind. It therefore holds that its institutions should in some sense be comparable to those of a liberal-democratic political system. The *general* nature of the problem is then clear: that is, there is insufficient democracy at EU level. In particular, the EP is too weak, the Commission is not elected, and the Council of Ministers and European Council are not properly controlled and accountable. The particular solutions advocated may vary, but fundamentally they are all predicated on the assumption that it is necessary to strengthen the democratic content at EU level. The alternative perspective rejects this view of the EU as a 'polity' and holds that the primary locations for decision-making and accountability remain within the 'nation-state'. Viewed in this way, the democratic problem looks quite different. Again, the proposed solutions vary but are based on the notion that it is necessary to secure or regain greater *domestic* control over the EU.

The above perspectives differ substantially both in their diagnoses of the problems and in their recommendations. The first two sections therefore discuss them in turn. Section three then raises questions about whether they are fundamentally contradictory or whether any synthesis between them is possible, and the final section offers some conclusions.

The democratic deficit at EU level

The EP was originally a wholly subordinate and peripheral body within the EU. Although it has certainly grown in importance and strength in recent years, most of those who hold that the primary location for the democratic deficit is at EU level continue to stress the relative weakness of the EP as the major problem. It is therefore necessary to begin with a brief outline of its development.

The evolution of the European Parliament.   The peripheral role of the EP (or 'Assembly' as it then was) in the Treaty of Rome was quite evident. Following the pattern set in the Coal and Steel community, its primary role was to provide a little extra legitimacy for the integration process and to act as a 'sounding board' for legislative proposals. The Council of Ministers was committed by the Treaty to refer to it in the 'consultation procedure' on a range of issues, but was not required to take any notice of its views. The EP also had the power to dismiss the whole Commission without having any role in the appointment of new Commissioners. Each MS could decide how to appoint its MEPs, and the governments' ability to ignore democratic considerations was demonstrated by the fact that until 1969 the Italian government refused to appoint any member of the Communist Party, despite its powerful presence in the domestic parliament. In most cases the original six MS nominated MPs from the centre of the political spectrum, thus establishing a pro-integrationist pattern for the EP, which has been maintained ever since the early days. This also consolidated another of its permanent features:

> It is interested in system change, i.e. in modifying the nature of the relationships that exist between it and the other Community institutions. Indeed, it is not possible to understand the workings of the Parliament without realizing that it is an institution concerned to alter the institutional *status quo*.[1]

[1] Francis Jacobs and Richard Corbett, *The European Parliament*, Harlow: Longman, 1992, p. 6.

The first breakthrough came with the change in the financing system of the EU in 1970, from one of national contributions to one of 'own resources' (see chapter 2). This led to a debate about budgetary responsibility, with the result that the Council alone remained empowered to determine the overall level of the budget, but that, within this, the Council and the EP jointly became the 'budgetary authority'.[2] These changes were then consolidated and formalised in a treaty revision in 1975, which gave the EP the following powers:

– the right to increase Community expenditure within defined limits without having to obtain the Council's approval;
– the opportunity to distribute the sums voted across the various sectors of the budget;
– the power to reject the whole budget; and
– the exclusive right to 'discharge' the Commission, i.e. to approve or disapprove the ways in which the Commission spends the money.

However, these budgetary responsibilities were limited by the distinction between 'compulsory' and 'non-compulsory' expenditure, the real purpose of which was to 'ring-fence' the CAP as compulsory expenditure so that it would be subject to minimal EP control. Nevertheless, the EP has constantly sought to increase the size of (non-compulsory) expenditure on social and regional policies, and to curb that on agriculture. This led to frequent clashes with the Council and the Commission over the budget.[3] However, the Delors I budgetary package in 1988 finally established the process by which the percentage of total expenditure devoted to agriculture began to decline, while the structural funds increased. EP pressure on the budget has been important both as an influence in shifting the spending priorities of the EU, and in elevating its own institutional status. Nevertheless, as Dinan argues, 'The EP may have acquired some budgetary authority, but as long as the budget remains relatively insignificant and Parliament cannot raise any revenue its power will remain correspondingly weak.'[4] The second critical

---

[2]
For details, see Michael Shackleton, 'The Budget of the EC: structure and process' in Lodge op. cit., *The European Union and the Challenge of the Future,* 1993; and chapter 12 in Jacobs and Corbett, op. cit.
[3]
The EP rejected the whole budget in 1979 and 1984, and refused to discharge the 1982 budget.
[4]
Dinan, op. cit., p. 273.

factor in increasing the role of the EP was the introduction of direct
elections for the first time in 1979. The four elections, which have
now taken place, have undoubtedly injected a greater sense of
purpose and determination into the institution, and a much stronger
basis of democratic legitimacy to argue for increased power, particularly with regard to legislation. The first directly elected parliament was almost immediately aided in this task by a judgment of
the ECJ in 1980 in the Isoglucose case.

Although the Treaty of Rome had required the Council to
consult the EP on twenty-two articles, it had not stipulated any time-
scale by which the EP had to give its views. In the Isoglucose case,
the ECJ annulled legislation because the Council had gone ahead
without awaiting the EP's response. This judgment effectively
provided the parliament with delaying powers, which it now
exploited by adopting a new procedure under which it suggested
and voted on amendments to a legislative proposal before considering its substance. In this way it hoped to pressurise the Commission
into accepting the amendments. Yet even if this strategy succeeded,
there was no guarantee that the Council would approve the amended
legislation and in the early 1980s it often chose to ignore the
amendments. However, the EP was now able to make a major
breakthrough – at the very least in terms of mobilising opinion – by
voting overwhelmingly in favour of the Draft European Union
Treaty pioneered by Altiero Spinelli in February 1984.[5] Spinelli's
initiative played a role in ensuring that the EP's demands were kept
on the Council's agenda and the Single European Act (SEA) led to
a very significant advance in the Parliament's role.

First, and most significant, it introduced a new legislative process,
the Co-operation procedure. This meant that in respect of the
proposals on which the Council was now to take decisions by
qualified majority voting (primarily concerning the single market),
a two-reading procedure was implemented which enabled the EP
to accept, reject or amend the Council's position. An EP rejection
or amendment (if accepted by the Commission) could then only be
overruled by a unanimous Council vote. Since the original legisla-

---

[5] The Draft European Union Treaty was a compromise between full federalism
and more cautious opinion in the EP and was adopted by 237-31 (with 43
abstentions). C.C. Piening, 'The Role of the European Parliament in the EC's
Integration Process, 1986-92', unpubl. MA thesis, University of Kent, 1992,
p. 33.

tive proposal would have been adopted in the Council by majority voting, and since it was quite likely that some of the MS would agree with the EP's amendments, the Co-operation procedure gave the Council a strong incentive to avoid conflict with the EP. Naturally, this increased the EP's bargaining power. It also strengthened the internal organisation of the EP, by providing an incentive to construct the alliances which would be necessary to secure a majority for amending or rejecting the Council's proposals. The result was that, between the implementation of the SEA in 1987 and the end of September 1992, of 259 acts adopted under the Co-operation procedure, the Council adopted 44% of the EP's first reading amendments and 26% of its second reading amendments.[6]

The second advance for the EP was to gain the right to ratify association agreements under an 'assent procedure' and also to approve the accession of new members. It has used these powers to delay association and co-operation agreements with Turkey and Israel, and in 1994, threatened to vote against enlargement so as to secure new powers. However, it refrained from so doing, as this would have been blatantly opportunistic and could have torpedoed an enlargement that was generally popular with MEPs.

Following the progress made under the SEA, the EP intensified its efforts to increase its power. In particular, it pressed hard to ensure that political union would accompany monetary union. It thus welcomed the establishment in June 1990 of the Inter-Governmental Conference (IGC) on political union and set out its own extensive demands in July 1990, translating them into treaty proposals in a resolution of 22 November 1990. These followed the lines of argument of Spinelli's draft European Union Treaty of 1984 and the more specific reports from the EP's inter-institutional committee. Apart from calling for foreign policy and immigration and asylum policies to be brought within the normal treaty framework, and the ending of the division between compulsory and non-compulsory

---

[6] The contrasting reactions of the institutions to the new system are also significant. In January 1993, the EP expressed general satisfaction with the working of the procedure, while identifying as major weaknesses the fact that the Council could still 'kill legislation by default' and adopt legislation, which the EP had rejected in full or in part. The Commission was also reasonably satisfied, but the Council much less so, believing that the EP used the new procedure to promote its own institutional agenda at the expense of effective decision-making. Dinan, op. cit., pp. 278-9.

expenditure, the most fundamental demands were for the EP and
the Council 'to be given equal rights and equal weight in the
legislative process' and for majority voting to become the norm for
all legislative decisions in the Council (except for treaty revisions,
enlargement or the expansion of the Community's responsibilities).[7]
Predictably, the EP was to be disappointed by the eventual outcome
in the Maastricht Treaty.

This brought about only a limited extension of majority voting
and, instead of granting the EP's demands on legislation, the new
treaty introduced yet another procedure – that of 'co-decision' – for
ten policy areas.[8] Under this procedure the EP secured the right to
a third reading, and a conciliation committee was established in
which the Council and EP, assisted by the Commission, would
attempt to reach agreement on draft legislation.[9] However, this does
not accord with the EP's understanding of 'co-decision' because it
does not require both bodies ultimately to *approve* the legislation.
Instead it simply grants the EP the negative right to block the
proposal in its entirety.

Maastricht also maintained and extended the co-operation procedure which had been established under the SEA formulation. This
has now become the most important legislative procedure and
covers fourteen policy areas.[10] The treaty also extended the fields in
which the EP is required to give its assent and it was granted the

[7] Report of the Committee on Institutional Affairs (Martin II resolution), PE A3-
166-90, quoted in Piening, op. cit., p. 96.

[8] Majority voting was extended to certain aspects of environment, development,
consumer protection, education and public health policy and trans-European
networks. Co-decision was introduced for free movement of persons (Art. 49);
right of establishment (Arts. 54.2; 56.2; 57); internal market (Art. 126); culture
(Art. 128); public health (Art. 129); consumer protection (Art. 129a); parts of the
policy on trans-European networks (Art. 129d); research and technological
development (Art. 130i); environmental action programmes (Art. 130s).

[9] See Dinan, op. cit., p. 281, for a useful table explaining the full procedure.

[10] Discrimination on nationality grounds (Art. 6.2); transport policy (Art. 75.1);
aspects of economic and monetary policy (Arts. 103.5; 104a.2; 104b.2; 105a.2);
European Social Fund (Art. 125); vocational training (Art. 127.4); parts of the
policy on trans-European networks (Art. 129d); implementation of decisions
relating to the European Regional Development Fund (Art. 130e); aspects of
environment policy (Art. 130s.1); development cooperation (Art. 130w.1).

right to ask the Commission to submit proposals for legislation (Art. 138b), thus putting it on a par with the Council in this respect.[11]

The EP's demands for Justice and Home Affairs and Foreign and Security Policy to be brought within the normal Community procedures were not granted. Instead the Council President was to 'consult' the EP on the main aspects of policy and to 'ensure' that the EP's opinions were taken into account. The EP's rights in these areas are to put questions, make recommendations and hold annual debates on progress.[12]

Maastricht also granted the EP the right to approve the Commission after the MS had consulted the EP on their choice of President. The term of office of the Commission is now also to run for five years, in harmony with the duration of the EP. The Parliament was also permitted to set up temporary committees of enquiry to investigate alleged contraventions or maladministration in the implementation of Community law, and to establish and select an Ombudsman.

The post-Maastricht EP is certainly not a negligible body. However, it remains dissatisfied with its position and, supported by many analysts, continues to regard its relative weakness as the principal component in the 'democratic deficit'. These arguments can now be elaborated.

The EP and the 'democratic deficit'.   Much discussion of the issue begins with the European Parliament's own definition of the deficit as a combination of two phenomena: (a) the transfer of powers from the Member States to the EU; (b) the exercise of these powers at EU level by institutions other than the EP, even though, before the transfer, national parliaments held power to pass laws in the areas concerned.[13] The suggestion is that the EP should now secure the powers which the parliaments within the MS have lost, and advocates of the EP have explored two possible strategies to bring this

---

[11] The right of assent was extended to aspects of citizenship law, the tasks and statute of the structural funds, the uniform electoral system, international agreements, and accessions to the Union. Piening, op. cit., p. 136.

[12] It has more extensive rights on visa policy. See chapter 6.

[13] EP Report on behalf of the Committee of Institutional Affairs on the Democratic Deficit. PE111.236/fin 1 February, 1988, pp. 10-11, quoted in Julie Smith, *Citizens' Europe? The European Elections and the Role of the European Parliament*, London: Royal Institute of International Affairs, 1994, p. 2.

about.[14] This first is the attempt to improve the existing institutional structure, without major treaty revisions. The main demand in this is co-decision in a full sense (rather than in the narrower Maastricht interpretation). As Juliet Lodge expressed it, 'Until it is given genuine co-decision rights with the Council across the board, the deficit will remain.'[15]

Since EU legislation cannot be changed by domestic parliaments once it has been adopted, the argument is that it needs effective democratic scrutiny by the EP *prior to adoption*. Co-decision, which would guarantee this form of control, could be achieved without treaty amendment if the Council undertook not to adopt acts which had been explicitly rejected by the EP, or if the Commission undertook to withdraw any such proposals. Secondly, the existing conciliation procedures could be extended to all important areas of legislation. Thirdly, the EP's budgetary responsibilities could be increased, and the distinction between compulsory and non-compulsory expenditure could be abolished. Fourthly, the EP could be given power to reject the several hundred implementing decisions taken every year by the Commission. Finally, the EP could be given the formal right to initiate legislation.[16]

The second strategy, which could be complementary to the first, is to adopt a wider 'gubernatorial' role, with more radical institutional change.[17] The main elements in this would be the right to elect the President of the Commission or, more radically, the whole team; and the requirement that the Commissioners should be approved by a vote of confidence before their appointment could be confirmed.[18] The EP's demands to have additional powers of this kind have been strengthened by the fiasco in the summer of 1994 in the Council when the British vetoed the Franco-German choice of successor to Delors, Jean-Luc Dehaene. This was followed in

---

[14] The distinction between the two strategies and the content of each is based on Jacobs and Corbett, op. cit., pp. 256-62.

[15] Juliet Lodge, 'Transparency and Democratic Legitimacy', *Journal of Common Market Studies*, 32, 3, Sept. 1994, p. 356.

[16] Jacobs and Corbett, op. cit., pp. 258-60.

[17] Ibid., p. 261.

[18] Some would go further than this and argue that the EP should have the right to petition for the dismissal of individual Commissioners. Shirley Williams, 'Sovereignty and Accountability in the European Community' in Hoffman and Keohane, op. cit., p. 171.

January 1995 by intensive questioning and criticism of some of the new Commissioners by the EP and the partially successful threat to delay or block the appointment of the whole Commission unless Jacques Santer agreed to MEPs' demands for an adjustment of his allocation of Commission portfolios.[19]

Problems in the EP's approach.   There is no doubt that the EP, and particularly some of its committees, have provided excellent evaluations and criticisms of many EU policies. It has also provided a forum for networking and cross-national lobbies, and has included a far higher proportion of women as MEPs than the majority of parliaments, and the percentage is still rising rapidly.[20] However, there are some difficulties in the suggestion that strengthening the EP should be the main means of democratising the EU.

First, it may be questioned whether its efficiency is adequate for the role which it is demanding. It has been aptly described as a kind of 'monthly road show', with MEPs spending three weeks per month in Brussels attending committees and political group meetings, one week per month in Strasbourg in plenary sessions, while much of the secretariat is based in Luxembourg.[21] This is hardly conducive to effective power. Secondly, although its internal organisation has greatly improved, party discipline and cohesion remain notoriously weak in comparison with most domestic parties. Thirdly, the calibre of some of the members has been questioned.[22] But far more important than any of these factors is the relationship between the MEPs and the domestic electorates and parties which they supposedly represent.

[19] 'Results of the hearings of the designated European Commissioners before the Committees of the European Parliament' *Europe Documents*, 1919, 18, Jan. 1995. The portfolios were not changed, but Padraig Flynn was forced to cede the position of Chair of the new Equal Opportunities Committee to Jacques Santer.

[20] 25.2% of MEPs elected in 1994 were women, compared with 19.9% in 1989, with the highest percentage in Denmark, at 43.8% and the lowest in Portugal, at 8%. *Women of Europe Newsletter*, 46, July-August 1994. The accession of Sweden, Finland, and Austria will reinforce this trend since these are all countries with relatively high levels of female representation. See J. Lovenduski and P. Norris, *Gender and Party Politics*, London: Sage, 1993.

[21] Dinan, op. cit., p. 259.

[22] Ibid., p. 263.

Democratic Deficits

As Table 7.1 shows, in each of the four elections since 1979 overall turnout has been disappointing in many countries with several showing a decline. Apart from the relatively low turnout, it

Table 7.1. EUROPEAN ELECTIONS TURNOUT (%)

	1979	1981	1984	1987	1989	1994
Bel	91.4		92.1		90.7	90.7
Den	47.8		52.4		46.2	52.5
Ger	65.7		56.8		62.3	60.1
Gr		78.6	77.2		79.9	71.2
Sp				68.9	54.6	59.6
Fr	60.7		56.7		48.7	52.7
Ire	63.6		47.6		68.3	44.0
It	84.9		83.4		81.0	74.8
Lux	88.9		88.8		87.4	86.5
NL	57.8		50.6		47.2	35.6
P				72.6	51.2	35.6
UK	32.3		32.6		36.2	36.4

Sources: European Elections 1994: Results and Elected Members: Provisional, 15 June 1994, DG for Information and Public Relations; and Julie Smith, *Citizens' Europe*, p. 13.

Note: The results for 1994 are provisional. It should be noted that, although there were increases in Denmark and France between 1989 and 1994, in Denmark 25% voted for anti-EU candidates and in France 22.5% voted for the Right-wing nationalist lists of Le Pen and De Villers. Voting is compulsory in Belgium and Luxembourg, and a 'civic duty' in Italy. However, the low turnout in 1994 in Portugal was probably because the elections took place during a national holiday.

is equally significant that in each election, in every country, the issues have primarily been about domestic politics rather than 'Europe'. The Euro-elections have thus tended to be equivalent to local elections, which are also normally dominated by 'national' preoccupations. Furthermore, the relationships between domestic and EU party organisations are, in most cases, relatively weak, and the national parties reinterpret the EU party manifestos to highlight issues which have salience at home, and sometimes virtually ignore the EU party position. Overall, there is little evidence that voters or even domestic parties are very interested in the EP's demands to strengthen its own position within the EU decision-making proces- ses. Of course, there are variations between the countries and the indifference must not be exaggerated, but it is probably fair to say that the EP and the Euro-elections are seen as adjuncts to domestic politics.

All this raises a fundamental question for proponents of enhanced

EP power as a means of reducing the 'democratic deficit'. Is it justified for an institution with comparatively weak democratic legitimacy to seek greater powers within the EU? It is often argued that the EP would achieve greater popular support if it secured greater powers. However, this is a debatable assumption given the evidence of increasing alienation from *domestic* systems – with declining electoral turnout, and diminishing support for parties and parliaments in several countries. Of course it is quite possible that the EP could use enhanced powers effectively vis-à-vis the Council even with its current electoral support. But it would be paradoxical to suggest that this could overcome the democratic deficit unless the EP also became embedded in popular consciousness and support.

Such considerations have led some commentators to argue that strengthening the EP may not be the most effective way of reducing the 'deficit' and that democratising the Commission might be more important.

Strengthening the democratic credentials of the Commission. In theory the Commission is the Executive of the EU, but its current democratic credentials are virtually non-existent. Governments may nominate whomsoever they please 'on the grounds of their general competence and whose independence is beyond doubt'.[23] There would therefore appear to be a *prima facie* case for democratising the institution. On the other hand, it has been suggested that this could be diversionary because the Commission is not the Executive in practice. Thus Juliet Lodge, for example, argues that the Council's emphasis on 'openness' and 'transparency' in the post-Maastricht era has scape-goated the Commission, and has attempted to set the EP and the Commission against one another, when the real culprits are the governments. In formal terms the Council may be the legislature, but in practice it is far more like an Executive since it is the ultimate decision-maker. It is also much less transparent and accountable than the Commission. It is therefore the Council, rather than the Commission, which really needs to be brought under democratic control.[24] There is undoubtedly much force in this argument, and the issue of the accountability of the Council will be

---

[23] Article 9 of the Treaty Establishing a Single Council and a Single Commission of the European Communities (Merger treaty), 8 April 1965.

[24] Lodge, 'Transparency and Democratic Legitimacy', op. cit.

considered below. However, the fact that some governments deliberately target the Commission for tactical reasons does not mean that there are no genuine grounds for concern about its democratic status. Yet while many agree that the Commission should be 'democratised', there are many practical and theoretical difficulties in deciding how this might be achieved. One radical proposal, made by Vernon Bogdanor, inadvertently highlights these problems.[25]

Bogdanor's wish to enhance the democratic status of the Commission is based on the view that this would be the most effective way of democratising the EU as a whole. Like the advocates of greater EP power considered above, he bases his recommendations on a conception of the EU as a potential liberal-democratic polity. However, he differs from them in suggesting that it is inappropriate to view it as a parliamentary system, particularly because of the weakness of transnational party cohesion and the continuing salience of domestic issues in Euro-elections. For Bogdanor the essential feature of liberal-democracy is the notion of alternative policies based upon divisions between government and opposition. This, he argues, is most obvious in two-party systems, but also exists in multi-party systems where there is normally an element of bi-polarity between a bloc of the Left and a bourgeois bloc.[26] However, at present it does not operate within the EU largely because there is no real sense of opposition to a 'government' and he does not believe that the EP is capable of playing an opposition role. Instead he suggests that the EU institutional structure is much closer to the US system than to other models of liberal-democracy as there is 'a separation of institutions, a separation of persons and a separation of powers' and 'no one institution can control the others'.[27] These powers are also interdependent in that 'effective policy-making requires that the institutions co-operate' to construct policies.[28] The

[25] Vernon Bogdanor, 'The Future of the European Community: Two Models of Democracy', *Government and Opposition*, 21, 2, 1986, pp. 161-76; see also Vernon Bogdanor, 'The June 1989 Elections and the Institutions of the Community', *Government and Opposition*, 24, 2, 1989, pp. 199-214; and Vernon Bogdanor and Geoffrey Woodcock 'The European Community and Sovereignty', *Parliamentary Affairs*, 44, 4, Oct. 1991.

[26] Bogdanor, 'The Future of the European Community', op. cit., p. 164.

[27] Ibid., p. 172.

[28] Ibid.

problem is that there is a lack of balance because the Council of Ministers and European Council are far too powerful in comparison with the Commission. The solution, he claims, is to introduce direct elections to the Commission for these would stimulate popular interest in the system, promote a greater sense of division between 'government' and 'opposition', and rebalance the institutions:

> Election of the Commission, the embryonic executive of a united Europe, would be by universal suffrage in the member states. Electors would be voting not for an individual candidate but for a ticket and they would not therefore be required to vote for an individual candidate of another country. Each party grouping would nominate its own team of Commissioners, comprising at least one candidate from each member state and headed by a candidate for the Presidency . . . . The multiplicity of parties in the Community would . . . require a two-ballot system . . . with the choice on the second ballot probably being between a broadly Left-leaning ticket and a Rightward one. . . . The election would be seen as fundamental to the allocation of political power in the Community. It would enable electors both to choose the government of the Community and to indicate what the future policy of the Community should be. It would therefore give the Commission both a democratic base and a legitimacy which it presently lacks.[29]

It may be reasonable to assume that direct elections to the Commission would be more likely to stimulate popular interest in the EU than that so far engendered by the elections to the EP. After all, the Commission is already a far more powerful body than the EP and prospective Commissioners might be able to detach themselves from domestic politics more easily than prospective MEPs.[30] Bogdanor may therefore be justified in arguing that this change would be more

---

[29] Bogdanor and Woodcock, 'The European Community and Sovereignty', op. cit., pp. 489-90.

[30] It is far more difficult for prospective MEPs to direct attention to EU issues because they are members of parties which are primarily concerned with winning domestic elections. Bogdanor's idea of prospective Commissioners fighting on a multi-national 'ticket' for EU policies should enable them to focus on European issues more effectively, although they would still be subjected to domestic pressures.

likely to transform attitudes to the EU than any incremental increases in the powers of the EP, and that:

> It would make the politics of Europe exciting to the voter who would come to feel that he was participating in a real choice, of importance to him and to his fellow-citizens of the Community. . . . Popular interest in Community affairs could be expected to increase, and the Community would come to be seen by voters not merely in terms of national interest but as a genuinely transnational enterprise. The election of the Commission would of itself play a part in helping to create that supranational party system without which Europe cannot be built.[31]

It is also probable that direct elections of a team would help to remedy one of the defects in the current system: the political incoherence and fragmentation of the Commission. (see Chapter 2). However, I believe that there are fundamental weaknesses in the whole argument.

In the first place, there are a series of considerations which suggest that the proposal is not based on practical politics. The very likelihood that direct elections to the Commission could have a transformative effect is surely a very good reason for concluding that it is extremely unlikely that they will be introduced? Once such elections took place the governments would be confronted by a body which could claim that its democratic basis was as solid as theirs: indeed on EU issues it would be able to argue that its legitimacy was deeper since it had been elected on European proposals, whereas they had come to power on a domestic agenda. The governments accepted the introduction of direct elections to the EP – long after the fundamental nature of the EU had been established – in the knowledge that the EP was, at that stage, a relatively impotent institution. Many of them have subsequently resented its gradual increase in power and in 1993 the Council as a whole argued that the EP had used the Cooperation procedure introduced in the SEA to promote its own institutional priorities at the expense of effective decision-making.[32] The Commission is in an entirely different position because it has always been seen as a potential rival anyway, and there have been frequent attempts by some of the governments

---

[31] Bogdanor, 'The Future of the European Community', p. 176.
[32] Dinan, op. cit., p. 278.

to 'cut it down to size' (see Chapter 2). There is therefore no question of the European Council accepting the idea of a directly elected Commission which could then present itself as a *real* EU Executive. Nor, of course, would the EP support the proposal since a directly elected Commission would also rival its democratic legitimacy. Indeed, since the Commission's powers are so much greater, it could even eclipse the EP.

Yet apart from these practical considerations, there are also important theoretical objections to Bogdanor's proposals. At present there are at least three sets of institutions which claim democratic legitimacy and which often dispute each other's credentials: the EP, national parliaments, and the governments. In many countries, there are also sub-central governments and parliaments, which also carry democratic mandates. Rather than simplifying the division between government and opposition, direct elections to the Commission would therefore further obscure the issues of power and responsibility. Moreover, a united team of Commissioners, elected on a two-ballot system, might reflect a temporary wave of opinion at the time of the election, and then seek to promote this agenda irrespective of the wishes of either the governments (which would have been elected at various different times) and a large minority of the European electorate. Elections by proportional representation would overcome this problem, but would also remove the original rationale for Bogdanor's proposal: the idea that direct elections could introduce a distinct sense of government and opposition into the EU system.

The practical and theoretical weaknesses in the radical suggestion of a directly elected Commission imply that any proposals for democratising the institution need to be more limited. It is therefore likely that discussions will continue to focus on the EP's rights in relation to the Commission, despite the 'diversionary' aspect noted above. It is, for example, quite probable that the EP will be granted more rights in choosing the Commission President in future. More generally, it is also likely that discussion of the 'democratic deficit' at EU level will continue to focus on the power of the EP. It is notable that the governments have made a limited concession in this respect. Thus while the EP was not represented on the IGC on Political Union before Maastricht, it had two representatives on the preliminary committee to prepare the 1996 IGC.[33] However, the

---

[33] This was agreed by the European Council at Corfu in June 1994 against the wishes

most likely outcome is incremental change rather than any dramatic breakthrough.

The above discussion has been predicated on the assumption that the 'democratic deficit' exists within the EU, conceived as a polity. It is now time to look at the issues from the alternative viewpoint, which stresses the problems of control and accountability within the MS.

The domestic democratic deficit and EU membership

Those who stress the *domestic* democratic deficit in relation to the EU do not necessarily disagree with the whole diagnosis of the problems discussed in the previous section. There is much common ground in arguing that the Council is relatively unaccountable, that the EP is comparatively weak, and that the Commission is undemocratic. However, there are differences of opinion over which problems are the most fundamental, and over where the solutions lie.

The major concerns of those preoccupied with the domestic democratic deficit is that the EU has involved, is involving, and will involve, transfers of power that diminish the internal accountability of the governments. The problems may be considered under three headings: those caused by acceptance of existing Community legislation (the so-called *acquis communautaire*), those resulting from the ongoing policy-making process, and those emanating from new stages in EU development.

The acquis communautaire.   There is a difference between the original 'six' and all later adherents to the EU in the sense that the original MS determined its nature (albeit with limited non-governmental involvement), while later Members had to accept the *acquis* as it existed at the time of entry. However, all newly elected governments and parliaments in all EU states are now in a similar situation in the sense that all existing EU law supersedes domestic law in cases of conflict. Moreover, the ramifications of the system have now penetrated deeply into policy areas that were previously

---

of both Britain and France. Michael Shackleton, 'Interparliamentary Cooperation and the 1996 IGC' in *The Changing Role of Parliaments in the European Union,* Maastricht: EIPA, 1995.

regarded as 'domestic'. None of this can legally be changed by any parliament in an MS. This means that the EU is structurally embedded into the domestic systems. However, this inter-penetration alters the parameters for parliaments, which have traditionally sought to control their governments. For they are now operating in a situation where the source of legislation is partially external, and where they cannot legally bring about any alteration in the *acquis* or even promote alternative policies or laws which would conflict with those of the EU.

The EU policy-making system.   One of the paradoxes about the EU is that, while membership constrains governments in various ways, it has simultaneously tended to reinforce their predominance over domestic parliaments. There are various reasons for this. First, irrespective of EU membership, modern parliaments are over-loaded with business, and have little chance of scrutinising more than a small proportion of legislation effectively. The EU has inevitably added to this problem by significantly increasing the amount of laws passed every year.[34] Moreover, EU legislation is classified in ways that differ from those used in many domestic systems, and its terminology is also distinct. It is therefore difficult for most politicians reared in domestic legislatures to understand, and this leads to new forms of bureaucratisation and hierarchy within parliaments, with specialist committees attempting to cope with EU legislation.[35] Secondly, there is no requirement in Community law for governments to consult domestic parliaments before agreeing to legislation. Although most parliaments have obviously tried to ensure that governments provide them with the necessary information, prior to Maastricht only the Danish parliament had secured any real control in advance of decisions being made at EU level.[36]

---

[34] In an average year there are now 7,000–8,000 instruments of all types adopted, of which approximately 4,000 are regulations, 2,500 are decisions, and 120 are directives. Nugent, op. cit., p. 215.

[35] For a summary of the situation in each of the EU12, see *The European Parliament and the Parliaments of the Member States: Parliamentary Scrutiny and arrangements for Cooperation*, European Parliament, Division for Relations with the Parliaments of the Member States, July 1994.

[36] However, in October 1990 the House of Commons had agreed to the introduction of a scrutiny reserve, which meant that ministers would not normally agree to legislation in the Council of Ministers on a proposal which was still being

Thirdly, most major policies are determined by the Council of Ministers and the European Council. But the Councils are extremely secretive and it is therefore very difficult for many domestic parliaments to know in advance (or even subsequently) what line their governments are taking. Moreover, the extension of Qualified Majority Voting since 1987 makes the possibility of domestic control and accountability far more difficult, even in principle: how is a government to be held responsible for a policy on which it was outvoted?

All these factors exacerbate the problem of accountability and, since an EU dimension is built into most policy areas to a greater or lesser extent, it follows that the EU has reinforced the general tendency towards Executive dominance. However, there is a further factor (discussed in Chapter 2), which exacerbates this problem: government re-organisation and the development of policy networks at EU level.

EU membership has precipitated administrative reorganisation in most countries so that they can cope more effectively with policy-making at this level. Some administrations are more successful than others, but there is a general tendency to seek high level policy-coordination within the domestic system. There is also the system of Permanent Representation at Brussels, with interchange of personnel between domestic and EU postings. Thus governments establish complex chains of interactions through which they are simultaneously seeking to promote their favoured policies within the EU, while working with other governments to uphold jointly agreed policies against potential opponents whether in the Commission, the EP, or at home. All this gives the Executive immense advantages over domestic politicians. Shirley Williams expresses it as follows:

> The 'democratic deficit' is the gap between the powers transferred to the Community level and the control of the elected [domestic] Parliament over them, a gap filled by national civil servants operating as European experts or as members of regulation and management committees, and to some extent by organized lobbies, mainly representing business. These civil servants are acquiring a detailed knowledge of the Community. . . .

examined by the Select Committee on European Legislation or which was awaiting consideration by the whole House. Ibid., p. 31.

National government ministers . . . are gaining a similar insight. But most national politicians . . . have no role in the Community. The national civil servants they scrutinize are building a knowledge and an influence over large areas of policy they cannot begin to match . . . . One of the unforeseen consequences of the Community, therefore . . . is the weakening of national parliaments vis-à-vis their own executives, even in those areas that lie outside Community competence at the present time.[37]

New stages in EU development.   Major new stages in the development of the Community, which have further weakened control, have normally occurred with comparatively little domestic debate. In particular the SEA, which not only extended the use of majority voting but also constituted a crucial development in opening economies, went ahead with little parliamentary involvement in most of the countries.[38] And, again in most countries, there was little domestic discussion of the Maastricht treaty before the Danish referendum result. There were, of course, some exceptions to this: in Britain there was considerable discussion because of the internal division in the Conservative party, in Germany the *Länder* ensured that major concessions were secured from the government, and, of course, there was a major debate in Denmark itself. Yet considering the extent to which the Maastricht treaty would limit future domestic policy options – particularly in monetary policy – the overall level of parliamentary involvement in the EU states as a whole was surprisingly limited. It thus took the Danish and French referendums and the currency crises of 1992 and 1993 to provoke the kinds of discussion which should have taken place much earlier.

Yet it would be wrong to imply that the process of deepening integration has occurred because governments have misled parliaments. Many of the MS parliaments have supported the EU as strongly as their governments and have perhaps not taken opportunities that were theoretically available to them to debate the issues or seek to impose controls. It is mainly in the 'Eurosceptic' countries – Denmark and Britain – that the question of domestic

---

[37] Williams, op. cit., p. 162.

[38] See Church and Keogh (eds), *The Single European Act*, op. cit., for an analysis of the debate in each MS.

democratic accountability has always been regarded as a major problem.

But if the EU has affected domestic control in all these ways, what remedies are proposed?

Proposed solutions for overcoming the domestic democratic deficit. Naturally, the most extreme proposal would be withdrawal from the EU, the restoration of the legal status quo prior to membership, and renegotiation of all links with the other MS. However, since the British Labour Party's crushing electoral defeat on such a programme in the 1983 General Election, no major party anywhere in the EU has advocated this policy. The general assumptions have been that it would be impracticable, undesirable, or electorally disastrous. In effect this means that parliaments have recognised a need to accept the bulk of the *acquis communautaire* and this also implies a *de facto* recognition of their limited ability to control the integration process (this will be discussed in the final section of the chapter). Less radical proposals than withdrawal involve the attempt to intervene in EU policy-making, either by breaking into the ongoing process in some way, or by ensuring that further major developments cannot take place without domestic consent. These may be considered in turn.

Most parliaments have attempted to secure commitments from their governments that they will be fully informed and consulted about EU policies and legislation but, as already noted, the Danish Parliament (*Folketing*) has gone the furthest in this. Its experience is therefore worth examining briefly.[39] The specific nature of the Danish control mechanism stems from two factors. The first is the tradition of very close co-operation between the Executive and the Parliament in policy-making. Because governments are normally in a minority or are coalitions they have always been obliged to compromise in a form of 'co-operative democracy', without a sharp division between executive and legislative power. Secondly, Denmark entered the EU primarily for economic reasons because the governing elites felt that they had little alternative once Britain made this choice. The decision was not based on any degree of political enthusiasm, and there were always strong feelings of separateness

[39] The following is based largely on Henning Sørensen and Old Vaever, 'State, Society and Democracy and the Effect of the EC' and Niels Jørgen Nehring, 'Parliamentary Control of the Executive' in Lise Lyck, *Denmark and EC Membership Evaluated*, London: Pinter, 1992.

and Nordic identity. Thus as soon as Denmark joined, its parliament had two equally strong reasons for establishing a new committee to scrutinise and control the policy-making process: it wanted to ensure that the Executive did not break the tradition of 'co-operative democracy', and it wanted to limit EU encroachment on Denmark as a 'nation-state'. It thus gave government two obligations: to inform Parliament and the new Committee about the agenda and policy of the Council of Ministers and, in specific cases, to follow instructions from the Committee as to how the Danish minister should vote in the Council. Subsequently, the Committee became more sophisticated in its procedures and is now the biggest and best staffed of all the Parliamentary committees in Denmark.[40] At times it has been so effective in mandating Danish ministers that EU sources have condemned it for holding up EC decision-making (although Delors praised it in a speech in September 1989).[41] Yet even with all these advantages the Danish experience before Maastricht was not dissimilar to that of the other parliaments. Thus it still lost part of its legislative role, it felt that it had difficulty in controlling the government and the EC, and it witnessed a growth of bureaucratisation, with increased relative power for the civil service. Furthermore, the Committee had only advisory status on foreign policy – which is a problem given that the distinction between foreign and domestic policy is hardly tenable in relation to the EU – and it found it difficult to control Danish Ministers in the European Council, where the procedures are less clear than those in the Council of Ministers.[42] Finally, it must be noted that the *Folketing* did not prevent the government from signing the Maastricht Treaty – a decision that was subsequently rejected by the electorate in the first referendum. In 1994 this led to a further extensive strengthening of Danish parliamentary rights in relation to the EU.[43]

If even the most rigorous system of parliamentary control has experienced these difficulties, all the others have naturally encountered still greater problems. The attempt to limit future developments without parliamentary consent has become far more general and has been given considerable impetus by Maastricht and the

---

[40] See Sørensen and Vaever, op. cit., for more details.
[41] Ibid., p. 9.
[42] Nehring, op. cit., pp. 80-1.
[43] *The European Parliament and the Parliaments of the Member States*, op. cit., pp. 18-19.

post-Maastricht crisis. It is notable that, in addition to the UK and Denmark, which negotiated formal 'opt-outs' from the Maastricht Treaty, both the German and Dutch Parliaments secured extensive new powers in relation to the EU and, in the German case, these were endorsed by the Constitutional court in October 1993, which also led to two new Articles (23 and 45) in the Constitution.[44] Moreover, in 1993-4 the traditionally weak French Parliament exploited the post-Maastricht crisis to secure new controls over the government's EU policy, which theoretically strengthened its position enormously and put it into a situation broadly comparable with that of the House of Commons.[45]

Overall, there are certainly signs of a hardening of parliamentary attitudes to further developments in many of the countries, including some that had previously been the most enthusiastic about the integration process. It is, of course, too early to know how much difference this will make, but it is unlikely that governments will want to risk a further crisis over the EU in the near future. They will probably try to ensure domestic support before undertaking major initiatives, even though this may make agreement in the 1996 IGC more difficult to secure. However, the fact remains that the development of the EU thus far has caused very considerable problems of domestic control.

The EP and domestic parliaments: contradictions or common action?

If the EU is interpreted *either* as a complete polity or as a conventional intergovernmental organisation, the two views of the 'democratic deficit' discussed above become irreconcilable. Thus if the EP claimed that *all* significant developments were now at EU level while domestic parliaments maintained the opposite viewpoint, there could be no agreement between them and no element of dual strategy. For some years, it appeared that this kind of irreconcilable contradiction was possible. However, it would now be extremely dangerous, from a democratic viewpoint, for either domestic parliaments or the EP to take such an extreme position.

---

[44] Ibid., pp. 19-21, 26-9. See also Michael Shackleton, 'Democratic Accountability in the European Union' in Brouwer, Lintner and Newman, op. cit., pp. 96-8.

[45] *The European Parliament and the Parliaments of the Member States*, op. cit., pp. 22-4; Shackleton, 'Interparliamentary Cooperation and the 1996 IGC', op. cit.

The EU has, in many respects, strengthened governments and powerful capitalist interests at the expense of those seeking to scrutinise and control them. The intergovernmental policy-making networks have already been discussed, but it is equally important to note the rather similar position of major economic actors. Thus, for example, the Commission constantly interacts with the organisations of powerful transnational companies.[46] This might not mean that such groups always get their way, but their influence is well documented.[47] Their overwhelming advantages in lobbying both the Commission and domestic decision-makers leads to a situation in which they have a good chance of influencing policy through two routes simultaneously.[48] Thus governments and major economic interests are able to operate on both levels, while domestic parliaments and the EP find this much more difficult. Yet one theorist of integration has effectively argued that this kind of power imbalance may be a positive feature of the EU:

> EC institutions strengthen the autonomy of national political leaders *vis-à-vis* particularistic social groups within their domestic polity. By augmenting the legitimacy and credibility of common policies, and by strengthening domestic agenda-setting, the EU structures a 'two-level' game that enhances the autonomy and initiative of national political leaders – often . . . a prerequisite for successful market liberalization.[49]

[46] Wyn Grant, 'Pressure Groups and the European Community: An Overview' and Sonia Mazey and Jeremy Richardson, 'Conclusion: A European Policy Style?' in Mazey and Richardson, *Lobbying in the European Community*, Oxford University Press, 1993.

[47] This was particularly evident in the period leading up to the Single Market Initiative. In the early 1980s Etienne Davignon, the Commissioner responsible for industrial affairs, held a series of meetings in the 'Round Table' discussion group, and in 1984 and 1985 several major companies argued in favour of completing the single market. The most influential advocate was the head of Philips, Wisse Dekker, who published *Europe-1990*, Eindhoven: Philips, 1985.

[48] This situation is naturally quite different from that of most voluntary groups and non-governmental organisations, for whom even the cost of an office in Brussels is prohibitive. Brian Harvey, 'Lobbying in Europe: The Experience of Voluntary Organisations' in Mazey and Richardson, op. cit.

[49] Andrew Moravcsik, 'A Liberal Intergovernmentalist Approach to the EC', *Journal of Common Market Studies*, 31, 4, Dec. 1993 p. 515. He thus also claims: 'The EC's "democratic deficit" may be a fundamental source of its success.' Ibid., p. 507.

Less euphemistically, this could be expressed as follows: 'governments force through the economic policies favoured by major industrial and financial organisations by using the EU to strengthen their hands against the sectors of society which will suffer as a result of these changes'. There is clearly a democratic requirement to prevent this from happening, which provides a basis for some common action between domestic parliaments and the EP. Similarly, as noted in the last chapter, Justice and Home Affairs policies are not effectively controlled either domestically or at EP level (and the same could be said for the Common Foreign and Security Policy).[50] Again, this suggests the advantages of inter-parliamentary co-operation.

There are some signs that such collaboration is developing. When the IGC on political union was meeting in the 'run-up' to Maastricht, the EP made considerable efforts to secure a united front with domestic parliaments on the 'democratic deficit'. This led to the so-called 'Assizes' meeting between MEPs and members of twelve domestic parliaments in November 1990, which adopted a resolution calling for the IGCs to take account of the parliaments' views and called for enhanced co-operation between the national parliaments and the EP.[51] Although this did not influence the IGCs' concrete proposals, the Maastricht treaty attached a Declaration inviting the EP and the national parliaments to meet as necessary as a Conference of the Parliaments (Assizes), promising that this would be consulted on the main features of the EU. A further Declaration encouraged greater involvement of national parliaments in the activities of the EU and a stepping up of the exchange of information between national parliaments and the EP. In fact, almost all domestic parliaments had already set up liaison offices with the EP, which also has a division which maintains constant contact with national parliaments. Officials from most domestic parliaments also attend each session of the EP and there is normally a biennial conference of the Presidents of the EP and of national parliaments. At its meeting in Athens in April 1994 this pressed for more active involvement by

[50] In May 1994 the French government specifically turned down a request for the new parliamentary control to be extended to these areas. Nor has there been any extension of such rights in the House of Commons. *The European Parliament and the Parliaments of the Member States*, op. cit., pp. 24, 30-1.

[51] *The European Parliament and the Parliaments of the Member States*, op. cit., p. 37; Shackleton, 'Interparliamentary Cooperation and the 1996 IGC', op. cit.

both forms of parliament in the preparations for the 1996 IGC.[52] There is also a twice yearly conference of the European Affairs Committees of the national parliaments and the EP (COSAC) and since April 1994 this has been considering practical proposals designed to improve parliamentary scrutiny.[53] Moreover, some parliaments involve MEPs in their own scrutiny procedures, although only Belgium grants the MEPs full voting rights.[54] Overall, it is evident that there is an increase in all forms of liaison between domestic parliaments and the EP.

Yet contacts between officials from parliaments, and even parliamentary committees, are likely to avoid ideologically sensitive issues. More effective political links are therefore also dependent upon strengthening relationships between 'partisan' organisations within the MS and at EU level, including those between national parties, their MEPs, and the party groupings. There are signs that some progress is being made on this. For example, many national parties now ensure the participation of MEPs in their policy-making bodies and party meetings, and the Party of European Socialists was able to agree a manifesto for the 1994 Elections without any of the national members formally dissociating themselves from its content. Yet considerable problems remain both in the relative lack of cohesion of the parties in the EP, and in the relationships with their domestic counterparts. Moreover, it is significant that there are tensions between MEPs and domestic parliamentarians even in countries which have been favourable to integration. Thus a survey of seventy-two out of the eighty-one German MEPs in 1987-8 found that almost of half of them felt that Bundestag MPs had very little interest in contacts with them, and three-quarters of them believed that their relationship was strained by feelings of rivalry in the domestic parliament.[55] When there is a gulf between MEPs and

[52] *The European Parliament and the Parliaments of the Member States*, op. cit., p. 36.
[53] Ibid., p. 37.
[54] Jacobs and Corbett, op. cit., p. 240. For an explanation of the Belgian committee, see Shackleton, 'Interparliamentary Cooperation and the 1996 IGC', op. cit.
[55] Survey by Hrbek and Schweitzer, cited in T. Saalfeld, 'Previous Research on the Bundestag and its Links with the EC' in a note prepared for the Research Group on National Parliaments and the European Union, Centre for Legislative Studies, University of Hull, 1993, and in Philip Norton, 'National Parliaments and the European Union', paper presented at the Workshop of Parliamentary Scholars and Parliamentarians, Berlin, 19-20 Aug. 1994.

the domestic parties over the attitude to adopt to the EU itself – as has recently been the case in the British Conservative Party and was previously evident in the Labour Party – the problems of cohesion are obviously intensified.[56] In these circumstances the EU-wide networking groups – such as the women's lobbies – may often be at least as important in simultaneously imposing pressures on domestic parliaments and the EP. Similarly, there are campaigns and policy issues on which there is a clear common parliamentary interest and on which joint action is most likely to be effective. One obvious example is the campaign against secrecy within the EU. Since information is a vital component of power, there is a clear democratic interest in ensuring that the EU operates in the most open manner possible. Had the Council adopted the kind of secrecy laws which were proposed in February 1992, much less information might have become available about the operation of the various inter-governmental organisations and committees dealing with asylum and immigration, and it is probable that other policy areas would become similarly secretive.[57] At the time of writing this matter remains unresolved, but it is widely agreed that a fundamental problem within the EU has been the lack of transparency of the Council of Ministers and the European Council.[58] There is therefore no reason for there to be any difference of opinion between the EP and the other parliaments on the need for a Freedom of Information Act, and on the demand that, at least when acting as a legislature, the Council of Ministers should sit in public. This would also be accepted by some governments – particularly those of the Netherlands, Denmark and Sweden – and will no doubt be an issue for the 1996 IGC.

There is therefore the possibility of considerable progress in

[56] Stafford T. Thomas, 'Assessing MEP influence on British EC Policy', with comments by James Elles, MEP and David Martin, MEP, in *Government and Opposition*, 27, 1, winter 1992.

[57] Tony Bunyan, 'Secret Europe', op. cit.

[58] The Dutch and Danish governments and *The Guardian* have taken the Council to the ECJ for failing to live up to its earlier promises on greater openness. Both Finland and Sweden included declarations in the Treaties of Accession on transparency, and the prospects improved with the submission of a memorandum by the Danish government on 6 March 1995 calling for open debates in the Council on all new legislative proposals, to be followed by automatic publication of the minutes. Shackleton, 'Interparliamentary Cooperation and the 1996 IGC' op. cit.; *The Guardian*, 31 Aug. 1994 and 6 March 1995.

forging stronger co-operative links between the different parliaments in the EU.[59] However, there are also some definite limits to this collaboration. The first difficulty is that, on crucial aspects of policy, there is a major difference between the priorities of the EP and those of many of the domestic parliaments. For example, the EP has always argued that the EU can be effective only if it adopts majority decision-making as its normal procedure. This, it believes, would speed up the processes (and would also strengthen its own role). But, while the Italian and Benelux parliaments may be prepared to accept this, others will continue to argue that it would reduce their control over EU decision-making and must be resisted. Similarly, the EP was dissatisfied with Maastricht because it did not go far enough towards political union while many of the domestic parliaments thought that it went too far.[60] Again, on the more specific issue of the EMU, the EP favoured monetary union (with some caveats), but was dissatisfied with the minimal rights of democratic control and accountability, while many of the domestic parliaments have been concerned about the process itself.[61]

All these are very fundamental divergences, which stem from rivalries between domestic and EU politicians, differing judgments about where power is located, and conflicts over future goals.

The EU has developed on the basis of considerable Executive autonomy with relatively weak democratic accountability. Since this is an unsatisfactory situation it is tempting to seek clear-cut solutions: for example, to suggest that the problem might be resolved if everybody accepted the need for supranational control by the EP, or at least saw a need for a clear division of labour between the EP and domestic parliaments. However, such outcomes are inherently unlikely. It may also be a mistake to presume that the current lack of clarity is totally negative.

The EP will probably continue to seek to propel the EU in an integrationist direction and some of the governments and parlia-

[59] For a sustained discussion, see Shackleton, 'Interparliamentary Cooperation and the 1996 IGC', op. cit.

[60] *Maastricht – The Treaty on European Union: The Position of the European Parliament*, Luxembourg: Office for Official Publications of the European Communities, 1992; Piening, op. cit.

[61] Shackleton, 'Democratic Accountability in the European Union', op. cit.

ments in the MS will also support this process. However, there are others which will remain reserved in their attitudes towards the EU and cautious about accepting reductions in their existing status. This diversity of attitudes certainly makes the policy-making process more complex, but *sometimes* acts as an effective form of democratic control. The post-Maastricht crisis may illustrate this.

After the result of the first Danish referendum on Maastricht, the author of *Denmark and the EC Evaluated* ended her book with a personal statement:

> The Danish 'no' has started a process which nobody today knows the end-result of, but I think I can speak for all Danes when I say I hope it will provide support for a democracy of the *peoples* of Europe and for widespread and open cooperation in Europe.[62]

Her hopes may well have been justified in the sense that the subsequent confusion had some positive results. In particular, it is likely that the political elites will take more trouble to build domestic support before embarking on further major steps in integration. A very small majority in one of the smallest MS may therefore have contributed a great deal to the eventual construction of a more democratic European Union. This would not have happened if all countries and parliaments had been equally enthusiastic or equally apathetic about the integration process.

---

[62] Lyck, op. cit., p. 243.

8

CONCLUSIONS: PEOPLES, STATES AND THE EUROPEAN UNION

This book began with an analysis of the political discourse normally used in the ongoing debate about the European Union. It suggested that both those who proclaimed the dawn of a United Europe and those who called for the defence of the 'sovereign state' were guilty of over-simplification. The subsequent chapters have shown just how complex the issues are, and how difficult it is to make judgments which have any universal applicability about the Members States and the European Union. Certainly, globalisation has affected *all* countries in the world, calling into question the notion of separate 'national' economies. Similarly, the increasing interdependence of the MS, underwritten by Community law, has meant that the European Union has had some common effects on all them. However, it would be as absurd to suggest that Luxembourg and Germany are equally constrained by the EU as to claim that Haiti and the United States are equally dominated by the international economy. Nor are all the members relatively weaker in international terms than they were in the early post-war era: the decline of British power is demonstrable, but Germany is clearly in a far stronger position than it was. Again, it would be misleading to imply that *all* are experiencing strong centrifugal pressures which are weakening internal cohesion and state power. Italy is certainly experiencing a crisis of internal legitimacy which is affecting both external and internal dimensions of state power, but there is no strong evidence of this process in the majority of EU states. In other words, there are so many specificities in the situation of each country that it is difficult to sustain a convincing argument that they are all subject to a universal tendency which will lead to a common destiny.

A comparable situation of complexity is apparent if the state-EU interactions are considered in relation to different policy-areas. It is evident that the EU has penetrated into many realms which would formerly have been regarded as the preserve of the state. Such

activities have created a formidable apparatus of interlocking interactions between the MS themselves and between those states and
EU officials. This has meant that new configurations of policy-
making networks have been established and that there is no clear
separation between the EU and domestic policy. Yet the impact is
uneven. In some spheres and, above all, in those concerning
commercial and competition policies, this penetration is very substantial. Taken in conjunction within the increasingly constraining
pressures of the international economy as a whole, there is thus a
substantial reduction in state economic autonomy. Economic and
Monetary Union would remove still more traditional levers of
macroeconomic policy-making from government control. Yet some
of the MS retain considerable scope both to influence the external
environment and to implement domestic strategies. In other policy
areas, such as the definition of citizenship by each state, the systems
of social security, and the internal distribution of authority between
the different tiers of government, the impact of the EU has been
much less substantial. And, while there is extensive inter-governmental
co-operation on Justice and Home Affairs, this has mainly taken
place outside the formal policy process of the EU.

Nor, of course, is it the case that the EU should be considered a
constraint on all forms of state power. For example, as argued in the
previous chapter, the policy-making system has tended to enhance
Executive power *vis-à-vis* domestic parliaments. Similarly, while the
process of integration has led to the erosion of some forms of legal
and economic autonomy, the creation of the EU may have reversed
a decline in other dimensions of state power that might otherwise
have taken place. This is particularly evident with regard to the
international economy, where the EU as a whole has greater weight
than the individual MS. But it is also true more generally that most
governments have perceived the EU as a buttress to state power,
and that it provides some of the smaller MS with an international
role that might otherwise not be available to them.

Overall, there is therefore little sign that states are withering away
despite the increasing density of their interactions in the EU. But
nor is there any consistency across all policy areas and all states. What
might therefore be concluded from this situation of complexity in
relation to democracy? Let us begin by asking whether the doctrine
of subsidiarity is helpful in this respect.

Subsidiarity suggests that decisions need to be made on a case to case basis about the levels at which policy may be devised and implemented the most effectively. It might therefore provoke thought and debate about the policies which need to be conducted at Union level and those that might be handled at lower levels. In principle, it could therefore lead to some readjustments between the competences of the EU, states, and sub-central governments, and to the introduction of regional tiers of government in centralised states. However, it would be utopian to believe that the doctrine of subsidiarity could overcome conflicts about the level at which policies should be decided or implemented. Consider, for example, the argument between a neo-liberal and an advocate of social regulation about the determination of wage-rates. According to the neo-liberal, these should be agreed by the employer and worker when striking their 'bargain' in the individual enterprise. The social-democrat, on the other hand, will insist that income levels should be controlled, at least to an extent, at a higher level by a public authority on the basis of some overall conception of social need and equity. In other words, the judgments are influenced by ideological considerations. Similarly, a belief about the legitimacy or otherwise of the 'nation-state' or participative democracy will permeate the argument about whether or not the MS constitutes the 'appropriate' policy-making level. Thus subsidiarity cannot transcend conflict about decision-making.

Discussion of democracy within the EU often concentrates on the issue of institutional reform. It is implied that a greater use of majority voting in the Council, and/or a stronger role for the European Parliament, and/or the introduction of regional government in centralised systems will be of fundamental significance in enhancing democratisation. It is certainly true that institutions and constitutions are of great importance, and both regional government and the problem of accountability have been addressed in earlier chapters. However, while institutional reform must certainly be an element in any strategy for democratisation, its impact should not be exaggerated. After all, the preservation of a veto power in the Council could conceivably mean that a particular state was able to defend an advanced welfare system against neo-liberal pressures. A strengthened EP might not become any more embedded in popular consciousness than it is at present. And in some circumstances regional government could strengthen corrupt local elites rather than empowering ordinary people. In other words, the issue of institutional reform has similarities with the debate over subsidiarity. It is obviously of crucial relevance to democracy to discuss *how* and at what *level* decisions should be made. But it is also insufficient to ask such questions without reference to the overall goals which are to be sought.

This book has been written on the dual assumptions that democracy is of fundamental importance, and that it comprises a constellation of procedures and values which need to be balanced against each other. The decision-making system cannot be detached from the goals of empowerment, equality, liberty, human rights and solidarity. However, these values are often in conflict with one another and judgments about the relative priorities are necessarily based on overall ethical frameworks. In earlier chapters some of the assumptions underlying the argument were made explicit. For example, the discussion of economic and social policies in Chapters 3 and 4 presumed that greater equality and the elimination of poverty were more important than the market freedoms celebrated by neo-liberalism; and the analysis of citizenship in Chapter 6 assumed that universal human rights should supersede other considerations even if there were a popular majority for policies of exclusion and racism. However, the EU has been treated as a 'vehicle' for particular policies. No view has been expressed as to whether its own maintenance and development should be regarded as positive goals. This approach is no longer adequate, for it is impossible to reach conclusions about democracy and the EU, without taking an explicit position on the latter.

The EU has some very negative features. It has been dominated by elites, it has elevated the competitive market above all other social and economic principles, it lacks effective democratic control, it has shown tendencies towards a 'Fortress Europe' mentality, and it has been protectionist against weaker economies which it should be aiding. However, it has also been one of the most successful experiments in international organisation ever created, it has helped to supersede previous enmities, it has made a valuable contribution in many areas by promoting good practice and EU-wide networks, and its continuation is probably vital if European stability and peace are to be secured. Integration should not supersede all other considerations, and attitudes to it must depend on the nature of its future development. Nevertheless, there are good reasons for arguing that the 're-nationalisation' of policies currently carried out by the EU would be highly retrogressive. However, before considering the EU and democratisation, two further factors must be discussed: the state of public opinion, and the increasing diversity of the MS.

It is always difficult to assess public opinion, particularly as survey evidence is so ephemeral. Nevertheless, recent signs of indifference to the EU cannot be ignored. Thus in the spring of 1993, on average across the twelve MS, only 54% of respondents recorded positive attitudes to the EU. Opinion in the Netherlands was the most favourable, with 68% recording positive attitudes, followed by Italy, with 67%. Britain was at the bottom of the list with only 40%, but it was more significant that in France only 52% were positive, and in Germany only 53%. There was also a high rate of ambivalent attitudes, with the EU average of 39% (45% in Britain) and negative attitudes at 7% (15% in Britain and 14% in Denmark).[1] This evidence must be balanced against the fact that most EU countries are also currently experiencing some problems in domestic democratic legitimation. Whereas 57% of respondents had been fairly satisfied or very satisfied with democracy in their own countries in March 1991, two years later this had fallen to only 42%. Whereas 40% were not very satisfied or not at all satisfied in March 1991, by March–April 1993 the figure had risen to 55%. As usual, the differences are as significant as the similarities. While 81% of Danish respondents were satisfied or very satisfied, 88% of Italians were not very satisfied or not at all satisfied.[2]

Such evidence might suggest that many people are equally disenchanted with their own political systems and the EU. However, the issue of *salience* is also very pertinent. In this respect Richard Sinnot's sophisticated disaggregation of the evidence which suggests strong support for EU intervention on particular issues, such as the environment, is important.[3] Yet it is also notable that in 1990, when popular enthusiasm for the EU was far higher than it was after

[1] For full details, see Nugent, op. cit., p. 425, adapted from *Eurobarometer*, 39, June 1993.
[2] *Eurobarometer*, 39, June 1993 and *Eurobarometer: Trend Variables, 1974-1992*, April 1993.
[3] Richard Sinnott, *Political Culture, Public Opinion and the Internationalization of Governance*, Dublin: University College Centre for European Economic and Public Affairs, 1992; Richard Sinnott, 'Integration Theory, Subsidiarity and the Internationalization of Issues: The Implications for Legitimacy', paper presented at the ECSA-World Conference, Brussels, 5-6 May 1994.

Maastricht, 88% of respondents felt attached to their country, 87% to their region, 85% to their town or village, but only 48% to the EC and 47% to Europe as a whole. 46% did not feel attached to the EC or Europe as a whole.[4] Such evidence raises questions about subjective feelings of identity.

The issue needs to be handled with great care, for emotions of this kind are often exploited to promote extreme nationalism and xenophobia. Indeed the sentiments themselves may sometimes be bound up with attitudes of superiority and imperialist nostalgia – and there are clearly elements of this in both Britain and France. Nevertheless, there are questions about identity which need to be considered dispassionately. For example, although Nordic countries are certainly not exempt from the general rise of racism in Europe, it would be illegitimate to ascribe the very reserved attitudes to the EU in those countries to chauvinistic sentiments. As two writers from the Centre for Peace and Conflict Research at the University of Copenhagen have argued, Danish attitudes can be explained neither by political apathy, nor any sense of economic exploitation:

> It is in the psychological field of society that we find the Danes' sense of loss on joining the EC. The feeling of losing something immaterial [i.e. non-material] – such as national identity, cultural significance, solidarity – deserves attention.[5]

Alan Branthwaite, who has explored the psychological basis of statehood, implies that such feelings are far more general. His conclusions on the EU are worth quoting at length:

> Attempts to change national identities . . . testify to their latent force and vigour. Aims to create a European identity among citizens of the European Community have not been notably successful so far. The most important line of cleavage in public opinion for or against European integration is based on nationality. This is a more important predictor of attitudes than national political affiliations, social class, age, occupations, or religion. A European identity is perceived as a potential threat to existing national identities and loyalty to the traditions and heritage of a country. So, at least among students, positive

---

[4] Cited in Karlheinz Reif, 'Cultural Convergence and Cultural Diversity as Factors in European Identity' in Garcia, op. cit., p. 138.

[5] Sørenson and Vaever, op. cit., p. 14.

attitudes to Europe are related to positive, secure feelings about one's nationality. Europe may be perceived positively if it is conceived of as compensating for weakness in one's own country; but still national attitudes predicate views of this wider union. There is little evidence of European unity being able to offer a compensatory identity to replace national identities, though it might be complementary. In general, a United Europe is perceived as an artificial entity for which there are no natural feelings or sympathy.[6]

Any conclusion that the 'nation' is to be regarded as the sole basis for identity must certainly be resisted. In reality, most so-called 'nations' are amalgams, which mutate over time, and many people have multiple identities. A democratic approach would foster these as a basis for a multi-cultural, internationalist Europe. Yet existing attitudes cannot be ignored on the false assumption that they will be eroded by rapid economic integration or institutional development. Rather, the pace of integration needs to take account of issues of identity. As Karlheinz Reif argues:

> Any conceivable 'European Political Union' would be and will remain a multinational and multilingual political system for handling affairs no longer manageable at national or regional level; it would not be transformed into a one-nation-state aimed at homogenizing societies and cultures.[7]

It is also necessary to ensure that:

> . . . there is enough political, economic and cultural self-confidence in Europe to remain open to the influence and impact of those other cultures which may not belong to what are generally regarded as the core European traditions but which are nevertheless present in our societies. An obvious example is European Islam [. . .] European identity is made up of a multiplicity of local identities.[8]

The implications of such observations are, I believe, that those who favour further integration need to respect subjective feelings of

[6] Alan Branthwaite, 'The Psychological Basis of Independent Statehood' in Jackson and James, op. cit., p. 60.
[7] Reif, op. cit., p. 51.
[8] Ibid.

identity. If premature political construction is advocated in a situation of economic insecurity, the extreme Right may find it easy to exploit such feelings and transform them into xenophobia and racism.

The second important factor to be taken into account – the growing diversity of the MS – is probably still more fundamental. The original conception of the 'six' was that the whole Community would move forward in unison towards 'an ever closer union' on the basis of common policies and common institutions. This notion continued to predominate throughout the 1970s and 1980s, but the strains of sustaining it have become increasingly apparent. The Maastricht Treaty, with its various 'opt-outs', was the first significant breach in the idea of uniform development. At first, the general assumption was that this was a purely temporary phase, attributable to internal divisions in the British Conservative Party. However, the concessions to Denmark before the second referendum, and the more general post-Maastricht crisis, soon led to further evidence of differentiation between the MS, particularly on the issue of monetary union. This was then compounded in the autumn of 1994, with both the German Christian Democrats and the French government openly advocating a two, or three tier EU, with an inner core moving far more quickly, and embracing more common policies, than the others. This caused alarm among MS which would be confined to the outer group, and the British government tried to respond with a proposal for a 'multi-level' EU, based on a free choice by each government as to which common policies to accept. Whatever the eventual outcome in the 1996 IGC, it is probable that the notion of different states moving at different speeds and levels in the integration process will set the pattern for the future.

The original 'six' had complementary economies and each regarded integration as beneficial for political reasons. Such circumstances no longer exist. There is now a far greater degree of economic differentiation between the MS, and a very wide range of differing priorities over practically the whole gamut of policy issues. Given the uneven development within the EU, the disappearance of the perceived common 'threat' in the former Soviet bloc, and the declining US interest in sustaining a rival economic power, it will be increasingly difficult to maintain common policies and uniform progress in the future. Moreover, the further enlargement in East-Central Europe, to which the EU is committed, will exacerbate all these problems.

It will introduce economies of a wholly different kind, and will probably make the current decision-making system unviable.

The growing complexity of the EU, and the need to respect the diversity in attitudes and subjective identities, thus suggest that, in future, 'variable geometry' will be built in to the EU system. For many of its long-term supporters this would be a matter for profound regret. The prospect of 'ever closer union' eventually leading to a federal Europe has been a compelling vision for many ever since World War Two and a 'multi-speed', 'multi-level' entity may appear much less alluring. It is also certainly true that this kind of EU involves dangers for peripheral areas, and for those facing the prospect of social exclusion. How, then, is it possible simultaneously to advance democracy and the EU, when both popular attitudes and divergent state interests appear to make a Europe of 'variable geometry' the most likely outcome of the current phase of development?

It will undoubtedly be extremely difficult, and the future could be bleak. However, this book has suggested *some* elements in a programme for democratisation, which could counteract many of the negative tendencies. This would include:

– a commitment to work towards full employment and to combat social exclusion;
– adherence to the Social Chapter and elaboration of a definition of social rights;
– a gradual increase (commensurate with GDP growth) of EU expenditure, with cohesion and redistribution as the major operating principles;
– incorporation of the European Convention of Human Rights into the domestic law of all MS and into EU law;
– acceptance of *jus soli* as the basis for citizenship;
– EU anti-racist legislation and the establishment of citizenship rights for non EU legal residents;
– an EU Freedom of Information Act;
– More effective accountability of the Council of Ministers and the European Council to both 'national' and European Parliaments; and
– the incorporation of Justice and Home Affairs (and the Common Foreign and Security Policy) into the normal EU policy-making process

If a programme containing these elements (and others not discussed in this book, such as environmental sustainability) were to prevail, a degree of 'variable geometry' could be countenanced. For it would then be possible to forge close collaboration and the development of a transnational consciousness in a Union which also respected diversity. Of course, there is nothing to ensure that the MS will implement these reforms, which would be anathema for some of the governments. Nor would such a programme preclude the danger of increasingly uneven development between the 'core' and the periphery. However, this would be preferable to a situation in which MS always strove to maintain uniformity with the most economically advanced no matter what the consequences for their populations. This kind of union would also leave considerable scope for different policies to be attempted within the MS, at both central and sub-central levels.

It is true that this would be a more complex Union than that outlined in federalist blueprints. Altiero Spinelli, and other founders of the 'European Idea', developed their views in the Fascist era in the belief that the 'nation-state' was inevitably an organ of expansion, which only a European Federation could prevent. Such ideas have been incorporated into the history of West European Integration and have played a role in constructing the institutions which have helped render unthinkable the idea of war between the former enemies. The Federal idea has thus played a key historical role, and it can continue to do so in other parts of Europe and in other regions of the world where traditional enmities remain to be overcome.

But it may be that, within the EU as a whole (though not within its MS), the time has now passed for the Federal model. In any case, it has never been demonstrated that all states, under all circumstances, are inevitably organs of aggression and expansion. Nor is it clear that regional supranational entities would necessarily be any less expansionist than the nation-states that they replaced.[9] It may be

---

[9] David Mitrany, a contemporary of Spinelli's, who advocated supranationalism on a functional basis, opposed European Federalism for this reason: 'There is little promise of peace in the mere change from the rivalry of Powers and alliances to the rivalry of whole continents, tightly organized and capable of achieving a high degree of, if not actual, self-sufficiency. Continental unions would have a more real chance than individual states to practise the autarky that makes for division.' David Mitrany, *A Working Peace System: An Argument for the Functional Development of International Organization*, London: National Peace Council Pamphlet no. 40 (4th edn, 1946), p. 20.

time to recognise that there is no single blueprint. The *primary* goal should not be supranationalism or the 'nation-state' or regionalism. These should all be regarded as subordinate to the more fundamental aim of constructing a Europe in which democracy and social justice exist at all levels. This is the challenge for the twenty-first century.

BIBLIOGRAPHY

Official EU sources

Commission of the European Communities, *Legal Instruments to Combat Racism and Xenophobia,* Luxembourg: office for Official Publications of the European Communities, 1993.

——,*1995 Annual Economic Report,* 1995 COM (94) 615 (final), 13 Dec. 1994.

——, Communication on Immigration and Asylum Policies, COM (94) 23 final, 23 Feb. 1994.

——, *Competitiveness and Cohesion: Trends in the Regions,* 5th Periodic Report on the Social and Economic Situation and Development of the Regions in the Community, Luxembourg: Office for Official Publications of the European Communities, 1994.

——, 'European Economic Area: Background Report', 13 Jan. 1994.

The European Parliament and the Parliaments of the Member States: Parliamentary Scrutiny and arrangements for Cooperation, Brussels/ Luxembourg: European Parliament, Division for Relations with the Parliaments of the Member States, July 1994.

European Parliament Report drawn up on behalf of the Committee of Inquiry into Racism and Xenophobia on the findings of the Committee of Inquiry (rapporteur: Glyn Ford), Luxembourg: Office for Official Publications of the European Communities, 1991.

European Social Policy: A Way Forward for the Union, Brussels: Commission of the European Communities White Paper, COM (94) 333 final/2, Brussels, 27 July 1994.

European Social Policy: Options for the Union (Green Paper) Luxembourg: Office for Official Publications of the European Communities, Nov. 1993.

Facts through figures: A Statistical Portrait of the European Union, Luxembourg: Office for Official Publications of the European Communities: EUROSTAT, 1994.

Groeben, Hans von der, *The European Community: The Formative Years: The Struggle to Establish the Common Market and the Political Union (1958-1966),* Luxembourg: Office for Official Publications of the European Communities, 1987.

Growth, Competitiveness, Employment, Brussels: Commission of the European Communities White Paper, COM (93) 700 final, 10 Dec. 1993.

Maastricht – The Treaty on European Union: The Position of the European Parliament, Luxembourg: Office for Official Publications of the European Communities, 1992.

Nomenclature of Territorial Units for Statistics, Luxembourg: Office for Official Publications of the European Communities, EUROSTAT, March 1992.

'Report of the Committee on Social Affairs, Employment and the Working Environment on the European Parliament's approach to the revision of the European Social Fund', European Parliament Session Documents, A3-0057/93, 18 Feb. 1993.

'Result of the hearings of the designated European Commissioners before the Committees of the European Parliament', *Europe Documents*, no. 1919, 18 Jan. 1995.

Treaty on European Union, Luxembourg: Office for Official Publications of the European Communities, 1992.

Trend Variables, 1974-1992, Luxembourg: Office for Official Publications of the European Communities, Eurobarometer, April 1993.

'Unemployment in Europe', Commission of the European Communities, COM (94) 381 final, 14 Sept. 1994.

Venturini, P., *1992: The European Social Dimension*, Luxembourg: Office for Official Publications of the European Communities, 1989.

Women in the European Community: Rapid Reports, Population and Social Conditions, no. 10, 1993, Luxembourg: Office for Official Publications of the European Communities.

Bulletins and newspapers

Agence Europe.
Eurolink Age Bulletin, November 1990.
European Information Service, 155, 19 Dec. 1994, (Local Government International Bureau).
The Guardian (London).
Women of Europe Newsletter.

Books

Amin, A., and N. Thrift, *Globalization, Institutions and Regional Development in Europe*, Oxford University Press, 1994.

Anderson, Svein S., and Kjell A. Eliassen, *Making Policy in Europe: The Europeification of National Policy-Making*, London: Sage, 1993.

Andrews, Geoff (ed.), *Citizenship*, London: Lawrence and Wishart, 1991.

Arblaster, Anthony, *Democracy*, Milton Keynes: Open University Press, 1987.

Aron, Raymond, *Peace and War: A Theory of International Relations*, New York: Doubleday, 1966.

Arter, David, *The Politics of European Integration in the Twentieth Century*, Aldershot: Dartmouth, 1993.

Austin, John, *The Province of Jurisprudence Determined*, New York: Humanities Press, 1965.

Batley, Richard, and Gerry Stoker (eds), *Local Government in Europe*, London: Macmillan, 1991.

Blainpain, R. (ed.), *Comparative Labour Law and Industrial Relations*, Deventer: Kluwer, 1985.

Bodin, Jean, *On Sovereignty* (ed. and transl. Julian H. Franklin), Cambridge University Press, 1992.

Brewster, Chris, and Paul Teague, *European Community Social Policy: Its Impact on the UK*, London: Institute of Personnel Management, 1989.

Brown, C. (ed.), *Political Restructuring in Europe: Ethical Perspectives*, London: Routledge, 1994.

Brouwer, Frank, Valerio Lintner and Michael Newman (eds), *Economic Policy Making and the European Union*, London: Federal Trust, 1994.

Bull, Hedley, *The Anarchical Society: A Study of Order in World Politics*, London: Macmillan, 1977.

Bulmer, S., and W. Wessels, *The European Council*, London: Macmillan, 1987.

Bulmer, S., and W. Paterson, *The Federal Republic of Germany and the European Community*, London: Allen and Unwin, 1987.

Bunyan, Tony (ed.), *Statewatching the new Europe: A Handbook on the European State*, London: Statewatch, 1993.

Camilleri, Joseph A., and Jim Falk, *The End of Sovereignty*, Aldershot: Edward Elgar, 1992.

Cafruny, Alan W., and Glenda G. Rosenthal, *The State of the European Community: The Maastricht Debates and Beyond*, London: Longman, 1993.

Caporaso, James A. (ed.), *The Elusive State*, London: Sage, 1989.

Carr, E.H., *Nationalism and After*, London: Macmillan, 1968.

———, *The Twenty Year Crisis: An Introduction to the Study of International Relations*, London: Macmillan, 1962.

Cash, William, *Against a Federal Europe*, London: Duckworth, 1991.

Church, Clive H., and Dermot Keogh (eds), *The Single European Act – A Transnational Study*, Dublin: Erasmus Bureau, 1992.

Church, C., and D. Phinnemore, *European Union and European Community: A Handbook and Commentary on the Post-Maastricht Treaties*, Brighton: Harvester Wheatsheaf, 1994.

Cobban, Alfred, *The Nation State and National Self-Determination*, London: Fontana, 1968.

Collins, D., *The European Communities: The Social Policy of the First Phase*, vol. II, London: Martin Robertson, 1975.

Collinson, S., *Beyond Borders: West European Migration Policy towards the 21st Century*, London: RIIA, 1993.

Corbett, Richard, *The Treaty of Maastricht: From Conception to Ratification: A Comprehensive Reference Guide*, London: Longman, 1993.

Cowie, Harry, and John Pinder, *A Recovery Strategy for Europe*, London: Federal Trust, 1993.

Dekker, Wisse, *Europe – 1990*, Eindhoven: Philips, 1985.

Dinan, Desmond, *Ever Closer Union? An Introduction to the European Community*, London: Macmillan, 1994.

Doughty, Peter J., and Michael T. Newton, *Spain: A Guide to Political and Economic Institutions*, Cambridge University Press, 1989.

Dunn, John, *The Political Thought of John Locke*, Cambridge University Press, 1969.

Dunn, John (ed.), *Democracy – The Unfinished Journey*, Oxford University Press, 1992.

Edwards, G., and D. Spence (eds), *The Commission of the European Communities*, London: Longman, 1994.

Edye, Dave, *Immigrant Labour and Government Policy*, Aldershot: Gower, 1987.

—— and Valerio Lintner, *Contemporary Europe*, Brighton: Harvester Wheatsheaf, 1996.

El-Agraa, A.M. (ed.), *Economics of the European Community*, London: Philip Allan, 1990.

Ellwood, D., *Rebuilding Europe: Western Europe, America and Postwar Reconstruction*, London: Longman, 1992.

Esping-Anderson, G., *The Three Worlds of Welfare Capitalism*, Oxford/- Cambridge: Polity Press, 1990.

Evans, P., D. Rueschmeyer and T. Skocpol (eds) *Bringing the State Back In*, Cambridge University Press, 1985.

Faber, M.J., *et al.*, *Nationalism and European Integration: Civil Society Perspectives*, Prague: Helsinski Citizens Assembly, 1992.

Friedman, Milton, *Capitalism and Freedom*, Chicago University Press, 1962.

Galbraith, J.K., *The Affluent Society*, London: Hamish Hamilton, 2nd rev. edn, 1969.

García, Soledad (ed.), *European Identity and the Search for Legitimacy*, London: Pinter, 1993.

Garton Ash, Timothy, *In Europe's Name: Germany and the Divided Continent*, London: Cape, 1993.

George, Stephen, *Politics and Policy in the European Community*, Oxford University Press, 1985.

Giddens, Anthony, *The Nation State and Violence*, Berkeley: University of California Press, 1985.

Gilpin, R., *War and Change in World Politics*, Cambridge University Press, 1981.

Haas, Ernst B., *The Uniting of Europe: Political, Social and Economic Forces, 1950-1957*, Stanford University Press, 2nd edn, 1968.

Haas, Ernst B., *The Obsolescence of Regional Integration Theory*, Berkeley: University of California Press, 1975.

Hall, John A. (ed.), *States in History*, Oxford: Blackwell, 1986.

Hall, Peter A., Jack Hayward and Howard Machin, *Developments in French Politics*, London: Macmillan, 1990.

Harvie, Christopher, *The Rise of Regional Europe*, London: Routledge, 1994.

Haworth, Alan, *Anti-Libertarianism: Markets, Philosophy and Myth*, London: Routledge, 1994.

Hayek, F.A., *The Road to Serfdom*, London: Routledge and Kegan Paul, 1944.

Heater, Derek, *Citizenship: The Civic Ideal in World History, Politics and Education*, Harlow: Longman, 1990.

Hebbert, M., and H. Machin (eds), *Regionalisation in France, Italy and Spain*, London School of Economics, 1984.

Held, David, *Political Theory and the Modern State*, Oxford: Polity Press and Blackwell, 1989.

—— (ed.), *Political Theory Today*, Oxford/Cambridge: Polity Press, 1991.

—— (ed.), *Prospects for Democracy*, Oxford/Cambridge: Polity Press, 1993.

Hine, David, *Governing Italy: The Politics of Bargained Pluralism*, Oxford University Press, 1993.

Hinsley, F.H., *Sovereignty*, 2nd edn, Cambridge University Press, 1986.

Hirst, Paul, *The Pluralist Theory of the State*, London: Routledge, 1989.

——, *Associative Democracy*, Oxford/Cambridge: Polity Press, 1994.

Hobbes, Thomas, *Leviathan* (ed. and intro. C.B. Macpherson), Harmondsworth: Penguin, 1968.

Holland, Stuart, *The European Imperative: Economic and Social Cohesion in the 1990s*, Nottingham: Spokesman, 1993.

Hurwitz, Leon, and Christian Lequesne (eds), *The State of the European Community: Policies, Institutions and Debates in the Transition Years*, Boulder, CO: Lynne Rienner, 1991.

Hutton, Will, *The State We're In*, London: Cape, 1995.

Hyland, James L., *Democratic Theory: The Philosophical Foundations*, Manchester University Press, 1995.

Jackson, Robert H., and Alan James (eds), *States in a Changing World: A Contemporary Analysis*, Oxford: Clarendon Press, 1993.

Jacobs, Francis, and Richard Corbett, *The European Parliament*, Harlow: Longman, 1992.

Jeffery, Charlie, and Roland Sturm, *Federalism, Unification and European Integration*, London: Cass, 1993.

Jenkins, Roy, *European Diary, 1977-1981*, London: Collins, 1989.

Joly, Danièle, *et al.*, *Refugees: Asylum in Europe*, London: Minority Rights Group, 1992.

Kearney, R., *Across the Frontiers: Ireland in the 1990s*, Dublin: Wolfhound, 1988.

Keegan, William, *The Spectre of Capitalism: The Future of the World Economy After the Fall of Communism*, London: Vintage, 1993.

Kennedy, Paul, *Preparing for the Twenty-First Century*, London: Fontana Press, 1994.

Keohane, Robert O. and Joseph Nye, *Power and Interdependence*, London: Harper Collins, 2nd edn, 1989.

Keohane, Robert, and Stanley Hoffmann (eds), *The New European Community: Decisionmaking and Institutional Change*, Boulder, CO: Westview Press, 1991.

E. Kirchner, *Decision-Making in the European Community: The Council Presidency and European Integration*, Manchester University Press, 1992.

King, Preston, *Federalism and Federation*, Beckenham: Croom Helm, 1982.

King, Russell (ed.), *Ireland, Europe and the Single Europe*, Dublin: Geographical Society of Ireland, 1993.

Laski, Harold, *The Foundations of Sovereignty*, London: Allen and Unwin, 1922.

———, *The Danger of Being a Gentleman and other Essays*, London: Allen and Unwin, 1939.

———, *A Grammar of Politics*, 4th edn, London: Allen and Unwin, 1938.

Laursen, Finn, and Sophie Vanhoonacker (eds), *The Intergovernmental Conference on Political Union*, Maastricht: Martinus Nijhoff, 1992.

Layton-Henry, Z. (ed.), *The Political Rights of Migrant Workers in Western Europe*, London: Sage, 1989.

Levi, Lucio (ed.), *Altiero Spinelli and Federalism in Europe and the World*, Milan: Franco Angeli, 1990.

Lindberg, Leon, *The Political Dynamics of European Economic Integration*, Stanford University Press, 1963.

——— and Stuart Scheingold, *Europe's Would-Be Polity*, Englewood Cliffs, NJ: Prentice-Hall, 1970.

Lintner, Valerio, and Sonia Mazey, *The European Community: Economic and Political Aspects*, Maidenhead: McGraw-Hill, 1991.

John Locke, *Two Treatises of Government* (ed. and intro. Thomas I. Cook), New York: Hafner, 1969.

Juliet Lodge (ed.), *The European Community and the Challenge of the Future*, London: Pinter, 1989.

——— (ed.), *The European Community and the Challenge of the Future*, London: Pinter (2nd edn), 1993.

J. Lovenduski and P. Norris, *Gender and Party Politics*, London: Sage, 1993.

Lyck, Lise (ed.), *Denmark and EC Membership Evaluated*, London: Pinter, 1992.

Macpherson, C.B., *The Political Theory of Possessive Individualism*, Oxford University Press, 1962.

McGrew, A.G. and Paul G. Lewis, *Global Politics*, Oxford/Cambridge: Polity Press, 1992.

McLellan, David (ed.), *Karl Marx: Selected Writings*, Oxford University Press, 1977.

Maddison, A., *Dynamic Forces in Capitalist Development*, Oxford University Press, 1991.

Marjolin, Robert, *Architect of European Union: Memoirs, 1911-1986*, London: Weidenfeld and Nicolson, 1989.

Marshall, T.H., *Citizenship and Social Class*, Cambridge University Press, 1950.

Mazey, Sonia, and Michael Newman (eds), *Mitterrand's France*, Beckenham: Croom Helm, 1987.

Mazey, Sonia, and Jeremy Richardson (eds), *Lobbying in the European Community*, Oxford University Press, 1993.

Meehan, Elizabeth, *Citizenship and the European Community*, London: Sage 1993.

Hugh Miall, *Shaping the New Europe*, London: Pinter/RIIA, 1993.

Miliband, David (ed.), *A More Perfect Union? Britain and the New Europe*, London: IPPR, 1992.

Milward, Alan, *The European Rescue of the Nation State*, London: Routledge, 1992.

—— *et al.*, *The Frontier of National Sovereignty – History and Theory*, London: Routledge, 1993.

Michie, Jonathan, and John Grieve Smith, *Unemployment in Europe*, London: Academic Press, 1994.

Mjøset, Lars, *The Irish Economy in a Comparative Institutional Perspective*, Dublin: National Economic and Social Council, 1992.

Morgan, R., and C. Bray (eds), *Partners and Rivals in Western Europe: Britain, France, Germany*, Aldershot: Gower, 1986.

Morgenthau, H.J., *Politics Among Nations*, New York: Knopf, 1960.

Murray, Robin, *Local Space: Europe and the New Regionalism*, Stevenage/Manchester: SEEDS/CLES, 1991.

Newman, Michael, *Harold Laski – A Political Biography*, London: Macmillan, 1993.

——, *Socialism and European Unity: The Dilemma of the Left in Britain and France*, London: Hurst, 1983.

Nicholls, David, *The Pluralist State*, London: Macmillan, 1975.

Nozick, Robert, *Anarchy, State and Utopia*, Oxford: Basil Blackwell, 1974.

Nugent, Neill, *The Government and Politics of the European Union*, 3rd edn, London: Macmillan, 1994.

Nuttall, Simon, *European Political Cooperation*, Oxford: Clarendon Press, 1992.

Oldfield, Adrian, *Citizenship and Community*, London: Routledge, 1990.

O'Nuallain, Colm (ed.), *The Presidency of the European Council of Ministers:*

Impacts and Implications for National Governments, London: Croom Helm, 1985.

Parry, G., G. Moyser and M. Day, *Political Participation and Democracy in Britain*, Cambridge University Press, 1992.

Pinder, John, *European Community – the Building of a Union*, Oxford University Press, 1991.

Plamenatz, John, *The English Utilitarians*, Oxford: Blackwell, 1958.

Pollard, S., Will Hutton, Robert Kuttner *et al.*, *Jobs and Growth: The International Perspective*, London: Fabian Society, 1994.

Putnam, R.D., *Making Democracy Work: Civic Traditions in Modern Italy*, Princeton University Press, 1993.

Redmond, John (ed.), *Prospective Europeans*, Brighton: Harvester Wheatsheaf, 1994.

Rhodes, R., *Beyond Westminster and Whitehall: The Sub-Central Government of Britain*, London: Unwin Hyman, 1988.

Roche, Maurice, *Rethinking Citizenship: Welfare, Ideology and Change in Modern Society*, Oxford/Cambridge: Polity Press, 1992.

Ross, George, *Jacques Delors and European Integration*, Oxford/Cambridge: Polity Press, 1995.

Rousseau, Jean-Jacques, *The Social Contract* (ed. and intro. Charles Frankel), New York: Hafner, 1947.

Rudden, Bernard, and Derk Wyatt (ed.), *Basic Community Laws*, Oxford: Clarendon Press, 1980.

Ronon, Dov, *The Quest for Self-Determination*, New Haven: Yale University Press, 1979.

Scharpf, F., *Crisis and Choice in European Social Democracy*, Ithaca, NY: Cornell University Press, 1991.

Semb, Anne Julie, *The Normative Foundation of the Principle of Non-Intervention*, Oslo: PRIO, 1992.

Shanks, Michael, *European Social Policy Today and Tomorrow*, Oxford: Pergamon, 1977.

Shonfield, Andrew, *Europe: Journey to an Unknown Destination*, Harmondsworth: Penguin, 1972.

Silverman, M., *Deconstructing the Nation: Immigration, Racism and Citizenship in Modern France*, London: Routledge, 1992.

Simonian, Haig, *The Privileged Partnership: Franco-German Relations and the European Community, 1969-1984*, Oxford: Clarendon Press, 1985.

Richard Sinnott, *Political Culture, Public Opinion and the Internationalization of Governance*, Dublin: University College Centre for European Economic and Public Affairs, 1922.

Smith, G., W.E. Paterson and P. Merkl (eds), *Developments in West German Politics*, London: Macmillan, 1989.

Spencer, Michael, *1992 and All That: Civil Liberties in the Balance*, London: Civil Liberties Trust, 1990.

Steiner, Josephine, *A Textbook of EC Law*, 4th edn, London: Blackstone Press, 1994.

Story, J. (ed.), *The New Europe: Politics, Government and Economy since 1945*, Oxford: Blackwell, 1993.

Taylor, Paul, *The Limits of European Integration*, Beckenham: Croom Helm, 1983.

Teague, Paul, and John Grahl, *Industrial Relations and European Integration*, London: Lawrence and Wishart, 1992.

Thomson, David, *Democracy in France since 1870*, Oxford University Press, 1977.

Tivey, L. (ed.), *The Nation State and the Formation of Modern Politics*, London: Martin Robertson, 1981.

Turner, Bryan S., *Citizenship and Capitalism*, London: Allen and Unwin, 1986.

Van Ham, P., *The EC, Eastern Europe and European Unity*, London: Pinter, 1993.

Vaughan, Richard, *Post-War Integration in Europe*, London: Edward Arnold, 1976.

Vincent, Andrew, *Theories of the State*, Oxford: Blackwell, 1987.

Wallace, William (ed.), *The Dynamics of European Integration*, London: Pinter/RIIA, 1990.

——,*The Transformation of Western Europe*, London: Pinter, 1990.

Waltz, K.N., *The Theory of International Politics*, Reading, MA: Addison-Wesley, 1979.

Wilde, Lawrence, *Modern European Socialism*, Aldershot: Dartmouth, 1994.

Williams, Merryn (ed.), *Revolutions 1775-1830*, Harmondsworth: Penguin/Open University Press, 1971.

Wills, Roy, *France, Germany and the New Europe*, Stanford University Press, 1968.

Wise, Mark, and Richard Gibb, *Single Market to Social Europe*, London: Longman, 1993.

Wright, Tony, *Citizens and Subjects*, London: Routledge, 1994.

Young, John W., *Britain and European Unity, 1945-92*, London: Macmillan, 1993.

Pamphlets and reports

Baskin, Gershon, *Jerusalem of Peace: Sovereignty and Territory in Jerusalem's Future*, Jerusalem: Israel/Palestine Centre for Research and Information, 1994.

Church, Clive, *Integration Theory in the 1990s*, London: University of North London Press, 1996.

Cini, Michelle, *European Community Competition Policy*, London: University of North London Press, 1992.

Edye, Dave, *1992 and the Free Movement of Labour*, London: University of North London Press, 1990.

Europe's Future: Four Scenarios, London: Federal Trust, 1991.

Held, David, *Democracy and the New International Order*, London: Institute for Public Policy Research, 1993.

Holtham, Gerald, *Economic Integration After Maastricht*, London: IPPR, 1993.

Galbraith, J.K., 'The Good Society Considered: the economic dimension', Annual Lecture of the Journal of Law and Society, Cardiff Law School, 26 Jan. 1994.

Klepsch, Egon A., 'A Europe of the Regions', inaugural Sunderland Lecture, 9 July 1993, London: UK Office of European Parliament, 1993.

Miles, Lee, *Enlargement of the European Union*, London: University of North London Press, 1995.

Mitrany, David, *A Working Peace System: An Argument for the Functional Development of International Organization*, London: National Peace Council Pamphlet no. 40 (4th edn, 1946).

Mjøset, Lars, *et al.*, *Norwegian Political Economy*, Report of the Institute for Social Research, Oslo, 1994.

Newman, Michael, *The European Community – Where does the Power Lie?*, London: University of North London Press, 1993.

Newton, K., *Is Small Really so Beautiful? Is Big Really so Ugly?* Glasgow: University of Strathclyde Centre for the Study of Public Policy, no. 18, 1978.

Put Europe to Work, Report of the Parliamentary Group of the Party of European Socialists, Brussels, 1993.

Smith, Julie, *Citizens' Europe? The European Elections and the Role of the European Parliament*, London: Royal Institute of International Affairs, 1994.

Colin Turner, *Trans-European Networks: The Infrastructure for the Internal Market*, London: University of North London Press, 1994.

Withdrawal from the EEC (and five background research papers), Labour Party, 1981.

Articles

Anderson, James, 'Problems of Inter-state economic integration: Northern Ireland and Irish Republic in the European Community', *Political Geography*, 13, no. 1, Jan. 1994.

—— and James Goodman, 'Northern Ireland: dependency, class and cross-border integration in the European Union', *Capital and Class*, 44, autumn 1994.

Angell, Valter (ed.), 'Norway Facing a Changing Europe', *Norwegian Foreign Policy Studies*, no. 1979, Oslo 1992.

Aron, Raymond, 'Is Multinational Citizenship Possible?' *Social Research*, 4, 1974.

Artis, M.J., 'The Maastricht Road to Monetary Union', *Journal of Common Market Studies*, 30, 3, Sept. 1992.

Baker, D., A. Gamble and S. Ludlam, 'Conservative Splits and European Integration', *Political Quarterly*, 4, 1993.

——, 'The Maastricht vote and Conservative MPs', *Parliamentary Affairs*, 2, 1993.

——, 'The Parliamentary Siege of Maastricht 1993: Conservative Divisions and British Ratification', *Parliamentary Affairs*, 1, 1994.

Benyon, John, 'Policing the European Union: The Changing Basis of Co-operation on Law Enforcement', *International Affairs*, 70, 3 July 1994.

Bogdanor, Vernon, 'The Future of the European Community: Two Models of Democracy', *Government and Opposition*, 21, 2, 1986.

——, 'The June 1989 Elections and the Institutions of the Community', *Government and Opposition*, 24, 2, 1989.

—— and Geoffrey Woodcock, 'The European Community and Sovereignty', *Parliamentary Affairs*, 44, 4, Oct. 1991.

Closa, Carlos, 'The Concept of Citizenship in the Treaty on European Union' in *Common Market Law Review*, 29, 6, Dec. 1992.

Corbett, Richard, 'The Intergovernmental Conference on Political Union', *Journal of Common Market Studies*, 30, 3, Sept. 1992.

Doogan, K., 'The Social Charter and the Europeanisation of Employment and Social Policy', *Policy and Politics*, 20, 3, July 1993.

Edye, Dave, 'Migration, Race, Asylum, Refugees', *Labour Focus on Eastern Europe*, 44, 1, Jan. 1993.

Endo, Ken, 'The Principle of Subsidiarity: From Johannes Althusius to Jacques Delors', *Hokkaido Law Review*, 44, 6, 1994.

Gaffikin, F., and M. Morrissey, 'In Pursuit of the Holy Grail: Combating Local Poverty in an Unequal Society', *Local Economy*, 9, 2, Aug. 1994.

John Grahl and Paul Teague, 'Economic Citizenship in the New Europe', *Political Quarterly*, 4, October 1994.

David Held and Anthony McGrew, 'Globalization and the Liberal Democratic State', *Government and Opposition*, 28, 2, spring 1993.

'The Hoover affair and social dumping', (no author's name), *European Industrial Relations Review*, 230, March 1993.

Kersbergen, Kees van, and Bertjan Verbeek, 'The Politics of Subsidiarity in the European Union', *Journal of Common Market Studies*, 32, 2, June 1994.

Koslowski, Rey, 'Intra-EU Migration, Citizenship and Political Union', *Journal of Common Market Studies*, 32, 3, Sept. 1994.

Lintner, Valerio, 'Monetary Integration, Recession and the Left', *Labour Focus on Eastern Europe*, 1, 1993.

Lingle, Christopher, 'The EC Social Charter, Social Democracy and Post – 1992 Europe', *West European Politics*, 14, 1, Jan. 1991.

Juliet Lodge, 'Transparency and Democratic Legitimacy', *Journal of Common Market Studies*, 32, 3, Sept. 1994.

Majone, Giandomenico, 'The European Community Between Social Policy and Social Regulation', *Journal of Common Market Studies*, 31, 2, June 1993.

Marquand, David, 'Reinventing Federalism: Europe and the Left', *New Left Review*, 203, January 1994.

Mazey, Sonia, 'European Community Action on Behalf of Women: The Limits of Legislation', *Journal of Common Market Studies*, 27, 1, Sept. 1988.

Meehan, Elizabeth, 'Citizenship and the European Community', *Political Quarterly*, 62, 2, April-June 1993.

Mingione, Enzo, 'Italy: the resurgence of regionalism', *International Affairs*, 69, 2, April 1993.

Mjøset, Lars, 'The Nordic Model Never Existed, but Does it Have a Future?', *Scandinavian Studies*, 64, 4, fall 1992.

Moravcsik, A., 'Preferences and Power in the European Community: A Liberal Intergovernmentalist Approach', *Journal of Common Market Studies*, 4, Sept. 1993.

Muller, W., and V. Wright, 'The State in Western Europe: Retreat or Redefinition?', *West European Politics*, 17, 3, July 1994.

Noel, E., 'The Permanent Representatives Committee and the Deepening of the Communities', *Government and Opposition*, 6, 4, 1971.

Pinder, John, 'The European Union After Maastricht: How Federal?', *New European*, 5, 3, 1992.

——, 'European Unity and the Nation State: A Case for Neo-Federalism?', *International Affairs*, 62, 1, Jan. 1986.

Rhodes, M., 'The future of the "Social Dimension": Labour Market Regulation in Post-1992 Europe', *Journal of Common Market Studies*, 30, 3, March 1992.

Scott, A., J. Peterson, and D. Millar, 'Subsidiarity: A "Europe of the Regions" v. the British Constitution?', *Journal of Common Market Studies*, 32, 1, March 1994.

Shackleton, Michael, 'Interparliamentary Cooperation and the 1996 IGC' in *The Changing Role of Parliaments in the European Union*, Maastricht: EIPA, 1995.

Smith, Alisdair, and Helen Wallace, 'The European Union: Towards a Policy for Europe', *International Affairs*, 70, 3, July 1994.

Streeck, Wolfgang, and Philippe Schmitter, 'From National Corporatism to Transnational Pluralism: Organised Interests in the Single European Market', *Politics and Society*, 19, 2, June 1991.

Thomas, Stafford T., 'Assessing MEP Influence on British EC Policy', with comments by James Elles, MEP, and David Martin, MEP, *Government and Opposition*, 27, 1, winter 1992.

Waever, Ole, 'Identity, Integration and Security: Solving the Sovereignty Puzzle in E.U. Studies', *Journal of International Affairs*, 48, 2, winter 1995.

Walby, Sylvia, 'Is Citizenship Gendered?' *Sociology*, 28, no. 2, May 1994.

Walker, R.B.J., 'State Sovereignty and the Articulation of Political Space/Time', *Millenium*, 20, 3, winter 1991.

Wallace, Helen, 'European Governance in Turbulent Times', *Journal of Common Market Studies*, 31, 3, Sept. 1993.

——, 'Remaking the EC', *International Affairs*, 67, 4, Oct. 1991.

Weiler, J.H.H., 'Journey to an unknown destination: A Retrospective and Prospective of the European Court of Justice in the arena of political integration', *Journal of Common Market Studies*, 31, 4, Dec. 1993.

Wessels, Wolfgang, 'Rationalizing Maastricht: The Search for an Optimal Strategy of the new Europe', *International Affairs*, 70, 3, July 1994.

Wincott, Daniel, 'The EC Social Charter: An Alternative Prospectus – A Response to Christopher Lingle', *West European Politics*, 16, 2, April 1993.

Witte, E., 'Belgian Federalism: Towards Complexity and Asymmetry', *West European Politics*, 15, 4, Oct. 1992.

Unpublished works

Armstrong, Harvey W., and Robert Read, 'Federalism and Subsidiarity: Lessons from European Micro-States and EC Autonomous Regions', paper presented at 2nd European Community Studies Associations-World Conference, Brussels, 5-6 May 1994.

Bache, I., S. George and R. Rhodes, 'The European Union and Subnational Authorities in the United Kingdom', paper presented at ESRC Research Seminar, 'State Autonomy in the European Community: National Administrative Styles and the EC Tier of National Policy Making', Christ Church, Oxford, 22 June 1994.

Burgess, Michael, 'Federalism, Subsidiarity and the European Community', paper presented at Eighth Lothian Conference, 'Subsidiarity and Federalism within the European Union', Royal Holloway and Bedford New College, 17-18 Dec. 1993.

Clark, Adrienne, 'Some Are More Equal Than Others: A study of European Community gender equality policies with particular reference to women in the United Kingdom and women in France', MA thesis, South Bank University, 1993.

Church, Clive, 'Theorising the Expansion of Western Europe', paper presented at 2nd European Community Studies Associations–World Conference, Brussels, 5–6 May 1994.

Crick, Paul, 'All Men are Created Equal? A Study of UK law in relation to the rights of gay men and lesbians, and its position and possible contribution to European Law', dissertation for Postgraduate Diploma in Modern European Studies, University of North London, 1994.

Ginderachter, J. van, 'The Belgian Federal Model', paper presented at Eighth Lothian Conference, 'Subsidiarity and Federalism within the European Union', Royal Holloway and Bedford New College, 17–18 Dec. 1993.

Hirst, Paul, 'Maastricht, The Missed Turning Point: The European Community Between Integration and Decline', paper presented at Eighth Lothian Conference, 'Subsidiarity and Federalism within the European Union', Royal Holloway and Bedford New College, 17–18 Dec. 1993.

Hueglin, Thomas O., 'Federalism, Subsidiarity and the European Tradition: Some Contextual and Critical Clarifications', paper presented at 2nd European Community Studies Associations–World Conference, Brussels, 5–6 May 1994.

Jachtenfuchs, M., 'Theoretical Reflections on the Efficiency and Democracy of European Governance Structures', paper presented at 2nd European Community Studies Associations–World Conference, Brussels, 5–6 May 1994.

Jeffery, Charlie, 'The *Länder* Strike Back: Structures and Procedures of European Integration Policy-Making in the German Federal System', paper presented at ESRC Research Seminar on State Autonomy in the European Community, Christ Church, Oxford, June 1994.

Kol, J., 'Subsidiarity: Concept and Application', paper presented at Eighth Lothian Conference, 'Subsidiarity and Federalism within the European Union', Royal Holloway and Bedford New College, 17–18 Dec. 1993.

Matlary, Janne Haaland, 'Integration Theory and International Relations Theory: What does the elephant look like today and how should it be studied?', paper presented at 2nd European Community Studies Associations–World Conference, Brussels, 5–6 May 1994.

Nakamura, H., 'Theory of European Integration and Democratic Decision-Making', paper presented at 2nd European Community Studies Associations–World Conference, Brussels, 5–6 May 1994.

Norton, Philip, 'National Parliaments and the European Union', paper presented at Workshop of Parliamentary Scholars and Parliamentarians, Berlin, 19–20 Aug. 1994.

Piening, C.C., 'The Role of the European Parliament in the EC's Integration Process 1986–92', MA thesis, University of Kent, Sept. 1992.

Sinnott, Richard, 'Integration Theory, Subsidiarity and the Internationalization of Issues: The Implications for Legitimacy', paper presented at 2nd European Community Studies Associations-World Conference, Brussels, 5-6 May 1994.

Spicker, Paul, 'Concepts of Subsidiarity in the European Community', paper presented at Conference on 'Democracy and Subsidiarity', University of Manchester, 12 Nov. 1993.

Thompson, Grahame F., 'Unitary State, Federation or Confederal Public Power: What Principles for European Political Unity?', paper presented at 2nd European Community Studies Associations-World Conference, Brussels, 5-6 May 1994.

Ugur, Mehmet, 'Integration Theory Re-Visited: State-Society Relations as Key for Understanding European Integration', paper presented at 2nd European Community Studies Associations-World Conference, Brussels, 5-6 May 1994.

Walters, Menno, 'The Principle of Subsidiarity in European Practice', paper presented at Eighth Lothian Conference, 'Subsidiarity and Federalism within the European Union', Royal Holloway and Bedford New College, 17-18 Dec. 1993.

INDEX

accession, of new members, 177, 179n11
accountability, 40, 110, 166, 173, 183, 188, 190, 192, 199, 203, 209
accounting, 88
acquis communautaire, 85, 188-89, 192
Adonnino, Pietro, 152
Africa, 161
agreements: 67, 94, 179n11; association, 177; employment, 86; Four Motors, 115; Luxembourg, 33, 33n14; regional, 115; Schengen, 164-5
agriculture: 30, 45, 175; CAP, 30, 33, 37n24, 68, 70, 72, 80, 175
aid: industry, 65, 65n45, 71, 72; regional, 37, 80, 114, 118, 131
Air France, 65n45, 72
Andorra, 65
Aron, Raymond, 147-50 *passim*
Asia, 55n11, 161
'assent procedure', 177, 179n11
'Assizes meeting', 196
association, right of, 80, 84, 85, 141
asylum policies: 162, 165, 165n73, 167, 177, 198; Dublin Convention on, 165n73
Atlantic area, 115
Austin, John, 6, 12
Austria, 41, 42, 63n34, 64

Bahl, Kamlesh, 171
balance of payments, 60, 61, 70, 74
banks, 68-9
bargaining, collective, 80, 84, 85
Belgium, 41, 89, 90, 112, 122, 126, 126, 126n48, 128, 130, 136, 152, 163, 197
Benelux, 72, 164, 199
Bjerregaerd, Ritt, 104n52
Bodin, Jean, 5, 12
Bogdanor, Vernon, 185-8 *passim*

Bonino, Emilia, 104n52
border controls, external, 167, 169 internal, 164-5
Brandt, Willy, 81
Branthwaite, Alan, 206-7
Brewster, Chris, 94
Britain: 1-3 *passim*, 35, 47n44, 55n10, 63, 64, 72, 77, 84-8 *passim*, 100, 102, 107, 113, 114, 119, 126, 129, 132, 135, 137, 139, 152, 159-61 *passim*, 163, 172, 180, 194, 201, 205, 206, 208; Act of Union, 147; British Nationality Act (1981), 156; Charter 88, 139, 139n3; Commission for Racial Equality, 171; Commonwealth Immigration Act (1961), 156; Conservative Party, 1-3 *passim*, 3n5, 34, 42, 53, 91, 99, 113, 119, 126, 135, 139, 191, 198, 208; and EMU, 37, 39; and EU budget, 2, 34, 35, 37, 82; Labour Party, 57, 90, 91n29, 113, 192, 198; and Maastricht Treaty, 39, 123, 124, 191, 194; 'opt-outs' from Treaty, 39, 98, 194, 208; and regional policy, 118-19; and social policy, 37, 40, 83, 86-95 *passim*, 85n20, 98, 99, 103; and subsidiarity, 123, 124; and voting, 41-2
British Telecom, 65n44
Brittan, Leon, 44, 71
broadcasting, 120
budget: EU, 2, 30, 34, 35, 37, 38, 70-1, 82-3, 88, 98, 133, 175, 180; 'own resources', 30, 175
bureaucracies, EU, 44-7; national, 43, 44, 46, 47n44, 190-1, 193

capital, 58, 59, 70
capitalism, 51, 52, 72, 142, 143
Carr, E.H., 17
childcare, 104

229